Mr & Mrs Smith
Hotel Collection

ITALY

PER DUE

This book is our love letter to Italy, inviting you to people-watch in its piazzas, scale its volcanoes, and go hunting for Renaissance masterpieces in its spectacular galleries. We've dipped into the turquoise waters of Sardinia, picnicked on powder-soft Puglian sands and hopped onto the obligatory Venetian gondola, to bring you a road-tested guide to the best of the big boot.

It was a daunting prospect – unearthing the most seductive boutique hotels in the country that pretty much invented passion – but Mr & Mrs Smith are never ones to turn down a challenge, and if we get to sample a few glasses of Brunello and the odd slice of *panforte* on the way, so much the better.

Feel part of *la famiglia* at a Tuscan farmhouse, dwell like a Doge at a palazzo, make like night owls in a slick city pad; wherever you choose to lay your hat, rest assured that we've been there, tested the beds, sampled the food, and put the service through its paces.

Our team of tale-telling tastemakers have reported back from the bedrooms of Treviso, Florence, Sicily, Milan and more, with entertaining anonymous reviews of every hotel featured. We dispatched editors from *Esquire*, the *Financial Times* and *Nowness* to cruise the Amalfi Coast and evade the crowds in Rome; sent fashion and retail figureheads Erdem and Mary Portas to live *la dolce vita* in Capri and Tuscany, kindled a love of Liguria in artist Natasha Law and asked architect Mario Mazzer to size up Sorrento.

Inspired by their stays? You can book any of the hotels featured (and hundreds more) at mrandmrssmith.com or through our expert Travel Team –wherever you are in the world (see page 5 for details). And don't forget: buying this book gets you six months' free membership of our BlackSmith travel club, your ticket to exclusive offers and discounts for every Smith stay you make. Now that's *amore*…

Best wishes and *buon viaggio*,

Mr & Mrs Smith

(take)
advantage of us

This is your own personal BlackSmith card, which entitles you to six months' free membership. The moment you register it at mrandmrssmith.com, you can access the members' area of our website, take advantage of exclusive offers from our hotels, and get money back every time you make a booking with us. The card also gets you members-only privileges whenever you book hotels and self-catering properties through us – such as free bottles of champagne on arrival, spa treats, late check-out, and more. Look out for this icon at the end of every review to see what you can get at each hotel featured: *Smith*

ACTIVATE YOUR MEMBERSHIP NOW

Register this card today at
**mrandmrssmith.com/
register-card**

- - - - - - - - - - - - -

Remove after
activation

Smith

ITM11117

REGISTER NOW

To access exclusive travel perks and hotel offers from Mr & Mrs Smith, activate your BlackSmith card by scanning the QR code with your phone, by ringing one of the numbers below, or by registering online at mrandmrssmith.com/register-card (it only takes a minute, we promise).

ROOM SERVICE

Activate your membership today and you'll also receive our fantastic monthly enewsletter *Room Service*. It's packed with news, travel tips, even more offers, and great competitions. We promise not to bombard you with communications, or pass on your details to third parties – this is strictly between you and us.

LOYALTY COUNTS

Let one stay pay for the next: once you join Mr & Mrs Smith, you get a percentage of every booking you make credited to your personal loyalty account, which you can put towards future Smith trips.

AND THERE'S MORE?

If all this isn't enough, you can upgrade your membership to SilverSmith or GoldSmith, which nets you even more money back and extra perks, such as access to VIP airport lounges, automatic room upgrades, flight and car-hire offers, and your own dedicated travel consultant. For more details and to upgrade, visit mrandmrssmith.com/members.

ON CALL

Thanks to our global Travel Team, Mr & Mrs Smith operates a 24-hour travel service, five days a week. Ring any of the numbers below to activate your membership today, and start planning your first Smith adventure.

From the UK 0845 034 0700
From the US and Canada 1 800 464 2040
From Australia 1300 896 627
From New Zealand 0800 896 671

From Mexico 55 4624 2406
From Brazil 11 3957 3947
From anywhere in Asia +61 3 8648 8871
From elsewhere in the world +44 20 8987 4312

Small print: all offers are dependent on availability and subject to change.

(contents)

(at a glance)

WEDDING BELLES

Borgo Santo Pietro	118
Ca' P'a (Casa Privata)	206
Capo la Gala	212
Casa Angelina	218
Castiglion del Bosco	124
Fontelunga	136
Il Salviatino	96
Palazzo Seneca	158
Petra Segreta	270
Sextantio Albergo Diffuso	168

SMALL SMITHS WELCOME

Bellevue Syrene	200
Borgo Santo Pietro	118
Castiglion del Bosco	124
Follonico	130
Fontelunga	136
JK Place Firenze	102
Lagació Mountain Residence	48
Palazzo Vecchietti	108
Residenza Napoleone III	186

SPA STAYS

Bellevue Syrene	200
Capo la Gala	212
Casa Angelina	218
Castiglion del Bosco	124
JK Place Capri	236
Hotel Signum	280
Il Salviatino	96
Lagació Mountain Residence	48
Palazzo Bontadosi	152
Petra Segreta	270
Villa Arcadio	38

COASTAL COOL

Bellevue Syrene	200
Ca' P'a (Casa Privata)	206
Capo la Gala	212
Casa Angelina	218
Hotel Signum	280
JK Place Capri	236
Maison la Minervetta	224
Petra Segreta	270
Villa Rosmarino	18

CITY SLICKERS

Babuino 181	180
Ca Maria Adele	70
Maison Matilda	58
Il Salviatino	96
I Qs	76
JK Place Firenze	102
Palazzina Grassi	82
Palazzo Vecchietti	108
Residenza Napoleone III	186
Straf Hotel & Bar	28

WINING AND DINING

Azienda Agricola Mandranova	290
Borgo Santo Pietro	118
Capo la Gala	212
Casa Angelina	218
Castiglion del Bosco	124
Fontelunga	136
Hotel Signum	280
Il Salviatino	96
JK Place Capri	236
JK Place Firenze	102
Locanda al Colle	142
Masseria Fumarola	256
Palazzo Bontadosi	152
Palazzo Seneca	158
Petra Segreta	270
Sextantio Albergo Diffuso	168
Villa Arcadio	38

OFF THE BEATEN TRACK

Azienda Agricola Mandranova	290
Borgo Santo Pietro	118
Castiglion del Bosco	124
Follonico	130
Fontelunga	136
Hotel Signum	280
Lagació Mountain Residence	48
Locanda al Colle	142
Masseria Fumarola	256
Palazzo Bontadosi	152
Palazzo Seneca	158
Petra Segreta	270
Sextantio Albergo Diffuso	168
Sextantio le Grotte della Civita	246

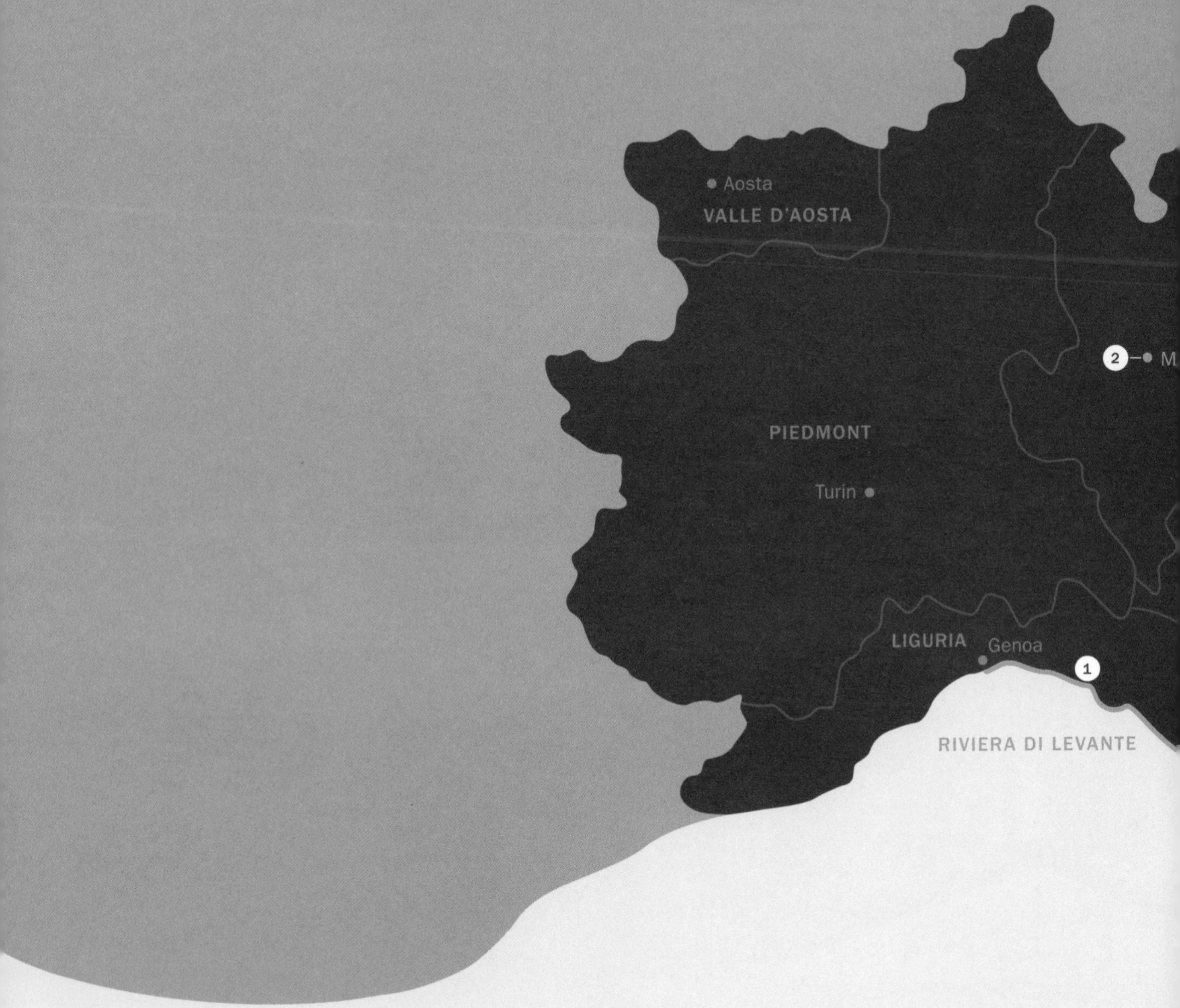
Aosta
VALLE D'AOSTA
2
PIEDMONT
Turin
LIGURIA
Genoa
1
RIVIERA DI LEVANTE

NORTH

RIVIERA DI LEVANTE

1 Villa Rosmarino

MILAN

2 Straf Hotel & Bar

LAKE GARDA

3 Villa Arcadio

SOUTH TYROL

4 Lagació Mountain Residence

TREVISO

5 Maison Matilda

VENICE

6 Ca Maria Adele

7 I Qs

8 Palazzina Grassi

RIVIERA DI LEVANTE

COASTLINE Rocky roads, pastel ports
COAST LIFE Bronzed, bold and beautiful

This exclusive sliver of golden coast is Italy's very own Côte d'Azur, a ravishing riviera of sunshine and mega-yachts. Flanked by France, poking into Piedmont and tickling Tuscany, Liguria's craggy shoreline pivots like a pair of compasses either side of its capital, Genoa. Di Ponente to the west is named for the sunset; easterly 'di Levante', for the sunrise. Winding roads climb rugged hillsides dotted with hidden beaches and Belle Epoque towns that have attracted literary luminaries for decades: the Gulf of Poets is named after its Romantic fan club. Fishing villages Portofino and Camogli – whose houses tumble down cliff-faces like so many playing blocks – have been given a stylish makeover: in summer, you can't move for super-size sunglasses. Get away from it all in the mountains, where sparkly-sea views come scented with citrus and pine.

GETTING THERE

Planes Genoa's airport (airport.genova.it) is 40 minutes by car from Camogli; it's just under an hour to Portofino.
Trains From Genoa, direct trains go to Camogli in half an hour and the journey to Portofino should take 45 minutes; see Trenitalia (trenitalia.com) for times and fares.
Automobiles These curvy cliffside roads are made for road trips, so get yourself some wheels, preferably vintage ones – just beware of the bends. There are plenty of car-hire desks to assist with coastal cruising, but if you're feeling flush, hit the Benelux desk at Genoa airport (beneluxcar.com) for Audis, BMWs or Mercedes.
Boats Tour the coast the traditional way – from the sea: Trasporti Marittimi Golfo Paradiso (golfoparadiso.it) runs ferries from Camogli to nearby hamlets Punta Chiappa and San Fruttuoso; there are departures from Genoa to Porto Venere and the villages of Cinque Terre, too.

LOCAL KNOWLEDGE

Taxis Busier seaside towns such as Portofino will have taxi ranks; otherwise, you're better off ringing one – in Camogli, try Taxi Autopubbliche (+39 0185 771143).

Siesta and fiesta Feel free to linger over lunch or sleep in the middle of the day: everyone else does. *Passegiata* is from 6pm, and dinner is around 8pm (later in summer). Santa Margherita Ligure has the latest nightlife.
Do go/don't go The region's balmy from April until October, but busy in July and August.
Packing tips Anything with a label to match the super-glam Italians; and a pair of dazzling white jeans for each day.
Recommended reads Try Laura Giannatempo's *Ligurian Kitchen* for regional recipes; or *Extra Virgin* by Annie Hawes, an expat's account of settling into Ligurian life; Dante and Petrarch were both fans of the Gulf of Poets.
Local specialities No coast is complete without its seafood stars; here, swordfish, sardines, tuna and sea-bass are popular. Ligurians love their home-made pesto with *trenette* (like linguine) and *trofie* (short and twisted pasta). Try a bit of sailor fare in port town Genoa: *fainà*, a chickpea-flour pancake, was historically a swift street-food snack for busy seafarers. Deep-fried treats are served in paper cones: *frisceu* (vegetable fritters), *cuculli* (chickpea ones), fried battered fish and strips of polenta-like *panissa*. *Pasqualina* has a paper-thin crust and is stuffed with beet

greens, eggs and cheese. Those in the know take their puddings with Sciacchetrà, a Cinque Terre dessert wine. And... The formerly isolated Cinque Terre villages were connected only by a steep coastal path through vines and olive trees. The area is now a Unesco heritage site.

WORTH GETTING OUT OF BED FOR

Viewpoint Head up to the hamlets Portofino Vetta or Ruta near the top of Mount Portofino, the rocky peninsula above the Gulf of Tigullio, and marvel at azure panoramas.

Arts and culture Liguria's capital, Genoa, is a city of art with one of the biggest mediaeval centres in Europe: an array of alleys lined with 16th-century villas, grand churches and Baroque shrines. On Via Garibaldi (aka Strada Nuova), there's a trio of museums: Palazzo Rosso, home to the Brignole-Sale family's collection of antiques and paintings; Palazzo Bianco, a notable art gallery; and exhibition space Palazzo Tursi (museidigenova.it). On Via Balbi, the Biblioteca Universitaria has a storied past: the Jesuit college library, decorated with 17th-century frescoes by Domenico Piola, had a radical makeover in the 1930s, when an impressive steel structure was installed to house more books (bibliotecauniversitaria.ge.it).

Activities Hire a *gozzo*, a traditional wooden boat, or a yacht with Italy Yacht Charters (+39 06 9818 1706; italyyachtcharters.com) and take to the seas, exploring the Levante's private coves. Set off on one of the many marked paths through Mount Portofino park and peninsula, picking from leisurely half-hour strolls or hardcore hikes (parcoportofino.it). In Camogli, B&B Diving will take you in search of coral and crustacea in the waters around the San Fruttuoso monastery (+39 0185 772751; bbdiving.it). In Rapallo, visit the castle in the sea right opposite the promenade, and take a ride on the funicular up Montallegro (setting off from Piazza Solari), where you'll be greeted with spectacular views of the bay below.

Best beach Punta Chiappa is a secluded outcrop of flat rocks leading to the sea, ideal for swimming and sunning. Cala degli Inglesi is a golden boulder-embraced bay that can only be reached by private boat or on foot; set off from Portofino for an hour-long stroll along the cliffs.

Daytripper Spend the day down in Portovenere, a pretty harbour town in the south of the Riviera. The Chiesa di San Pietro on Piazza Spallanzani was built in the 13th century, on the site of a sixth-century chapel, and an even older temple to Venus before that. On the headland below the church, you can visit the Grotta Byron, the pile of rocks where the Romantic bounder composed 'The Corsair' (and swam off to meet his mate Shelley in Lerici). There's lots of art to admire at Chiesa di San Lorenzo.

Walks Take the two-hour trek from San Rocco di Camogli to the abbey of San Fruttuoso, a perfectly preserved building built by Greek monks in the 10th century. Its warren of corridors and rooms lead to cloisters, vaults and a Byzantine church (sanfruttuoso.eu). There's a buzzy bay to stroll along once there, too.

Shopping Seghezzo on Via Cavour in Santa Margherita Ligure stocks an amazing array of wine, oil, cheese and chocolate (+39 0185 287172). Portofino is where to find the high-end houses: Hermès, Gucci and Armani all have outposts on Via Roma; for designer eyewear, peek into Ocularium on Via Roma in Genoa (+39 010 543388). Further down the coast, the town of Zoagli is known for its textiles; at Tessitura Artigianale Giuseppe Gaggioli on Via dei Velluti you'll see the ateliers in action, spinning silks, damasks and velvets (+39 0185 259057).

Something for nothing Walk to Paraggi from Santa Margherita Ligure along the decked path which wends along the sea, arriving at dusk as the evening gets going.

Don't go home without... heading to the town of Recco to taste its cheese-filled take on *fugassa* – a thin slice of salt-sprinkled focaccia with a generous dousing of olive oil and a layer of mild, soft stracchino cheese. Try them deliciously warm, straight from the oven, at Panificio Moltedo on Via XX Settembre (+39 0185 74046).

RAVISHINGLY RIVIERA DI LEVANTE

Liguria is the home of pesto, humble herb paste and now larder staple. Pasta's dream partner is made with garlic, pine nuts, parmesan, pecorino, coarse sea salt and lashings of local extra-virgin olive oil, along with the fragrant basil produced by the region's magic microclimate; a wooden pestle and a marble mortar see to the rest. The name comes from *pestare*, 'to pound', as does the word pestle, meaning, obviously, 'pounder'.

DIARY

Late April Join in at the beach party in Portofino on the 23rd – the town celebrates St George's Day with a colourful procession, live music and a big bonfire by the sea. Mid-May Camogli stays true to its fishing-village roots with its annual festival on the second Sunday of the month: enormous pans are used to cook enough fish to feed the extended population, all in honour of patron sain of fishermen, San Fortunato. Late July Levanto near Cinque Terre welcomes thousands of revellers to enjoy the Feast of San Giacomo on the 25th. July–August atch one of the classical concerts held at the atmospheric abbey of San Fruttuoso during Rapallo's Summer Festival (+39 0185 64396; omniaeventi.com).

Villa Rosmarino

STYLE Modern-art mansion
SETTING Portofino Peninsula village

'Through the gentle strobing of palm trees
in the gardens, our balcony is treated to
an eyeful of Camogli Bay. It's perfect'

Deep blue sky, even deeper azure sea flanking a leafy hillside of sun-faded yellow, pink and terracotta houses: the view from our shower thanks to a perfectly positioned window. Through the gentle strobing of palm trees in the gardens, our balcony is treated to the same eyeful of Camogli Bay. We may be in the Terrace Room (one of Villa Rosmarino's humbler bedrooms) but, to me, it's perfect.

I know lucky individuals with pals that hand over keys to renovated palazzos with swimming pools, staff and easy access to the sea. Anyone not so blessed: consider Villa Rosmarino's owners Mario and Fulvio those kinds of friends instead – their warmth and attention to detail make staying here like being lent a home. On arrival, Mario gives you keys so you can come and go as you wish, and a detailed map marked with insider essentials.

Villa Rosmarino is the kind of place you can spend time doing a) a lot; b) not very much; or c) absolutely nothing. Genoa is half an hour away, there are excellent coastal walks, and there's a swimming pool with sunloungers, magazines and espressos on tap to keep you from going anywhere. My plan? To enjoy as much pasta, focaccia and ice-cream as possible – guilt-free. And anyway, pounding up the steps to hilltop San Rocco for supper tonight is surely equivalent to a good Stairmaster workout?

The season hasn't properly begun and still all six rooms are taken – yet over the weekend we rarely collide with another guest. We admire fabulous artworks amid clean, modern lines, and witty touches such as a red vintage kids' scooter. Leather sofas and a long refectory table (which heaves under fruit salads, yoghurts, breads and croissants at breakfast-time) deck out a ground-floor room that opens out onto lemons, rosemary, lavender, roses and pomegranates. Another sitting room offers shelves of art, design and photography books, testament to the owners' previous careers in advertising.

Camogli's *panificios* fill the snack-sized hole left in our afternoon. You can't miss the bakeries – they crop up every few shops, wooing you in with their aromas and breads laid across large trays. Revello on the seafront is the pasticceria where the local sweet cream-filled *crostate* pastry originated. I choose an olive oil-, salt- and oregano-sprinkled focaccia; Mr Smith pounces on a thin slice with melted cheese. They're all the more delicious eaten on a beach surrounded by Italians, equally appreciative of the spring weather, shedding layers and bringing out their bambini to soak up the sunshine.

Dusk falling, we pick up the path to San Rocco, following winding steps up past gardens and dry stone walls. Lights twinkle on across the hillside and a gentle mist falls. As we turn corners and more stairs appear, my mental pedometer pats me on the back while mutterings of 'Oh God' emanate from an under-the-weather Mr Smith. 'What do you mean there's a bus that takes you from outside the villa to San Rocco in one stop?' he asks as we reach the top 30 minutes later. Just then, hewn into the cliff-face, we find the perfect tonic: a bar. Perched at a candlelit table, we toast our climb with a

pre-dinner glass of Ligurian red and some saltines before taking our table for dinner at a cosy, family-run trattoria.

La Cucina di Nonna Nina is the kind of restaurant you dream of stumbling across. A sweet waitress translates the Ligurian-dialect menu and soon we're devouring *ancioe pinn-e* (anchovies cooked like whitebait), Nonna Nina's special fish ravioli, a beany Genoese minestrone and *coniglio alla Genovese*.

Revived by wine and oven-roasted rabbit, we make it down again and up back to Rosmarino. Lamps glow from the garden room, music plays softly and the honesty bar awaits. Over a nightcap, I suggest walking back up that hill tomorrow, along the less hair-raising path to San Fruttuoso. A by-now-sniffly Mr Smith doesn't take it well. We reach a compromise: painkillers and a boat ride.

Waiting for ferry tickets at a café in the boat-bobbing harbour the following morning, we hear from a local how the little port got its name. Ca' mogli is from *casa delle*

'Galvanised by crab and fish cooked the Ligurian way with potatoes, parsley and garlic, we snoop around the abbey'

mogli meaning 'house of the wives', a reference to the ladies left running the village while their fishermen were away. Seafaring inspired its festivals too, a waiter chips in. He gestures to a vast frying pan set on the harbour wall used to cook for the Sagra del Pesce, a street party in May that honours patron saint of fishing folk, San Fortunato. Then in August, a special mass is held for Stella Maris when candles in paper cups are nudged out to sea to remember lost sailors. A rainstorm breaks and Mr Smith eyes the water suspiciously.

Amid thunder and lightning, we reach the tiny cove of San Fruttuoso at the foot of Mount Portofino. I am told that the statue of Christ of the Abysses is below us – sadly it's only just visible when the waters are calmer, so we head straight for lunch at La Cantina, another Mario tip. Galvanised by crab and fish cooked the Ligurian way with potatoes, parsley and garlic, we snoop around the Benedictine abbey. Above is a tower used by 16th-century monks as a pirate lookout. We ponder more exploring but those heading up the hill have big boots, metal poles and crampons (although I hear the Italian ladies do it in high heels). I pause instead to sketch a monk-like Mr Smith. 'I'm pondering mortality,' he tells me, looking contemplative. But knowing how good Mario and Fulvio's hospitality has been, I suspect he's casting his thoughts ahead to cocktail hour on Villa Rosmarino's terrace. And who could blame him?

Reviewed by **Natasha Law**, artist

NEED TO KNOW

Rooms Six.

Rates €140–€240, including Continental breakfast.

Check-out 11am. Earliest check-in, 2pm.

Facilities Library, gardens and free parking. In rooms: free WiFi, Comfort Zone bath products and not a TV in sight.

Poolside The infinity pool is surrounded by sun-bleached teak decking, sweet-smelling geraniums in dusky pots and elegant wooden sunloungers.

Children Over-eights can stay, but only in the Garden Room, which can have an extra bed added for €50 a night.

Also During high season (April to October) and at weekends, a two-night minimum stay usually applies. In-room spa treatments can be arranged.

IN THE KNOW

Our favourite rooms What the top-floor Terrace Room lacks in size, in makes up for in views – spectacular ocean panoramas from both its eponymous terrace and the shower. The room names give the game away: if you want somewhere large, it's got to be the Large Room; this light, airy suite has the most space (but no sea view, sadly). The shady Garden Room is on the ground floor, with marble mosaics, stripy velvet chairs and a polished wooden day-bed.

Hotel bar Nothing formal, just a houseboy-tended honesty bar of wines, spirits and juices in the kitchen.

Hotel restaurant None, but guests can catch up with their hosts over an expertly made espresso in the communal kitchen. The grey stone space spans an entire floor, and leads out to a sunny breakfast terrace. The long table inside is scattered with books, maps and interiors mags, and the room features a low leather BB Italia sofa, a pair of powder blue Marco Zanuso 'Lady' chairs, a vintage Castiglioni lamp and Murano glassware set on an antique kilim.

Top table Poolside for prosecco, and out on the terrace along the side of the house for breakfast. Slip away upstairs for a punch-packing ristretto in the library.

Room service None.

Dress code You're up against a super-stylish host couple from Milan, so get those labels out.

Local knowledge If Mario and Fulvio's collection has inspired a little envy, call in at Via Garibaldi 12 in Genoa (viagaribaldi12.com) and raid this 16th-century palazzo-turned-concept-store.

LOCAL EATING AND DRINKING

Stock up on pizza and pastries at Revello Pasticceria e Focacceria on Via Garibaldi in Camogli (+39 0185 770777). On the same road, silky-smooth gelato and icy granitas await at Gelato e Dintorni (+39 339 655 3007), or pop a few doors down to its smoothie-making counterpart, 5 Frutta e Gelato (+39 0185 773934). Bistingo Sea Bar on Piazza Colombo is the perfect pitch in the sunny square from which to watch the wooden boats bobbing on the marina (+39 0815 773357). Head to La Cucina di Nonna Nina on Viale Franco Molfino for Ligurian cuisine in a cosy, pastel-hued villa on Mount Portofino (+39 0185 773835; closed Wednesday). Try the spaghetti *vongole* or *al sugo di pesce* at Ristorante da Paolo on Via San Fortunato (+39 0185 773595). Fish is chosen by weight and then grilled or baked in salt, and served Ligurian-style with olives, pine nuts and potatoes.

GET A ROOM!

Hotel details 38 via Enrico Figari, 16032 Camogli (+39 0185 771580; villarosmarino.com).

To book Ring our expert Travel Team (you'll find all our numbers with your membership card on page 5) or go to mrandmrssmith.com/villa-rosmarino.

 Two glasses of local wine.

MILAN

CITYSCAPE Grand designs
CITY LIFE One long catwalk

Cosmopolitan, commercial, glittering – sure, Milan may lack the fecund fields of rural Italy, or the blue-gold glamour of the coast, but this city has its own claim to fame: it never goes out of fashion. Label-lovers walk the Golden Triangle clutching bags from big-name boutiques, hipsters jostle for vintage treasure in the flea markets, and canny consumers come for the designer outlets. There was life before shopping, though: sport, art and culture have flourished here for centuries. Sit in the bowels of the San Siro Stadium, relish the anticipation, and cheer on the nimble-kneed football stars. Be moved to tears by a soprano at La Scala, or Leonardo's *Last Supper*. Wonder at the Gothic Duomo, or Giò Ponti's architectural peak: the soaring shark-fin of the Pirelli tower. Like a supermodel with a PhD, there's more to Milan than meets the eye.

GETTING THERE

Planes Milan's largest airport is Malpensa, around 40km north-west of the city centre. Linate is smaller, but closer to downtown Milan (sea-aeroportimilano.it). Bergamo airport, further out, handles budget flights from the UK.
Trains The Malpensa Express runs every half-hour and connects to Milan's Cadorna station, near the Castello Sforzesco, in about 40 minutes (malpensaexpress.it). Linate doesn't have a train connection, but you can hop on a bus to the city's main rail hub, Milan Centrale. Within Italy, Trenitalia connects Milan to popular spots, including Rome, Florence and Bologna (trenitalia.com).
Automobiles A car will cramp your style – city parking issues mean it's easier to explore the main sights on foot; the apricot-yellow trams are pretty fast, too.

LOCAL KNOWLEDGE

Taxis As you'd expect, it's easy to flag taxis at airports and stations. Alternatively, give Radio Taxi a call (+39 02 8585; +39 02 6969; 028585.it).
Siesta and fiesta Lunch is enjoyed between 12.30pm and 2.30pm; dinner, 8pm–10.30pm. Don't worry if you're hungry before then, most bars provide snacking bites for happy hour (6pm–9pm). Shop to your heart's content between 9.30am and 7.30pm. Few shops close for lunch, but many shut on Monday mornings and Sundays.
Do go/don't go Bargain-hunters should hit Milan's January sales. Body-swerve February and September's *molto*-busy fashion weeks (unless you have front-row seats, of course). The city blooms in spring. Urbanites throng to the lakes in high summer, so the city can feel deserted then.
Packing tips Bloggistas, bring your iPad for timely fashion updates. Sunglasses are as crucial as passports.
Recommended reads Mark Twain gives a lively account of Milan in *The Innocents Abroad*. *Designer Bargains in Italy* is the English version of *Lo ScopriOccasioni*, Theodora van Meurs' famous shopping bible, now in its sixth edition (scopriocasioni.it). Ernest Hemingway's short story 'In Another Country' is also set in Milan.
Local specialities The region is renowned for its liberal use of butter, and super-strong espressos. A favourite place to tackle the Lombardy kitchen is snug little Antica Trattoria della Pesa on Viale Pasubio (+39 02 655 5741; closed Sundays): trademark alla Milanese dishes include

saffron-flavoured risotto; plate-sized breaded veal *cotoletto*, minestrone (a broth made from greens, rice and bacon) and *ossobuco* (braised veal shank). We also have Milan to thank for the light and airy peel-peppered *panettone*, which graces the country's Christmas tables.

WORTH GETTING OUT OF BED FOR

Viewpoint Milan's Duomo is one of the world's largest, most eye-boggling Gothic cathedrals. It's a muscle-aching climb to the top – 166 steps (or a speedy ascent in the lift), but worth it for the eyeful. If you can handle heights, explore the roof, with its intricate tangle of architecture and statuary. Want Duomo views with cocktails, too? Sip some in the rooftop restaurant at upmarket department store La Rinascente (rinascente.it), by the cathedral.

Arts and culture Santa Maria delle Grazie's former refectory houses Leonardo da Vinci's iconic *The Last Supper* (book in advance; milan-museum.com). Pinacoteca di Brera (brera.beniculturali.it) is a fine-art must, with pieces spanning pre-Renaissance to Post-Impressionist. The Prada Foundation (fondazioneprada.org) hosts biannual exhibitions at Via Antonio Fogazzaro, and has a permanent art installation at the church of Santa Maria Annunciata in Chiesa Rossa. Treat yourselves to a ballet, opera or orchestra performance at one of the world's greatest theatres, La Scala (teatroallascala.org). You're expected to look the part: jackets and ties are compulsory for Mr Smith (black tie for premieres). A tour of the opera house is no substitute for a performance, but still illuminating.

Activities If it's warm, follow locals to Milan's man-made lake, Idroscalo (idroscalo.info). Seek out Milan's best coffee with a café crawl: Zucca (Caffè Miani) in Galleria Vittorio Emanuele II is gorgeously grand (+39 02 8646 4435); Pasticceria Marchesi on Via Santa Maria alla Porta has tux-clad barmen, and potent espressos (+39 02 876730). Have a treatment at the iconic Gianfranco Ferré spa (+39 02 7601 7526; carolihealthclub.com) on Via Sant'Andrea. Achille Castiglioni, the influential industrial designer, died in 2002, but you can still peek into his studio on Piazza Castello, which remains exactly as he left it (+39 02 805 3606; achillecastiglioni.it).

Perfect picnic Pick up panini and pastries from über-deli Peck on Via Spadari (+39 02 802 3161; peck.it) and take them to the Indro Montanelli Gardens, by Via Palestro.

Daytripper Head for one of Italy's great lakes: chic Como, gastro-glamorous Garda, Lugano or Maggiore. Garda's southern shores are just a 90-minute hop; have a lunch of lake-fish in the port of Salò, or on a hillside villa terrace.

Walks Explore the aristocratic gardens and paths of Parco Sempione, between Sforza castle and Piazza Sempione.

Shopping It's all about high fashion: Gucci, Prada, D&G and Bottega Veneta occupy privileged perches in the Golden Triangle (Via della Spiga, Via Sant'Andrea, Via Monte Napoleone). The Armani concept store sells everything from skirts to sushi in Giorgio's mini-mall on Via Manzoni (armani.com). Fashion editors flock to 10 Corso Como (+39 02 654831): set in a converted garage, it has a gallery, bookshop, café and wallet-emptying stash of fashion and design lust-haves. Milan's cut-price outlets are famous: many are outside the city, but Il Salvagente (+39 02 7611 0328) is on Via Fratelli Bronzetti. Pick up a pair of satin-soft leather gloves from Sermoneta at 46 Via della Spiga (+39 02 7631 8303). Rummage for vintage bargains (retro Ray-Bans, Prada bags, original Halston and the ilk) at the Navigli flea market, held on the last Sunday of every month (except July and August).

Something for nothing Visit the macabre chapel of San Bernardino alle Ossa: its walls are sculpted from human skulls and bones. The ossuary was built to house remains when a nearby cemetery ran out of space in the 1200s.

Don't go home without… feasting on marshmallow-plump mozzarella at Obikà, a sleek little mozzarella bar. There are several outposts to choose from – we like Brera's best, at the corner of Via Mercato and Via dei Fiori Chiari (+39 02 885 2453; obika.it).

MAGNIFICENTLY MILAN

Galleria Vittorio Emanuele II is one of the world's oldest shopping arcades. Designed in 1861, it took 12 years to build. Today, it sparkles from a recent renovation, and boasts bandbox-neat boutiques, lively cafés and a plush hotel (there's also a McDonald's, but nobody's perfect). It's a great place to pick up top-notch hats, star-stylish sunglasses, and Prada pieces (although the brand's four other branches involve less tourist-tussling).

DIARY

February The two-week long Carnevale Ambrosiano, with floats and crowds processing to the Piazza del Duomo, ends on the first weekend in Lent. **Late February** The first of Milan's biannual fashion spectacles begins. **Mid-April** Preview design trends at Milan's massively influential furniture fair, the International Salone del Mobile (cosmit.it). **May** The area along Alzaia Naviglio Grande canal bustles with artists and canvas-collectors, for the Pittori sul Naviglio outdoor art show (naviglilive.it). **Late September** Fashion week (spring/summer collections) returns in style. **December** Pick up Christmas presents from Milan's festive markets: Oh Bej! Oh Bej! is held near the castle in early December; L'Artigiano in Fiera is a week-long craft fair (artigianoinfiera.com).

Straf Hotel & Bar

STYLE Set in concrete
SETTING Duomo on your doorstep

'A splodgy black artwork has an acid-yellow lozenge on it: the room's sole hit of colour. The bathroom is a vision of oxidised brass. It's surprisingly sexy'

The architect and artist behind Hotel Straf is meditating atop a mountain peak in a toga, chewing goji berries and ruminating on his future hotel's interior design. He fingers his mala beads. 'Coloured soft furnishings? Pah. Wallpaper? So last season. Carpet, schmarpet. Door knobs? *Such* bad energy.' He turns to a gnomish devotee beside him, and intones: 'My one indulgence shall be: the Wellday massage chair – more knot-kneading than a thousand masseuses, more relaxing than a thousand bubble baths. And – the people – they shall come.' With that, he levitates.

Now, I can't verify that Vincenzo de Cotiis actually designed Straf *quite* like that. But it's how the minimalist and modern interiors *should* have been conceived. When Mr Smith and I arrive at the hotel's secretive, beetle-black entrance, we trip over a smiley man in a hoodie and trainers, who opens the glass door for us. 'Wow, what polite staff – even off-duty,' we muse. Turns out he's wearing the front-desk uniform. We're in Milan, remember: a hoodie here is as smart as an amorphous garment can be.

Minutes later, our room-inspection routine is underway. Surroundings are surveyed. Soft furnishings: nil. Walls: concrete, putty-coloured. Floor: concrete, putty-coloured. Bed: low, topped with putty-coloured cover. A splodgy black artwork has an acid-yellow lozenge on it: the room's sole non-putty hit. Soaps have batch numbers. The bathroom is a vision of oxidised brass. (I later discover that showering here is like bathing in a giant tin. And it's surprisingly sexy.)

Such aesthetic severity does funny things to Mr Smith. I can hear mutterings from our metallic bathroom: 'What? That's the tissue dispenser?' Locating the minibar is tantamount to seeking out the Holy Grail. We stand helplessly before a giant sliding glass door. 'It must be hidden down a trap-door,' we conclude. 'A secret underground passageway that leads to the Duomo perhaps?' suggests a getting-carried-away Mr Smith (our hotel is steps from the sacred stone behemoth). Thirty minutes later, we reach an anticlimactic conclusion: the glass panel is stuck. With an almighty shove, Mr Smith uncovers a little fridge, stocked with wine and nibbles.

Snacks demolished, and massage chair tested (I'm saving up for one; they're only $2,795), we venture out. I wasn't sure I'd like Milan. I'd heard it was industrial, unsightly, even hostile in parts, and I'd read somewhere that if you aren't wearing Gucci, waiters actually cannot see you. Yet coming here proves like falling in love with a friend's ex-boyfriend: they've warned you against him, but all you can see is his sexy side.

Strolling around, we unwrap Milan bit by bit. Cherry trees in blowsy blossom billow by the cathedral. Friendly and funny waiters feed us delicious pasta. The fashion capital is of course full of shops (and retail is my religion). The sun shines. Galleria Vittorio Emanuele II glitters with fripperies, and there are people wearing dandified uniforms. There's a moment of panic when I realise I'm *sans* sunglasses (this is akin to going without trousers in Britain). I purchase some. Disaster averted.

We shoot up to the top of the Duomo in a lift. The roof is slanted like a giant Toblerone. A billion feet (roughly) above ground, I make an inconvenient discovery: I suffer from vertigo. We come down again, sharpish. We wander inside the Gothic cathedral and watch a service. A lady sings like an angel, and a shockingly embarrassing thing happens: whenever her voice soars into the silence, rivers of tears run down my face. Worried I might start speaking in tongues, and unable to fight the spiritual tremors, I quickly drag Mr Smith into the secular security of outdoors.

Religious highs give way to fleamarket thrills. At Fiera di Senigallia, in the canal district, hipsters mingle and vintage Prada luggage costs €100. We pretend to be Italian. We are in love. We are also at our most glamorous. For my funeral I want pictures of us in Milan emblazoned across my coffin. I shall pretend this is how I always looked: clad in black cape and skinny jeans, black pumps, Chanel bag, giant sunglasses, and a bouffant up-do that is admired (bizarrely) by an Italian stallholder. (Him, pointing at my head: 'Thees ees from your miiind?' Me: 'Sorry? What?' Him: 'Youu cam up with thees look from your miiind?' Me: 'Er. Yes.' Him: 'I liiiiike. Iz niice!' Me: 'Thanks. Goodbye.')

'It's testament to Straf's greatness that, amid Milan's many distractions, we miss our neat-as-a-bento-box boudoir'

After obliterating our earnings, it's time for an utterly futile mission. A minibreak wouldn't be complete without one fruitless pilgrimage. We trundle around: footsore, thirsty, seeking a phantom restaurant. An hour later, we arrive. It's closed. We perk up with espressos at Pasticceria Marchesi, followed by Campari and olives at Resentin. Because we're hungry, we linger. Since landing in Milan, I've been dreaming about risotto Milanese. We order big bowls, and tuck in. The saffron lends a flavour I can only describe as mediaeval – try it, you'll understand.

It's testament to Straf's greatness that, amid Milan's many distractions, we miss our neat-as-a-bento-box boudoir. We hop on an apricot-yellow tram, and 10 minutes later, I'm back in *that* massage chair, being rubbed robotically, and listening to opera on the TV's inbuilt stereo. I'm so happy, I start bawling like a baby. (Again.) Mr Smith has no choice but to order a bottle of prosecco.

Our stay in Milan has had the emotional range of a Shakespearean drama: tears, laughter, lust (luggage-induced) and love. I've felt my knees wobble with fear, and I've cried buckets. It rained. Twice. Despite this, here at Straf Hotel, Mr Smith and I have had a blast. Vincenzo de Cotiis – *grazie mille*.

Reviewed by Mr & Mrs Smith

NEED TO KNOW

Rooms 64, including three suites.
Rates €344–€729, including Continental breakfast.
Check-out 12 noon, but flexible, subject to availability and a charge (half the daily room rate between 2pm and 5pm; a full day's rate after 5pm). Earliest check-in, 2pm.
Facilities Fitness room, valet parking, free WiFi throughout. In-rooms: flatscreen TV, minibar.
Children Welcome: extra beds are free for under-12s; €88 a night for teens.
Also Little dogs (the fashionable kind) are invited, too.

IN THE KNOW

Our favourite rooms Book a Wellbeing Room (we heart 504) for its bold burnished brass bathroom, minimal monochrome decor, glittering glass surfaces and, above all, electronic massage chair. These rooms also have an aromatherapy and chromotherapy corner (a suite of mood-improving gadgets which, when activated, change the lighting colour, and emit puffs of scented air). Suite 604 has a moody black stone bathroom; 605's is dazzling white (both rooms have Duomo-facing balconies).
Hotel bar Dark, compact and edgy Straf Bar is a magnet for the fashion set, drawn here by the retro good looks (aged leather sofa, acid-green lightshade mushrooming from the ceiling), potent cocktails and generous nibbles. Drinking sessions officially end at midnight, but it's often open later.
Hotel restaurant Breakfast and lunch are served in a neat little room, with glossy white table tops, square leather seats and textured colour-block canvases. The novel Euro-Asian fusion à la carte lunch menu has dishes such as Thai pasta or salmon with black rice. Dinner isn't on offer, but a complimentary Milanese finger-food buffet is laid out at 6.30pm.
Top table Sit in the corner booth by the glass wall for the most privacy. For easy access to the buffet at breakfast, sit at the other end, closest to the spread.
Room service It's drinks-only by day: try one of the exotic teas (sweet pan yong golden needle, or kimono: green tea with rose petals and cherry) from 7am. In the evening, a selection of Italian staples can be ordered until 10.30pm.
Dress code As directional as the decor: Jil Sander for the ladies, Alexander Wang for the gents.
Local knowledge Visit Sforzesco Castle (+39 02 8846 3700; milanocastello.it), a leisurely 15-minute stroll from the hotel; there's a museum of ancient art on the ground floor of the Corte Ducale, a stash of antique furnishings, and a selection of musical instruments on the first and second floors of the *rocchetta* (little fort).

LOCAL EATING AND DRINKING

La Libera on Via Palermo (+39 02 805 3603) is an unassuming little restaurant (it calls itself a beer cellar plus kitchen) with dark wood decor and accomplished comfort cooking. Try the mustardy veal kidneys or the excellent seafood. Sparkling-white Chatulle on Via Piero della Francesca (+39 02 342008) serves imaginative Italian cuisine in sophisticated surroundings. Locals are justly proud of Antica Trattoria della Pesa on Viale Pasubio (+39 02 655 5741). Go there to sample Milanese favourites – risotto, plate-sized breaded veal and osso bucco with gremolata. Gioia 69 on Via Melchiorre Gioia (+39 02 6671 0180) has a moodily magnificent restaurant and black-velvet lounge bar. Stay up late for Bar Basso (+39 02 2940 0580) and its potent cocktails at 39 Via Plinio.

GET A ROOM!

Hotel details 3 via San Raffaele, 20121 Milan (+39 02 805081; straf.it).
To book Ring our expert Travel Team (you'll find all our numbers with your membership card on page 5) or go to mrandmrssmith.com/hotel-straf.

 A free drink of your choice at Straf Bar, and a platter of seasonal fruit.

LAKE GARDA

COASTLINE Sea of tranquillity
COAST LIFE Soft-tops and speedboats

Largest and most laid-back of the Italian Lakes, Garda is flanked by vineyards and olive groves, cradled by snow-capped mountains and adored by weekending lovers, motorbikers and showboaters in equal measure. Once an Austrian territory, and marking the start of the Alps, the northern reaches of Lake Garda sport a hint of chalet chic; further south, the sunny microclimate imposes a nonchalant Riviera feel along serpentine roads suspended from the rock face. To vroom along here is to follow in the tyre treads of James Bond; and the super-star villas above the lake have luxury trappings that would impress a retired jewel thief. Spend your days idling on the water, touring vineyards or mooching in markets – Lake Garda's amazing natural splendour has earned it admirers from Catullus to Clooney, and it'll bowl you over, too.

GETTING THERE

Planes For south or east Lake stays, Verona airport is best (aeroportoverona.it), but more flights land at Milan Malpensa or Linate (seamilano.eu; both about 90 minutes from Salò). Bergamo is also an option (sacbo.it).
Trains Desenzano del Garda station has regular rail connections to Venice, Milan, Verona, Brescia and other Italian cities (trenitalia.com). SIA buses (840 620 001) can connect you to lake-edge towns such as Salò.
Automobiles A car is a must for exploring, but if you're staying put, you can do without. From Milan, take the A4 to Venice; exit east at Brescia. Brescia and Verona are both around half an hour from the lake's southern tip.
Boats Car ferries zip between Desenzano and Riva del Garda several times a day, stopping at various ports en route (including Sirmione, Salò, Gargnano and Limone); pedestrian boats and catamarans ply more routes and are more frequent. See navigazionelaghi.it for timetables.

LOCAL KNOWLEDGE

Taxis Most towns will have ranks, but cabs can still be elusive. If you're on a schedule, ask your hotel to book one.

Siesta and fiesta In high season, shops are generally open daily until 7pm or so, but some close for a couple of hours around lunch. Many hotels (and most tourist sites) will be closed over winter, reopening in time for Easter.
Do go/don't go Spring and autumn are fantastic, especially if you're lounging on a sun-warmed terrace on a bright clear day. Cool mountain air makes summer pleasant along northern shores, but temperatures can soar in the south. July and August bring busy roads and packed restaurants.
Packing tips Outdoorsy gear for biking or rambling up hills or among vines; deck shoes, shades and binoculars for lake jaunts; swimsuits if you plan on testing the waters.
Recommended reads Dip into *Catullus: The Complete Poems* – Lake Garda is where the poet was supposedly inspired to pen his most explicit erotic works. A key scene in Thomas Mann's *The Magic Mountain* was inspired by the dramatic Varone Waterfall (cascata-varone.com).
Local specialities Menus make the most of the region's bountiful natural resources, with freshwater lake fish such as pike, carp, trout, eel and perch hogging the culinary limelight. The supporting cast includes mountain-dwelling wild boar; bright citrus fruits; vivid herbs and aromatic

olive oils. The eastern shores are flanked by miles of carefully tended vines, with Valpolicella and Bardolino heading up the vintage hit list, while the Lombardy region to the west produces Garda Classico DOCs. Make an appointment to visit centuries-old producer Azienda Agricola Comincioli in Puegnago sul Garda to see how they make fragrant extra virgin olive oil, wine and grappa (+39 0365 651141; info@comincioli.it).

WORTH GETTING OUT OF BED FOR

Viewpoint At Lake Garda, any view is a great view, but the higher you climb, the more you'll see. Take Malcesine's futuristic cable-car (funiviedelbaldo.it) to the top of Monte Baldo for a vertiginous vista of the whole lake; in just 10 minutes, you'll climb almost 1,800 metres – the second stage of the ascent is completed in 360° rotating cabins.

Arts and culture Mansion-turned-museum Il Vittoriale degli Italiani (vittoriale.it) in Gardone, the former residence of interventionist writer Gabriele d'Annunzio, is a fascinating estate of follies, gardens and rivers. The jaw-dropping Palazzo Bettoni in Bogliaco di Gargnano houses an important art collection, with prized paintings by Canaletto and Veronese and a Rococo staircase.

Activities Fresh air and incredible scenery will inspire even the laziest couple to seek outdoor pleasures, be it kayaking or canyoning or careering along mountain-bike paths. Head for the hills of the Alto Garda Bresciano national park and seek out pastures new. Speed across the water in a polished mahogany launch: a lake tour aboard Villa Arcadio's classic motorboat will make you feel quite the 1960s film stars. The wind-tickled waters at the top of the lake make Riva, Torbole and Malcesine a magnet for windsurfers and kite-surfers; Surf Segnana in Torbole can kit you up and teach you the basics (surfsegnana.it) – they also rent out catamarans and bicycles.

Best beach Most beaches here are of the pebbly kind – the best being to the north of Garda – but for sunbathing, you can recline siren-like on the rocks at Sirmione; there are soothing views of mountain peaks from here, too.

Daytripper Verona's artistic and architectural legacy runs the historic span from Roman to Renaissance. The well-preserved amphitheatre in the city's Unesco-listed centre hosts the world-famous Verona Opera Festival (arena.it); there are Pisanello frescoes and ancient tombs in the peaceful church of Sant'Anastasia; the Basilica di San Zeno Maggiore dates back to the fifth century; and,

on Via Capello, you'll see the famous Casa di Giulietta ('Juliet's house'), a big draw for Shakespeare fans.

Walks Hit the culture trail: a walk through the historic town of Salò will reward you with the 15th-century Palazzo della Magnifica Patria, and the Palazzo Fantoni. All roads lead to the high-gothic Duomo, Santa Maria Annunziata, complete with wonderful artworks, but explore a little further and you'll find enchanting side streets and scenic lakeside lookout points.

Shopping If you're looking for clothes, go to Verona or Milan; the kind of browsing and buying that quickens hearts here is done at a local market. Seek out regional cheeses from Taleggio to Grana Padano at Gavardo's covered market; elsewhere, some of the best markets are held on Saturday in Salò; Tuesday in Limone; Wednesday in Gargnano; Thursday in Bardolino and Friday in Garda. Hunt for antiques on the first Sunday of the month in Desenzano's Piazza Malvezzi; every second Sunday in Brescia; or every third Sunday in Bardolino and Mantua.

Something for nothing Bardolino's Museo del Vino is worth a peek: Cantina Fratelli Zeni (zeni.it) gives you a glimpse into the world of wine-making. It's free to visit, and you can even sample a few glasses in the Vinoteca.

Don't go home without... something sweet from Pasticceria Vassalli, a renowned pastry shop and chocolatier on Via San Carlo in Salò (+39 0365 20752). Among its specialities are products made exclusively with citrus fruit grown around Lake Garda, including lemon and quince jam, candied orange peel and Cedrina, a limoncello-like liqueur.

LITERALLY LAKE GARDA

The massive lake suface (almost 400 square kilometres) means a climate of mild winters and balmy summers that's perfect for olives, grapes and Riviera-reminiscent sub-tropical gardens. The André Heller Botanic Garden (hellergarden.com) combines eco reserve with sculpture park: contemporary pieces by the likes of Keith Haring and Roy Lichtenstein are dotted among a 2,000-strong plant collection that includes rare bamboo, cacti and orchids.

DIARY

Late April/May Garda con Gusto, the month-long Lake Fish Food Festival, whets appetites annually in Toscolano Maderno. **June–September** The renowned Verona Opera Festival is a season of star-quality spectacle set in the city's phenomenal Roman amphitheatre (arena.it). **September** Engines roar (and so do the crowds) when F1 Ferraris scream round the course at the Italian Grand Prix in Monza, just north of Milan (formula1.com). The power of nature is harnessed in the mid-month Centomiglia sailing regatta, when hundreds of boats navigate the perimeter of Lake Garda from Gargnano (centomiglia.it). **Early October** The annual Bardolino wine festival at the start of the month brings fireworks, fiddlers and alfresco finger food to the mediaeval lakeside town.

Villa Arcadio

STYLE Classic, monastic, fantastic
SETTING Wooded lake-view hillside

'The view is mesmerising. When it is misty, it's hard to know where the world ends. When it is clear, snow-capped peaks loom majestically in the distance'

Mr Smith and I like to consider ourselves seasoned travellers. You know: sophisticates with well-stickered 'weekend' luggage, versed on which local *aperitivo* to order, and dedicated to staying in so-stylish-you-wouldn't-know-it's-a-hotel-without-SatNav kind of places. The type who gad about Lake Garda on a speedboat, swapping trattoria tips with the captain. Not the sort who get sunburn on the first day. Or look the wrong way when they cross the road. No, no, no. Or stand filming the very fast and shiny catamaran from what they think is the ferry terminal, only to watch it sail past into the next pretty bay. Never. Not us.

But, you see, holidaying in Italy is relaxing. And holidaying at Lake Garda, without your tantrumming toddler in tow, and with sunshine, mountain vistas and non-stop fabulous food and wine, is especially relaxing. In fact, so enchanting is holidaying here, it's brain-befuddling, stupidity-magnifying – turning even the most *seasoned* travellers (sophisticates with special weekending bags!) into craven half-wits.

Thankfully, during our stay at the exclusive Villa Arcadio hotel, staff are professional enough to overlook poolside narcolepsy, dangerous toaster mismanagement, and other breakfast-buffet blunders (which we blame on them, for placing an ice-bucket of champagne right next to the fresh blood-orange juice).

They also provide the kind of subtle prompts that allow off-duty parents and loved-up fools to swagger about like bona fide minibreak gurus. Would Signor Smith perhaps like a 'spritz'? It's that prosecco, Aperol and soda cocktail he has no doubt seen the pastel-chino-shorts crowd drinking in Salò's fashionable lake-front bars. The one he perhaps naively mistook for bright-orange IrnBru? Yes, that one. Would Signorina (why, thank you) perhaps like chef to whip up some handmade gnocchi with tomato ragu for lunch today, to soak up last night's multi-spritz-spree in aforementioned lake-front bars? And (in mezzopiano tones) would Signor like the table dressed with a posy of wild flowers plucked from the hotel grounds, because it is also Mother's Day, which he has forgotten? *Tutto va bene.*

Elbows suavely propped on immaculate linen and enjoying a sensational alfresco meal, we pause to fully appreciate our surroundings. From this handsomely restored monastery, set on a wooded hillside overlooking the town of Salò, the view is mesmerising. When it is misty, it's hard to know where the world ends. When it is clear, snow-capped peaks loom majestically in the distance. Little boats buzz across the water; songbirds flit busily among olive trees; the owners' spaniel, Diana, bounds through buttercup-sprinkled grass with a blackbird in her muzzle. It's all very… Arcadian. I've already taken about 4,000 pictures. At least.

We've enjoyed the view from the bed, designer sofa and dressing area of our junior suite (admittedly we enjoyed it less at 6am – we'd forgotten to close the light-stopping wooden shutters at bedtime. I still took a few pictures, though). Our room is serene, and blissfully free of unnecessary trinkets (most refreshingly, there are no plastic fire engines to trip over). The beams overhead may be new, but they marry harmoniously with original architectural features, terracotta flooring and creamy linen drapes.

A single, striking modern canvas packs a colourful punch amid an otherwise neutral palette – undoubtedly taken from the owners' enviable stash of art and antiques.

Jaana and Francesco have an unerring eye for quality: their collection – generously shared around Villa Arcadio's 18 bedrooms, dining rooms, bar and lounge – spans bronze figurines, 18th-century etchings, frescoes, Alvar Aalto glassware and contemporary carvings by Loris Marazzi. They also own a boat. Not just any boat: a vintage Aquariva launch. Calling it 'a boat' is a bit like calling a hand-built Bugatti 'a runaround'. They even let you charter it.

As we polish off lunch with some local Bardolino and ristrettos, my of-Italian-descent Mr Smith declares this the sort of terrace Merchant Ivory would have picked for the scene where the brooding farmhand is overcome with desire for the English governess. He says it quite suggestively, and throws in 'mi amore', for good measure. I ignore him, partly because he forgot Mother's Day, but mostly because I want to go and explore. And have another spritz.

'Staff provide the kind of prompts that allow off-duty parents and loved-up fools to swagger about like minibreak gurus'

Sirmione – which we (eventually) reach aboard the very fast and shiny catamaran that leaves from Salò's Lungolargo promenade – is a spindly peninsula packed with café-cornered piazzas, gelaterie and touristy trinket shops. It's Grand Tour gold. The town's star attractions (apart from Maria Callas' holiday home) are the so-called grottoes of Catullus, and the moated mediaeval fortress, all swallow's-tail crenellations and reflections of ducks. Tennyson's been; and Ezra Pound bumped into James Joyce here.

But, for us, draw of the day is a Riva-style cruiser. OK, it's just a water taxi, but still. Approached by a rakishly handsome Italian speaking in a seductively incomprehensible rolling staccato, I thought my luck had turned, but Paolo is simply offering us a spin in his nice boat, on the cheap, since it's quiet. He navigates us round the tip of the peninsula, letting the engine idle and the wheel spin so he can take a snap of us as we pass the Augustan Roman villa on the headland. He waves his arms, gesticulating for us to get closer (to each other, presumably, not the perilous rocks).

It turns out to be the perfect picture: romantic, sunlit, elegant. It makes us look like the type who gad about Lake Garda on a speedboat, swapping trattoria tips with the captain. You can barely notice the sunburn.

Reviewed by Mr & Mrs Smith

NEED TO KNOW

Rooms 18, including four suites.

Rates €230–€450, including tax, a generous Continental buffet breakfast, on-site parking and WiFi.

Check-out 12 noon; late check-outs are possible, subject to availability (and a €50 charge). Earliest check-in, 2pm.

Facilities Landscaped grounds with olive groves and orchards, terrace, gym, Finnish sauna and treatment rooms. In rooms: flatscreen TV, air-conditioning, minifridge, Erbario Toscano olive-oil toiletries, robes, slippers, hairdryer.

Poolside With daydreamy views across Lake Garda, the outdoor infinity pool is flanked by lounger-sprinkled decking.

Children Welcome (this is Italy, after all). Extra beds (free for under-eights; otherwise €40–€80 a night) and cots (€20) can be added to suites. The restaurant is child-friendly, and nannies can be drafted in with a week's notice (€30 an hour).

Also Ayurvedic treatments, Shiatsu massage, Nordic walking, yoga and Pilates all available on request. Small pets welcome (€15 a night).

IN THE KNOW

Our favourite rooms Rooms are all decorated with the same light touch: neutral colours and simple, stylish furniture serve to highlight, rather than distract from, original beamed ceilings, terracotta floor tiles and 14th-century frescoes. Any one's a winner – ask for a lake view. Marble bathrooms are petite but practical, with walk-in showers and twin sinks.

Hotel bar Take top-notch tipples in the sophisticated wooden bar area, snugly set between the lounge and terrace. You can call for cocktails until midnight. Dip into a bottle of local Groppello, Bardolino or Soave from the excellent wine list.

Hotel restaurant Chef Walter Zanoni sources seasonal regional ingredients (some straight from the villa's kitchen garden) to create typical dishes with a twist: don't miss fresh pike plucked from the lake, delicious handmade gnocchi and zingy gelati. Two elegant rooms – vaulted stone ceilings, grand marble fireplaces and 18th-century prints – lead out onto a pretty terrace: the perfect place to drink in those *bella* vistas and bellinis.

Top table In summer, you'll want to dine alfresco: the terrace at night is enchanting, with soft-toned lanterns swinging among the vines and candles on every wrought-iron table.

Room service Dishes from the main menu can be ordered in-room between 8am until midnight – staff aim to please, so there's no harm in asking if you have a specific snack in mind.

Dress code This genteel hideaway inspires old-fashioned chic: discreet designer dresses, caramel cashmere, crisp linens.

Local knowledge The pretty port of Salò is just a short drive away, and there are plenty of eateries, bars and browsable boutiques to keep you entertained. Regular ferries sail from Salò to Sirmione, Garda and Limone, among other ports.

LOCAL EATING AND DRINKING

Top picks in Salò include Antica Trattoria alle Rose on Via Gasparo (+39 0365 43220), which has been serving up regional delights for 25 years, and its simpler sister outpost, wine bar Osteria dell'Orologio on Via Butturini (+39 0365 290158). Locanda del Benaco (+39 0365 20308) on Salò's lakeside promenade is perfectly positioned for *passegiata* pitstops; the lakefish tartare with black truffle is unmissable. Tucked down a cobbled alley in the town centre, Osteria di Mezzo (+39 0365 290966) is a local favourite for its fresh pastas and unswerving focus on Gardese ingredients and wines; the cheese trolley is fantastic. La Dispensa, a 10-minute drive away in San Felice di Benaco (+39 0365 557023), provides a mouthwatering Modern Italian menu care of chef Michele Bontempi, and the occasional live jazz set.

GET A ROOM!

Hotel details 2 via Palazzina, 25087 Salò (+39 0365 42281; hotelvillaarcadio.it).

To book Ring our expert Travel Team (you'll find all our numbers with your membership card on page 5) or go to mrandmrssmith.com/villa-arcadio.

 A bottle of local wine in your room; or, for members staying three nights or more, a three-course dinner for two (excluding alcoholic drinks) on one night of their stay.

SOUTH TYROL

COUNTRYSIDE Lofty peaks, lowly pines
COUNTRY LIFE Gourmet with altitude

Italy's northernmost region is dominated by the Dolomites, majestic mountains topped by towering slabs of rosy-hued rock. There's drama in its history, too: part of Austria until 1919, Südtirol is a characterful land where region trumps nation – a trait reflected in its language, culture and cuisine. In winter, the Sella Ronda circuit is a wonder: a dozen ski resorts dot the massif, including Alta Badia at its heart. In summer, *via ferrata* trails lure hikers and climbers with their natural highs. Both the spa town of Merano and ancient Bolzano are surrounded by mountains, shaped by turret- and dome-topped buildings, and share a smattering of museums recording the region's archaeology, nature and history – and both play second fiddle to their Dolomiti backdrop, a splendid year-round playground for gourmets and gadabouts.

GETTING THERE

Planes Innsbruck is the nearest internationally served airport, around two hours from Val Badia, or you can fly into Bolzano (75km away) via Rome.

Trains For South Tyrol's northerly resorts, Brunico is the main station, two and a half hours from Innsbruck, or Fortezza is an hour by car from Val Badia. In the south, direct trains from Venice to Belluno, or from Verona to Bolzano, take around two hours (trenitalia.com).

Automobiles Roads are straightforward – the A22 is the main north-south access road – then it's mountain winders all the way to Val Badia, so choose a car that can handle hairpins. Hire wheels at Bolzano or Innsbruck airports.

LOCAL KNOWLEDGE

Taxis Outside of regional railway stations, you'll need to book a cab, rather than hail one. Taxi Fedo is based in San Cassiano (+39 333 369 6535); Taxi Badia is a nearby alternative (+39 335 737 3981; taxibadia.it).

Siesta and fiesta Lunch is the main event here, so shops shut between noon and 2pm–3pm. Do your shopping before 7pm, and catch restaurant kitchens before 9pm.

Do go/don't go The ski slopes open from December to March. From May until autumn, the upland pastures are popular for walking, biking and riding. The turn-of-season shutdowns are post-Easter and in November.

Packing tips Swimming kit for spa moments; boots made for walking; a hip flask to fill with reviving sips of grappa.

Recommended reads Run for the hills, with Tim Parks' novel *Cleaver;* with Solomon, the pachydermal peak-crosser in *The Elephant's Journey* by José Saramago; or with legendary Tyrolean mountaineer Reinhold Messner, in his account of Himalayan triumph, *All 14 Eight-thousanders*.

Local specialities South Tyrol's Austrian genes mean fist-sized *canederli* or *knödel* (dumplings) have every course covered, served savoury with meat or cheese, as well as sweet with berry fillings, apples or apricots. Try the hearty *schlutzkrapfen* – Tyrolean spinach and ricotta ravioli. *Vinschger paarl* (rye bread rolls) are chewy and spiked with caraway; smoked speck is a tender and delicate ham. Sultanas and pine nuts make South Tyrolean pancakes, aka *kaiserschmarrn*, dangerously moreish.

And... What does a 5,000-year-old corpse have in common with Brad Pitt? Ötzi the Ice Man is on display at the South Tyrol Museum of Archaeology in Bolzano (iceman.it); he's also inked onto Brad's forearm.

WORTH GETTING OUT OF BED FOR

Viewpoint Take the Piz Sorega gondola lift from San Cassiano up to the Rifugio to enjoy a *cioccolato caldo* on the terrace with views over the village (pizsorega.it).

Arts and culture The nearest you'll get to a gallery in the Alta Badia region is the Galleria del Lagazuoi – this network of World War I tunnel-trenches is part of the open-air museum I Musei della Grande Guerra (+39 0436 2863), reachable by cable car at Passo Falzarego. Consider a trip to any of Reinhold Messner's Mountain Museums: the Museum in the Clouds (MMM Dolomites) is at 2,000 metres on Monte Rite – a former fort where artworks from the Romantic period to the present vie for your attention with the snow-dusted mountain scenery (+39 0435 890 996; messner-mountain-museum.it).

Activities The Alta Badia ski area offers 130km of red- and blue-graded slopes, perfect for intermediates (altabadia. org). Die-hard skiers and boarders will want to access the 500km of piste on the Sella Ronda circuit (dolomitisuperski. com). Heilig Kreuz arranges ski tours with palate-pleasing pit-stops (+39 0471 839645; santa-croce.it). The peaks, valleys and plateaux of Alta Badia are crisscrossed with mountain trails, patrolled by snowshoers and cross-country skiers in winter, and walkers in summer. Adrenaline Xtreme Adventures (+39 331 418 8007; adrenalineadventures.it) organises speedy cable slides 100 metres above the valley. Let the snow-melt warm up a little and, during summer months, tackle the rapids rafting, canyoning or kayaking with Peter Mair's River Tours (+39 347 442 8020; suedtirol-river-tours.com).

Perfect picnic Load up with salami, speck and goat's milk camembert from Delizius at 51 Micurà de Rü Strasse in San Cassiano (+39 0471 840155) and head to Corvara. From the Boé cable car, take the pretty path towards Colfosco, through the Borest woodland, and end up at the foot of the Pisciadù falls. Graze at leisure, then walk back via Colfosco and Pescosta.

Daytripper Follow the wine route west of Bolzano from Appiano south towards Salorno. Stop in Caldaro for tasting and lunch. The vine-striped slopes of the Ritterhof estate are topped by a chalet winery: sip gewürztraminer and try the lake's namesake Kalterer See reds (+39 0471 963298; ritterhof.it). Come summer, Castel Ringberg

opens up its lake-view terrace to diners, where you can feast on Stefan Unterkircher's seasonal menu, shaded by almond trees (+39 0471 960 010; castel-ringberg.com).

Walks From the top of the Piz Sorega chairlift, well-marked trails will take you towards Corvara or La Villa. To get away from it all, opt for routes that venture into the wooded plains of the Pralongiá plateau: high above San Cassiano, it has breathtaking branch-framed views. From Corvara, follow the riverside trail to the village of Pedraces. For more intrepid hikers, the Sella massif is home to a network of *via ferrata*, aka high mountain routes fixed with cables and ladders. You can download detailed itineraries, sorted by level of difficulty, at dolomiti.org.

Shopping Don't expect D&G to move to the mountains any time soon. Super-chic Cortina d'Ampezzo is your best bet for designer après-ski threads, with 250 boutiques and stores centred around Corso Italia. From late November, visit Bolzano's festive Christmas market for gingerbready stocking fillers, wooden toys and Alpine linens.

Something for nothing The *waalwege* footpaths trace ancient irrigation channels in the Vinschgau valley near Merano, cutting through picturesque orchards and chestnut woods to Juval Castle: make a day of it.

Don't go home without… having a hay bath. Südtirolers discovered hay's anti-rheumatic, joint-soothing qualities while snoozing on it in barns; now you can steam in it, infused with Alpine herbs, to ease stiffness, relieve tension and boost circulation. You'll find it on most local spa menus, including the one at Lagació Mountain Residence.

SUITABLY SOUTH TYROL

Ladin is a romance language once spoken widely across the Alps, as far as
Switzerland, now confined to 40,000 speakers in South Tyrol – to impress, greet them
with 'Bun dé'. Living mostly in Val Gardena, Val Badia and Cortina, the region's trilingual
locals speak Ladin, German and Italian, five per cent of them claiming Ladin as their
first language. A Ladin museum in San Martino documents its history (museumladin.it).

DIARY

Mid-January The Chef's Cup is a week of culinary events and ski races in Alta Badia (chefs
cup.it). Afterwards, vintage cars career around the Dolomites in the Winter Marathon
(wintermarathon.it). **Early March** Madonna di Campiglio residents camp it up as ye olde
aristocracy for the annual Habsburg Carnival (campigliodolomiti.it). **June** Bolzano's Old Town
hosts live music and foodie displays for the South Tyrol Gourmet Festival (suedtirol.info).
September Make a beeline for Bressanone's Piazza Duomo and carbo-load at the Bread
and Strudel Market (suedtirol.info). **November** The Merano Wine Festival and Culinaria
are twin comestible festivals (meranowinefestival.com). **December** Downhill daredevils
descend on Val Gardena and Alta Badia for the Men's Skiing World Cup (fis-ski.com).

Lagació Mountain Residence

STYLE Chalet-chic apartments
SETTING Deep in the Dolomites

'Forget Alpine clichés: wooden shutters and chintzy woodcarvings are out; sharp corners are in. See-through sides invite you to take a bloody good look at that Südtirol scenery'

There's something about travelling to Italy via Austria that's like watching a stripper who begins their act wearing a welder's mask and Crimplene pantsuit. However, as our plane swoops between the mountains, searching out Innsbruck's runway, notions of national distinctions give way to an appreciation of general European mountainy-ness.

To catch this early flight, Mrs Smith and I were are up at 4.30am, having rented a cell in an economy airport hotel. An oxymoronic start to a period of relaxation, perhaps, but the paucity of passengers at least offsets the usual security hell. Restorative dozing through a two-hour flight and two-hour hotel transfer makes us chipper by the time we arrive at Lagació Mountain Residence.

Forget Alpine clichés: in this tiny north-east Italian hamlet of San Cassiano, wooden shutters and chintzy woodcarvings are out, and sharp corners and glass panels are in. Lagació's see-through sides demonstrate the owners' appreciation that, however incredible their

hotel is, its guests are really here for what's outside. And they invite you to get a bloody good look at all that stunning Südtirolean scenery.

Environment and sustainability is important at Lagació, but never at the cost of luxury. Everything is natural. Take the fossils, for example. They're all over the gaff. Handpicked from these very mountains, the stony motifs show Margareth and Pio Canin's dedication to fusing eco-consciousness with local relics. They appear everywhere, from room numbers to floor signs – a cute design touch, but also a bizarre memento mori. They call to mind childhood revelations that our planet has played host to bygone beings; odd monsters and dark creatures. Intended to inspire us to push ourselves harder on the slopes or to indulge without guilt, perhaps? Mrs Smith and I do both, just to be on the safe side.

Thanks to our early flight, we are up a mountain by late morning – me on my snowboard and my lady with snowshoes. Then, after the thrills of the piste, we throw ourselves into Lagació's epicurean delights. A short walk away at Rosa Alpina, there is the excellent Grill and the Michelin-starred St Hubertus. Mrs Smith and I soon learn that we prefer our restaurants less fussy, our food less pernickety, and our meals to cost less than €500. Taking the advice of Lagació's receptionist, we discover we are financially better off next to the Piz Sorega bubble lift in the strip-lit, diner-style Ski Bar – where we enjoy some of the most delicious pizza ever.

Many guests, though, cook lunch and evening meals themselves. Baskets of organic produce can be pre-ordered to stock your cupboards. There are five classes of apartment available at Lagació; we are in the second smallest, yet the intelligent layout and posh fittings make it feel larger than your usual suite. A pine-clad hall leads to an open-plan kitchen-cum-salon, with a glass wall at the end framing that staggering Piz Sorega view. And an enormous double bed – crisp white cotton sheets, an excess of pillows – is all that stands between us and the two-person bath.

The bathroom is that special mix of black slate and designer fixtures that makes a simple shower feel like a deleted scene from *American Psycho*. Not a murdery moment, mind; a bit where you'd go, 'Ooh, isn't his apartment nice?'

Being rubbed, buffed and scrubbed is another feature of a Lagació stay, thanks to spa La Palsa. Mrs Smith opts for a Dr Hauschka facial and shouty-looking Relaxing Full Body Massage, whereas I, being a terribly manly sort, have a Full Body Sports Massage in an attempt to put right some of my self-inflicted snowboarding damage.

And the saunas! They are, well, saunas (you know the sort of thing: tongue-and-groove, hotter than hot), but these bad boys border on preternatural, location-wise. Huge slices of rock act as modesty screens, and ice cascades into a stone font for therapeutic rubbing. A dark slate steam room feels very grown-up and, dare I say it, sexy. Next-door, a relaxation lounge with ergonomic eco-furniture and a surfeit of herbal infusions leads to a

'Sliding down the Dolomites at high speed and masseuse-applied ylang-ylang prove a heady mix'

second outdoor sauna and a giant water-filled barrel for that all-important pore-closing sub-zero dip. Just thinking 'I've never jumped into a big barrel of cold water before' is enough to make you want to try it. A word of advice: allow extra time after your sauna for your internal and external organs to return to their usual locations.

Piste-activated adrenalin and masseuse-applied ylang-ylang prove a heady mix, and Mrs Smith and I pat ourselves on the back for leaving our offspring in the bosom of his London-based grandparents. As an urbanite, the opportunity to tit about in nature is a rare treat indeed. I imagine that any trip here is very much focused on sliding down the Dolomites at high speed – and for that Lagació Mountain Residence makes the ideal base. The Fairtrade cherry on this organic panettone? Being able to step directly from the piste's powdery playground into unabashed luxury.

Reviewed by **Rufus Hound**, comedian

NEED TO KNOW

Rooms 24 suites.

Rates €146–€890, including Continental breakfast, tax and shuttle rides to and from the Alta Badia ski resort.

Check-out 11am; later check-out may be possible, but there's a day's charge. Earliest check-in, 3pm.

Facilities Ski shop; ski room with boot dryer; spa with treatment rooms, saunas, crushed-ice well and fitness room; free WiFi throughout. In rooms: kitchenette (refrigerator, dishwasher, microwave, Nespresso machine); balcony; flatscreen TV; hairdryer; felt bag containing bathrobes, towels and slippers.

Children The apartment-style lodging is ideal for families – cots or extra beds cost €15; €50 for over-threes. Alternatively, choose a two-bedroom suite: Claraia and Daonella have bunk beds in one room; the Ammonite suite has two double bedrooms and a terrace. Babysitting can be arranged.

Also Each suite has its own natural drinking-water fountain, fed by a spring. The reviving La Palsa spa offers facials, massages (some using honey and chocolate), Ayurvedic therapies and body peels.

IN THE KNOW

Our favourite rooms Marvel at the Dolomites from the comfort of east-facing Claraia's sleek couch. Honeymooners should book Bellerophon, which has a terrace running the length of the apartment and Lagazuoi mountain views. Ammonite has a seductive leather-upholstered bed, an open fireplace in its living room and a Kneipp shower.

Hotel bar Begin the day with a couple of coffees in the slate-floored, terracotta-walled Lagació Bar, before hitting the slopes or hiking the hills in summer. Return in the evening for potent mountain aperitifs and the sounds of jazz fusion; in winter, there are hearty organic South Tyrolean bar snacks available on request.

Hotel restaurant A 'best of' breakfast buffet spread highlighting the region's freshest natural fare is laid out in the Stube, a set of three rooms all panelled in reclaimed wood; throw your five dailies into the noisy juicer.

Top table Aim for a table by the floor-to-ceiling windows, to make the most of the light and elbow room.

Room service Order up cheese, cured meats, cakes, toast and pie until 11pm. Select organic goodies (including baby food) and supplies from the hotel's in-house list two weeks before you arrive; the groceries will be left in your kitchen.

Dress code Post-slopes comfort: designer denim and casual cashmere.

Local knowledge Rent or buy equipment from the hotel's onsite ski shop; have the concierge arrange your ski passes. The Alta Badia area offers winter sports activities for beginners and pros, including toboggan runs and a snowboard fun park.

LOCAL EATING AND DRINKING

St Hubertus (+39 0471 849500), at the Rosa Alpina hotel in San Cassiano, has garnered two Michelin stars. The same hotel's Wine Bar & Grill is less formal, serving hearty meat dishes and superb pizza from its wood-fired oven. Take a table on the terrace overlooking the market, and listen to the brass band as you sample aged prosciutto and buffalo mozzarella. Casually elegant La Siriola (+39 0471 849445), where Fabio Cucchelli fashions basic local ingredients into culinary fireworks, is a three-minute drive from Lagació, at Hotel Ciasa Salares; there's a fantastic wine bar, too, serving *cicchetti* (and more) alongside a good range of biodynamic wines. Take the cable car from the centre of San Cassiano to the top of Piz Sorega, where you'll find Utia Punta Trieste (+39 0471 836643), an all-wood mountain refuge on the Pralongia plateau above Corvara. Set the mood by sipping prosecco in the wine-tasting hut outside.

GET A ROOM!

Hotel details 48 via Micurà de Rü, 39030 San Cassiano, Alta Badia (+39 0471 849503; lagacio.com)

To book Ring our expert Travel Team (you'll find all our numbers with your membership card on page 5) or go to mrandmrssmith.com/lagacio-mountain-residence.

 Welcome drinks; 10 per cent off spa treatments; and a 10 per cent discount on equipment and rentals from the hotel's Alta Badia ski shop (altabadiaskirental.com).

TREVISO

CITYSCAPE Little lanes, big reflections
CITY LIFE Calm café culture

Looping mediaeval alleyways, frescoed façades, well-stocked galleries and shimmering canals: so far, so Serenissima – but this is Treviso. Venice's compact cousin is a more peaceful proposition: instead of tourists, cobbled streets yield Gothic gargoyles and cloisters; instead of gondolas, the waters reflect leafy willows and waterwheels. Treviso has its own riches – mighty churches and vivid Renaissance art, ancient palaces and stylish citizens. Artists' hearts will sing with inspiration here: there are peachy-pink buildings, borage-blue skies and plenty of inspiring scenes to choose from: the lively *pescheria*, where locals have haggled for fish since the 1800s, or the colourful canals, which are still the city's veins. Like Treviso's two signature treats, prosecco and tiramisu, a stay here is a sweet, indulgent pick-me-up.

GETTING THERE

Planes Treviso's international airport just 15 minutes outside the city (+39 0422 315111; trevisoairport.it). Alternatively, Venice's Marco Polo airport (+39 041 260 9260; veniceairport.it) is 30km away.

Trains Treviso Centrale is a 10-minute walk from the city centre, and has regular connections to Venice, Padua, Milan, Trieste, and other popular stop-offs. Marco Polo is half an hour and a handful of euros away (trenitalia.com).

Boats Start as you mean to go on, by entering the city on a water taxi. The passage from Venice costs around €55 (shuttleforyou.com).

Automobiles Gadding about by foot or water is the most enjoyable way to see the city, but if wheels are non-negotiable, the A27 connects Venice and Treviso (a drive of approximately an hour). From further afield, the E70 crosses the top of Italy, leading into Turin and Switzerland.

LOCAL KNOWLEDGE

Taxis Try VIP Service (+39 393 808 0801) or Radio Taxi Treviso (+39 0422 431515; taxitreviso.it).

Siesta and fiesta Shops shut for a leisurely lunch between 12.30pm and 3pm, opening again until 7pm, when shopping makes way for contemplative fizz-sipping and olive-nibbling. Check before visiting a restaurant on a Sunday or Monday: many are closed then.

Do go/don't go Treviso is an all-year charmer but, as you'd expect, the streets are liveliest in the summer.

Packing tips A capsule wardrobe that spans boat trips, bike rides, gallery jaunts and nocturnal gallivanting.

Recommended reads The ubiquitous Benetton label hails from Treviso – read the brand's rag-to-riches story in Jonathan Mantle's *Benetton*; Victoria Moore's *How to Drink* (a useful companion to any boozy holiday) has an insightful section on prosecco; swot up on frescoes and paintings with Evelyn Welch's *Art in Renaissance Italy*.

Local specialities Sample *sopressa* (garlicky pork salami), served with velvety polenta and earthy funghi. Risotto features *bruscandoli* (hop shoots), or Treviso's peppery raddichio. Order bowls of golden *sopa coada*: roast pigeon, in a soup enriched with wine and bread. Unsurprisingly, pasta features heavily: try *bigoli*, a rough-cut spaghetti, and pasta e *fagioli* (with beans). Familiarise yourself with the region's *cicchetti* (small plates) at the warm-hearted L'Antica Osteria al Cavallino (+39 0422 412801) at 52 Borgo Cavour. Order prosecco di Conegliano-Valdobbiadene (the hilly Veneto regions of the same names are famous for their fizzy nectars).

WORTH GETTING OUT OF BED FOR

Viewpoint Unsurprisingly for a city built on pancake-flat plains, canals and cycle paths are more common than vistas over the city. That said, the Ponte Dante bridge and Buranelli canal both offer picture-perfect water views.

Arts and culture Santa Caterina (+39 0422 544864) on Piazzetta Mario Botter is a former church and convent blessed with Tommaso da Modena frescoes; the town's stash of archaeology and statuary is also housed here, in the Civic Museum. Casa dei Carraresi (+39 0422 513150), a beautiful 13th-century building overlooking the Botteniga river and the Pescheria on Via Palestro, hosts temporary art exhibitions. Visit the Duomo for its Titian altarpiece, time-worn crypt and Byzantine-frescoes. The City Museum L Bailo, set in a former Jesuit monastery on Borgo Cavour, has three main themes: architecture, art from the Renaissance to the 19th century, and modern works by local artists.

Activities Hire bikes from Pinarello (+39 0422 543821) at Borgo Giuseppe Mazzini, and wend your way along the banks of the Sile. Oenophiles should explore Veneto's L'Anello del Prosecco: the 'prosecco ring' is a 10km footpath connecting villages and vineyards. Follow in the footsteps of Robert Browning and visit Asolo, an arty town outside Treviso that holds a wonderful antiques market on every second Sunday (except July and August). Villa di Maser is a 16th-century masterpiece designed by Andrea Palladio set in gorgeous grounds – no wonder it's a Unesco heritage site (+39 0423 923004; villadimaser.it).

Perfect picnic This city is designed for café crawls, but if you're intent on an al fresco pitch, hunker down on the spot of grass off Via Giuseppe Tonioli, overlooking the Sile. There are plenty of *pasticcerie* to pick up supplies from, but if you want something pre-assembled, grab a meaty panino and some wine from Dai Naneti on Vicolo Broli.

Daytripper It would be a crime against culture to miss Venice, given that it's just 25km away. If you've been there/done that/got the T-shirt, drive to Padua to admire the mind-bogglingly beautiful Giotto frescoes in the Cappella degli Scrovegni (cappelladegliscrovegni.it). The chapel's walls, ceilings and floors are decorated with 38

dramatic scenes. It's popular: early booking is essential.

Walks Amble along the city's mediaeval walls: the section between the San Tommaso and Santi Quaranta gates showcases some of the city's finest historic architecture. Or try a leisurely stroll along the riverbanks, admiring the rustic red-brick houses and green gardens.

Shopping Lined with fashion and homewares boutiques, Treviso's smartest shopping streets are Via Calmaggiore, Corso del Popolo and Via XX Settembre. Benetton is honoured with a monumental flagship store on Piazza Indipendenza. Don't miss fashion and lifestyle shop Pot-Pourri, stocked with beautiful clothes, equestrian-style leather accessories, candles and cushions. There are three boutiques, in Asolo (the closest), Mestre and Venice (+39 0423 529374; potpourri.it). If you prefer antiques to labels, try the Borgo Cavour market, held on the fourth Sunday of every month (except July). Join the throngs at open-air fruit, flower and clothes markets on Tuesdays and Saturdays (7.30am–1.30pm) at Viale Burchiellati, Piazzale Bartolomeo Burchiellati, Borgo Mazzini or Piazza Matteotti.

Something for nothing Admire the evocative 14th-century frescoes in the church of San Nicolò, including a tender rendering of the Madonna and her attendant angels by Tommaso da Modena.

Don't go home without... visiting the lively fish market, held every Tuesday on Isola della Pescheria, a little island connected to the city by two bridges. Expect to see an international array of salty specimens (including mullet, scorpion fish, sea bream and crabs).

TASTEFULLY TREVISO

There are two tales behind the origin of tiramisu, Treviso's trademark dish: the first is that it was a prostitutes' booster; in the second, when weary new mum Alba Campeol tried her mother-in-law's coffee-laced zabaglione, she liked it so much she recreated it on her restaurant menu. Alba's son Carlo now heads up Ristorante Beccherie Di Campeol Carlo on Piazza Ancilotto Giannino (+39 0422 540871), and still serves up her original recipe.

DIARY

February–June Primavera del Prosecco is a four-month celebration of the sparkling stuff, with tastings and exhibitions across the region (primaveradelprosecco.it). **March** On the second Sunday of the month, a marathon takes place between Vittorio Veneto and Treviso. Concerts in the city centre spur on contestants and keep the crowds entertained (trevisomarathon.com). Trevisani proudly honour their white asparagus season, with tastings and displays at the end of the month (trevisoinfo.com/asparagusfestivals). **June** The Buranelli Party is a traditional festival held by the *pescheria* on the last weekend of the month, with puppet shows, concerts, plenty of succulent seafood, and comedically speedy serving staff, competing to deliver trays of drinks unspilled in the waiters' race.

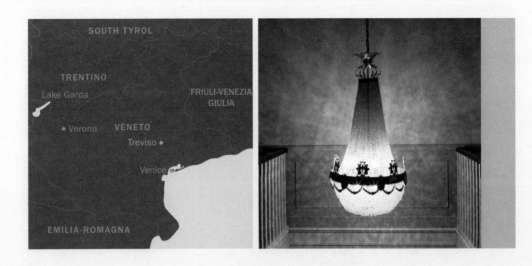

Maison Matilda

STYLE *Casa famiglia*
SETTING Venice's tranquil twin

'There's a beautiful terrace, chandeliers, wooden beams, opera on a little stereo in the room. What more could you want? Turtles in a tank? They've got those, too'

I want to be an Italian man. I'd live in Maison Matilda permanently. I'd definitely be less bald. I'd wake up every morning, pour *balsamico* all over my sturdy torso, run my hands through my thick black forest of equine hair, argue passionately with Mrs Smith, then make love to her like I've never made love before. (Longer than two minutes.)

Maison Matilda is turbo-brilliant. Hang on – we'll get back to this – let's start with Treviso. Why would you want to visit this town in northern Italy? I'd never heard of it. Gentle research revealed it's the birthplace of tiramisu. That in itself is a perfectly good reason to visit a place. And, it turns out, Treviso is a clever person's way of going to Venice: it's 20 minutes away by train but you don't have to hang around with all those tourists. (But we'll come to that later. This is getting a bit disjointed: I've already got two stories on hold. Stay with me – I'm just a bit excited.)

So, why is Maison Matilda so brilliant? It's small, which I like; there are only six rooms. It's the perfect display of modern Italian design. It makes you want to steal things.

I was walking around working out what I would fill my suitcase with (I calculated two lamps, if I went for the smaller vase and threw out my socks and underwear). Would it be ridiculous to check out sweating and sobbing under the weight of a hat that looks suspiciously like a solid marble horse? It's got to be worth a go.

There are even secret doors. You know the ones – where it just looks like a bit of wall? Maison Matilda has loads of them. Our rooms were behind one of them. Yep, you heard me: *rooms*. Plural. We had two bedrooms, a bathroom, a dressing area and a little study, all behind our secret door. The bed is massive. There is literally prosecco coming out of the taps. (I actually mean that unliterally. But you do get a free glass of it on arrival.) They make you breakfast whenever you wake up. There's a little area with free biscuits. (I love the way that, even though we're paying €300 or so a night, I still feel like I'm winning if I can stuff three complimentary biscuits in my mouth without anyone seeing.) There's a beautiful terrace, chandeliers, wooden beams, opera on a little stereo in the room. What more could you want? Turtles swimming in a tank? They've got those, too.

Treviso itself is pretty good. I confess I feared it was a bit rubbish at first. Don't be deceived by the big-retail-park look; as you get inside the old city wall, everything comes over all *Godfather.* We went to Antico Ristorante alle Beccherie on the first night, and our meal was delicious. It's the restaurant where tiramisu was invented; the creamy coffee dessert was created here as a little snack to perk up prostitutes between shifts, to give them a 'sexy energy boost'. (I find this very hard to believe, as it seemed to have the opposite effect on Mrs Smith.)

After supper, we went to the bar opposite where they only serve wine and ham. If you go to Treviso you *must* spend a night here. By the early hours I was slow-dancing to David Bowie with a very affectionate man (he had a great head of hair), while Mrs Smith was being serenaded by a slightly

scary Italian version of Il Divo (all with great heads of hair). Things started to turn quite surreal after that, so we staggered home where I fell asleep to the chiming bells of Treviso and the belching of a woman who'd eaten too much tiramisu.

I can't express just how pleasant it is to wake up in Maison Matilda. There's no set time for breakfast: you just pad out of the room in comfy clothes whenever you like. We were properly hungover, and would have paid to have damp rags dragged across our lips; the waiter couldn't press oranges fast enough. We also met the lovely owner – Elena, who named the hotel for her daughter Matilda – and she told us all the amazing furniture was picked up at auctions across Italy and France. Elena then gave us a Venice train timetable and waved us off for a romantic day in the sun.

You know that thing where you're running for a train, with a hangover, and the words 'Venezia' and

'Vicenza' suddenly look exactly the same? 'Trust me, this is our train,' I rasped as I hurled Mrs Smith onboard. Twenty minutes later we were expecting to see some water. Venice is an island, right? ('Archipelago, actually,' sighed Mrs Smith.) Whatever: outside were fields. After half an hour, we realised we were going in the wrong direction; we ploughed into mainland Italy for over an hour before alighting at Vicenza. Not a lot goes on in Vicenza, as we found out. By the time we got to Venice, the 'quick' journey had taken four and half hours; Mrs Smith and I by now were communicating with hisses.

I won't bother banging on about Venice: you've seen the films. It's charming. Except, well, it's just the tourists. They're *everywhere*. Like a long stream of leafcutter ants holding up huge cameras and cooing at anything with a gargoyle on it. I just wanted to be back in Treviso. This could well have been because Mrs Smith kept going on about a stolen kiss she had with a Spanish man called José while she was interrailing. 'It was definitely on this bridge… oh no, actually I think it was that bridge,' and so on. There are more than a hundred bridges in Venice. I hate José.

We went back to Maison Matilda. (Is it embarrassing to admit we watched *X-Factor* on my laptop curled up in our beautiful bed? It's probably worse to admit that we had to wake up the manager to get the WiFi password in order to do so. It's awful being English. He didn't mind. He's got such a thick head of hair, I'm sure he doesn't mind anything.) So our story ends with the two of us curled up in a bed bigger than my flat, in a chrysalis of Egyptian cotton. Simon Cowell's beetroot face casts dancing shadows across the marble ornaments while the gentle tapping of charming Italian men striding home in leather shoes occasionally drowns out the awful singing. On a holiday that offered gondolas, architecture and fine dining, that was the bit I'll remember forever. *Grazie mille*, Matilda.

Reviewed by **Oli Beale**, advertising creative

NEED TO KNOW

Rooms Six, including one suite.

Rates €160–€350, including all-day home-made breakfast.

Check-out 12 noon, but you can stay a little longer if there's no-one else booked in. Earliest check-in, 1pm.

Facilities Library, free WiFi throughout. In rooms: flatscreen TV, CD player, Tivoli radio, Ortigia bath products, Nespresso coffee, Mariage Frères tea and soft drinks.

Children Cots are provided free; extra beds for 8–14-year-olds cost €50 a night (otherwise they're €80).

Also In-room beauty treatments can be arranged.

IN THE KNOW

Our favourite rooms True to its name, La Romantica is a love den worth swooning over for its red lacquered four-poster bed that's king-size but feels bigger, high ceilings with white wooden beams, parquet flooring, shower for two, and peaceful private terrace with views over the courtyard. Cosy and inviting, La Musica – taking up the whole top floor – has a treehouse-y feel and is teched out with a Bang & Olufsen sound system (hence the name). 'Best Bathroom' prize goes to La Suite, which dazzles with its Carrera marble-clad number.

Hotel bar There's no bar, but there's an in-room soft-drink stash, and staff will serve stronger refreshments anywhere in the hotel. The owners often host cocktail evenings.

Hotel restaurant None, but Maison Matilda's only a stroll away from some great restaurants. Breakfast can be served at any time of day in your bedroom, by the fire in the living room, on the terrace, or in the courtyard.

Top table Shotgun the sunloungers on the terrace, or settle in with a book on the sleek ivory sofa.

Room service Nothing formal, but staff will do whatever they can if you ask.

Dress code Match the decor: start with vintage, supplement with neutral, and embellish with contemporary.

Local knowledge Taste the province's finest prosecco with a trip north to the Follador winery, an estate that sits between Conegliano and Valdobbiadene in Col San Martino and has been producing fine fizz since 1769 (+39 0438 989566; folladorprosecco.com).

LOCAL EATING AND DRINKING

Hit Piazza dei Signori, five minutes' walk away, if you're in need of an aperitivo or digestivo; safe bets are Bar Biffi (+39 0422 178 5458) and Bar Beltrame (+39 0422 540789). Just beyond the piazza on Vicolo Broli, local secret Osteria Dai Naneti has a vineyard's worth of wine bottles, hams hanging from the ceiling and the finest cheeses and meats in town. Take a 10-minute stroll from the hotel and wine/dine overlooking the peaceful mill at Vineria Università on Largo Umanesimo Latino (+39 0422 419787), or a 10-minute drive to its scenic out-of-town sibling on Via Castellana (+39 0422 210460). Also close, the kitchens of Antico Ristorante alle Beccherie on Piazza Ancilotto are the stuff of legend: tiramisu was created here (+39 0422 540871). Try the signature Venetian-style sardines at perpetually packed-out Toni del Spin on Via Inferiore (+39 0422 543829).

GET A ROOM!

Hotel details 44 via Jacopo Riccati, 31100 Treviso (+39 0422 582212; maisonmatilda.com)

To book Ring our expert Travel Team (you'll find all our numbers with your membership card on page 5) or go to mrandmrssmith.com/maison-matilda.

 A glass of prosecco each and free parking.

VENICE

CITYSCAPE Archipelago of alleyways
CITY LIFE Walking on water

It may seem curious in a city that sits out in the sea and is characterised by glittering waterways, but it's walking you'll do most of when you visit Venice. A beautiful city that prompts planet-wide superlatives, it's an atmospheric maze in which to lose yourself (despite high-season throngs). Built right on the water's edge, La Serenissima hides the snap-happy sightseers well; drift down canals by gondola and float back in time as you admire Byzantine, Renaissance and Baroque architecture. Give film-familiar Piazza San Marco a chance to sink in, then follow the locals off the main drags to the best restaurants, hidden churches and lively markets. With so many *palazzi* and *piazze* to discover, this is a place for early nights and misty mornings spent wandering charming, traffic-free alleys – it is the romance capital of the world, after all.

GETTING THERE

Planes Marco Polo (veniceairport.com) and Treviso (treviso airport.com) are the city's two airports: from Marco Polo take the ferry, or arrive in style on a speedboat (around €100 each). From Treviso, it's a 25-minute taxi journey (€70); or 80 minutes on an ATVO Eurobus (€5).
Trains Of the city's two main stations, Santa Lucia is city central; mainland Venezia Mestre is the stop for through trains (grandistazioni.it). Take a sleeper service from Munich (citynightline.de) or Paris (artesia.eu); the Orient Express offers the ultimate rail ride (orient-express.com).
Automobiles Cars are redundant here: park on the mainland if you've hired wheels to explore beyond Venice.
Boats Venice's *vaporettos* (water buses) provide an easy, inexpensive way to get from A to B (actv.it). They all take the same route, but differ in how many stops they make.

LOCAL KNOWLEDGE

Taxis Use water buses (€6.50 a journey; €16 for a one-day travelcard); for private transfers, hail a (pricier) water taxi.
Siesta and fiesta Business hours are standard 9am–5pm, extending to banks, attractions and museums; shops close around lunchtime and reopen 4pm–8pm. Book restaurants to dine between 8pm and 10pm.
Do go/don't go August is hot, sticky and crowded. Autumn can be lovely; November is quietly fabulous when the city is cloaked in fog. February is great if you're going to a carnival ball, but trying to find a hotel room then is no picnic; September's film festival is similarly challenging.
Packing tips Bubble wrap for protecting fragile purchases; sleeved tops and at-least-mid-length skirts or trousers to cover up while visiting the city's holy sites.
Recommended reads Tears before bedtime in Thomas Mann's classic *Death in Venice*; macabre goings-on in *The Comfort of Strangers* by Ian McEwan; or a romp through time in *A History of Venice* by John Julius Norwich.
Local specialities Venetians work many intriguing wonders with the fruits of the sea: *risotto nero*, stained black with cuttlefish ink; silky marinated sardines and hearty fish soup. Bloodier fare also hails from these shores: carpaccio was conceived at Harry's Bar and named for the painter whose visceral works deck the Gallerie dell'Accademia. Recipes often include ingredients recalling Venice's merchant days (pine nuts, raisins, pomegranates). Veneto

wines include soave, valpolicella and prosecco: quality varies, so look for reliable vineyards such as Anselmi (try the San Vicenzo; robertoanselmi.com), Pieropan (for soave classico; pieropan.it), and Allegrini (for valpolicella; allegrini.it). Venetian tapas – *cicchetti* – are little savoury mouthfuls, best enjoyed around 12 noon with a thimbleful of wine. **And…** Venice comprises 117 islands, 409 bridges and some 150 canals; it's the only city centre in Europe to function entirely without cars; even ambulances float here.

WORTH GETTING OUT OF BED FOR

Viewpoint Piazza San Marco, aka St Mark's Square, is the heart of the city; get a 360-degree sunset-enhanced vista from the top of the Campanile. For a different perspective, book a tour of 16th-century clock tower, Torre dell'Orologio, overlooking the square (vivaticket.it).
Arts and culture Venice is packed full of churches, galleries and museums: top of every tourist's hit list are the Gallerie dell'Accademia, a former convent housing works from the 14th to 18th centuries (gallerieaccademia.org); the Basilica di San Marco, which has golden mosaics trumped only by a Pala d'Oro altarpiece (basilicasanmarco.it), and the adjoining Doge's Palace, ornate Gothic seat of Venice's former republic (museicivicivenezani.it). We love the Peggy Guggenheim Collection in Dorsoduro (guggenheim-venice.it) and International Gallery of Modern Art at Ca' Pesaro (+39 041 721127; San Stae waterbus stop).
Activities Cross the lagoon by speedboat with Consorzio Motoscafi Venezia (+39 041 522 2303; motoscafivenezia.it), or fly figures of eight above it in a chopper (heliairvenice.com). See everyday Venice on an early morning stroll through the Rialto Fish Market (Tuesday–Saturday): once a bazaar for treasures from the Orient, it now sells fresh everything-from-the-sea. Have a private cooking lesson in an art deco villa on the Lido, or taste wines in a palazzo, with Venice Gourmet (venicevenetogourmet.com). Listen to Baroque music played on period instruments at the jaw-dropping, Tintoretto-decked Scuola Grande di San Rocco (+39 348 190 8939; musicinvenice.com). Journey into a romantic otherworld on a gondola ride; negotiate prices first, though – they can be very steep.
Best beach You can rent cabanas and umbrellas for the day on the private stretches of Venice's beach, the Lido, but they don't come cheap. There are public beaches at either end of the island; rent bikes on Gran Viale from Venice Bike Rental (venicebikerental.com) or Lido on Bike at 21b Santa Maria Elisabetta (lidoonbike.it) and explore, or find quieter shores at Sant'Erasmo near Burano.
Daytripper The island of Torcello is the classic place to go for an afternoon of peace when La Serenissima is less than serene: for calm upon calm, sit in its 11th-century cathedral, Santa Maria Assunta. To get there, take the LN vaporetto line to Burano, then the T to Torchello.
Walks Unplanned meanders and corner-peeking are a must in Venice, but if you like treasure hunts, you'll love *Venice: The Ruyi* (whaiwhai.com/en), an interactive app tour of the city based on a coded book: SMS the hidden codes you find at each historic location to get clues.
Shopping You'll find designer labels around San Marco, and especially on Calle Larga 22 Marzo. Boutiques and gift shops line the streets between Piazza San Marco and the Rialto. Don't buy souvenirs in tourist areas: go to Dorsoduro for masks from Ca'Macana on Calle delle Botteghe (+39 041 277 6142); or buy a *forcole*, the wooden oar-rest from a gondola, from Saverio Pastor's workshop on Fondamenta Soranzo (forcole.com). For Murano glass, visit the island itself; ditto for Burano lace.
Something for nothing Get a taste of what it feels like to be on a gondola for (next to) nothing: follow 'Traghetto' signs leading to the water; the shuttle service costs just 50c. The real thing will cost €100 an hour; singing is extra.
Don't go home without… having a *caffè* in Piazza San Marco. The price will set your heart racing faster than a ristretto will, but there's a reason tourists flock here – it's beautiful. Caffè Florian (caffeflorian.com) is legendary.

VERY VENICE

There's no fee for turning up during carnival, but you need tickets to attend a ball. Tragicomica (tragicomica.it) is the *mascarero* and costumier behind the Mascheranda ball (carnivalofvenice.com). Venetian-born Antonia Sautter, another respected costume designer, organises the opulent Ballo del Doge (ilballodeldoge.com). Tickets for events are expensive (€300–€600), but if you are going to go to the ball, it's best to go all out.

DIARY

February Venice Carnival unleashes masked-ball mayhem (carnevale.venezia.it). **May/June** The start of the Venice Biennale, an extravaganza of art, dance, theatre and more, held every two years (labiennale.org). **July** Flamboyant fireworks commemorate the end of the 16th-century plague at the Fiesta del Redentore (redentorevenezia.it). **August–September** The Venice Film Festival brings cinema greats from Hollywood and Europe to the Lido for 10 days of events and screenings (labiennale.org/en/cinema); make sure you've booked your accommodation well in advance. On the first Sunday of September, the Regata Storica is a spectacular boat race: see gondoliers in full regalia line up to compete in their magnificent traditional vessels (regatastoricavenezia.it).

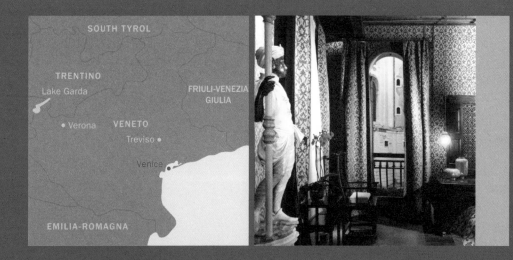

Ca Maria Adele

STYLE Baroque elegance
SETTING Canalside charm

'Ancient oak beams cross a high ceiling, above a bed the height of Olympus, as wide as the Grand Canal. And the view! We could take mass from under our duvet'

s it how Venice lies along the gulf like an ageing courtesan on her chaise-longue, being caressed by the Adriatic? Maybe it's the continual rocking of the pontoons. Either way: Venice is sexy. Especially when you are away from family, paperwork and *Newsnight* in bed for a whole weekend. Ah, Ca Maria Adele – even saying the name of our proposed place of repose is as pleasurable as a kiss of Mrs Smith's neck.

Splashes from water taxis fuelled by diesel and espresso-pumped young men elicit squeals of pleasure and the occasional '*Vaffanculo*'. I cover Mrs Smith's ears. No need for us to rush – an idling introduction is what this glamorous getaway needs, and we jump aboard Vaporetto 1 to cross the Grand Canal to Salute.

A few islands later, San Marco comes into sight. Mrs Smith hugs me tightly. Santa Maria della Salute's fleshy, muscular saints loom next – a soothing contrast to the tourist-besieged San Marco. Here in the bosom of this glorious building lies Ca Maria Adele. A private dock

coaxes us to its elegant reception, resplendent in gold marble and deep African teak. We pass dark velvet wall-linings, gold picture frames, yellow flowers and rich oak. 'Venetian rock star crossed with gothic Withnail,' muses Mrs Smith. We can't wait to see our room.

Too early for check-in, we forgo a coffee in the hotel, and take a stroll around Dorsoduro. The neighbourhood is quiet and serene; within a few hundred yards, Mrs Smith and I are alone in shoulder-wide alleys that end at canals. Washing hangs from lines draped across courtyards. We pause in a bar full of chattering locals enjoying cold white wine and crusty bread with prawns before returning to our bellboy, by now poised to show us to our top-floor boudoir.

Ancient oak beams clad a high ceiling above a bed the height of Olympus, as wide as the Grand Canal. At its foot is a gondola-sized bath. Mrs Smith is beside herself. And the view! Santa Maria della Salute looms so large we could take mass from under our duvet.

Reluctantly, we prise ourselves away – the Peggy Guggenheim Museum, former home of the ex-flapper socialite and art passionista, beckons. Minutes later, we're surrounded by Peggy's 20th-century collection of Pollocks, Picassos, Mirós and Magrittes. It feels wonderfully naughty to wallow in modern art while touring this historic waterside city.

Masterpieces ogled and appetites whetted, we consult Alessandro at Ca Maria Adele about dinner and he books us into the Linea Dombra on Canale della Giudecca. In a bid to freshen up, I set my sights on the Jacuzzi, and discover, to my delight, that our tub lights up like a Seventies disco. Mrs Smith soon tires of my pyrotechnics and demands attention before we take the two-minute skip to our high-end supper spot.

Leaving the restaurant lighter-headed (and light-walleted), we're ready to see more of the city by moonlight. Mainly, Piazza San Marco. The late hour means fewer people, delicate lighting and the gentle strains of music from the cafés. Salute, too, has no one around, and it feels as though it's ours alone. There's just the sound of lapping water and a distant cat as we stroll back to our hotel.

With its assortment of spirits, ice and lemon slices, a beautifully laid-out honesty bar makes a nightcap on the terrace irresistible. Overlooked by a clocktower (mercifully quiet at night), its palm trees, Moroccan shutters and tables lit from within lend warmth and exoticism. White rose petals sprinkled over a breakfast list on our bed beg us to think of food again… Cheese omelette with bacon and fruit salad, freshly squeezed orange and Jasmine tea will be the boost we need for tomorrow's touring.

What a wonderful city it is that has you stumbling through an open door into a schoolroom-sized space full of beautiful paintings. We linger in a secret world for 10 minutes until an old gentleman chucks us out. And it isn't long until we're eating again, this time tempted into a noisy local trattoria at the end of Via Garibaldi, the widest street in Venice, where a greengrocer's barge floats in front.

Then it's on to Harry's Bar – Mrs Smith is intrigued. We'll save you the trouble: it's a bit expensive and the waiters should visit Ca Maria Adele for a lesson in how charming staff can be. Inevitably, our hotel's seductive lounge draws us back. Mrs Smith picks through coffee-table books and international papers while I sneak off to the corner of our room that has a leather chair in the eaves. Here, in what Mrs Smith dubs my Venetian 'man shed', I learn some of my lines before bed.

Mrs Smith has one insistence for our last day. Her heroine is Katharine Hepburn. Our task? To find where she fell into into the canal in 1950s film *Summer Madness*. As luck would have it, it's nearby, at the Campo San Barnaba. After a photo session (and some strange looks), we settle on the water's edge for our final lunch: a couple of rolls liberated from breakfast, and half a bottle of wine. We dine like young student lovers listening to the throb of liners and car ferries leaving the lagoon. We linger as long as we can, but Alessandro has ordered our water taxi. Plotting our return, we hope it won't be long until we once again savour solitude in a crowded city.

Reviewed by **Danny Webb**, actor

NEED TO KNOW

Rooms 12, including two suites.

Rates €310–€700, including American à la carte breakfast, minibar soft drinks and service. Tax is an extra 10 per cent.

Check-out 12 noon, but later departures may be arranged. Check-in, 2pm, but flexible if the room is not booked.

Facilities Private landing stage, CD/DVD library, free WiFi throughout. In rooms: plasma TV, CD/DVD player, Gilchrist & Soames bath products. Personal shoppers and in-room massages can be arranged, too.

Children The hotel's better suited to over-14s; the apartment suite, with its extra bedroom, is the one to go for if you're travelling en famille.

Also There's a two-night minimum stay in high season. Pets are welcome on request. The hotel organises tailored tours around the city and you can take a gondola ride across to the Grand Canal to view the Royal Palace.

IN THE KNOW

Our favourite rooms We loved the themed rooms, in particular the seductive Sala Noire, the resplendent red and gold Sala del Doge and Sala del Camino for its huge fireplace. Overlooking the canal and the church, Deluxe room 332 and the Sala dei Mori have the best views. Modern, wood-beamed Suite 336 has a Jacuzzi tub at the foot of the bed.

Hotel bar You can order evening drinks anywhere in the hotel. We suggest the breakfast room or the Moroccan Terrace on the second floor; in summer, you can have a tipple brought to you outside. After 9pm, there's an honesty bar, stocked with prosecco, spirits and a selection of soft drinks.

Hotel restaurant Only breakfast is served. Italian-style afternoon tea is available on the terrace, weather permitting.

Top table Find a spot on the ponyskin sofas in the cosy living room, and take your tea there. You're almost at water level, so the fascinating view of the nearby bridge and church is unlike any you'll see from the upper floors.

Room service A light, limited menu of salads, snacks and tasting plates is available from 11am until 11pm.

Dress code Ducal and decadent.

Local knowledge The neighbourhood, Dorsoduro, is arty in the extreme: as well as the Peggy Guggenheim collection (+39 041 240 5411), it's home to the exhibition spaces of the avant-garde Fondazione Emilio e Annabianco Vedova (+39 041 522 6626) – a 'floating gallery', where paintings aren't hung on the walls, but suspended from the ceiling.

LOCAL EATING AND DRINKING

Linea d'Ombra (+39 041 241 1881) on Ponte de l'Umiltà is a great restaurant on the canal, and the perfect plot to head to in summer, thanks to the lovely terrace with views across to the Giudecca, and the chef's modern take on classic Venetian dishes. Ai Gondolieri (+39 041 528 6396), close to the Guggenheim, is popular with local and visiting carnivores for its meaty Veneto dishes of game and pork, and is famed for its gnocchi and polenta. There's a decent wine list, too. Waterside on the Zattere, La Piscina is the eatery attached to the historic *pensione* La Calcina, and makes for breezy terrace dining from a delectably down-to-earth menu (+39 041 520 6466). For a cosy, wine-bottles-on-the-wall kind of osteria, try Cantina Canaletto (+39 041 521 2661) in Castello.

GET A ROOM!

Hotel details 111 Dorsoduro, 30123 Venice (+39 041 520 3078; camariaadele.it).

To book Ring our expert Travel Team (you'll find all our numbers with your membership card on page 5) or go to mrandmrssmith.com/ca-maria-adele.

 A bottle of Valpolicella.

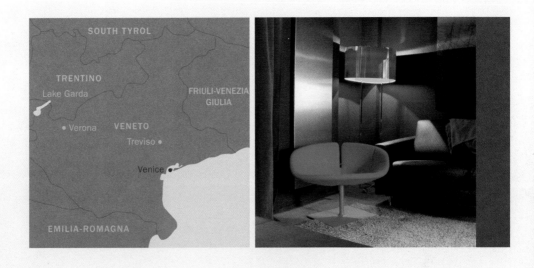

I Qs

STYLE Modern Italian Gothic
SETTING Beyond the Bridge of Sighs

'Every window pane faces one of two intersecting canals, both of them blessed with the sounds of gondoliers singingly plying their trade. For us, it's pure romance'

Gazing out of my office window on a rainy day, it strikes me like a brick: the only thing harder than organising a milestone birthday is organising the follow-up. While a 30th is all about celebrating the reigning reveller, 30 plus one is focused on forgetting that you've handed your crown to fresher-faced milestoners. I have a flash of inspiration: a weekend in Venice. It's on Mrs Smith's shortlist of dream destinations and I can impress her with secrets I've gleaned from previous visits to this watery city.

A few weeks later, we're in the Piazzale Roma, main gateway to the archipelago. As a result of boarding the incorrect *vaporetto*, instead of gliding down the stunning Grand Canal, as intended, we're chugging along the Canale della Giudecca. It's like entering Venice through the tradesmen's entrance; Mrs Smith is not impressed.

Hopping from ferry to terra firma, I claw back some Venetian street cred (or should that be canal cred?) by swiftly navigating the maze of alleys to I Qs. Calling the property discreet is an understatement: I Qs doesn't give any indication it's a hotel. If you've managed to find your way to its iron gate, across the private bridge and through the heavy wooden doors, then you've definitely earned a room at the inn.

Dark-toned walls, drapes and furniture, and a very low-slung bed – our boudoir sets the mood for a weekend of mischief. We've been treated to room number 4, a huge suite with an abundance of windows (even the walk-in wardrobe has one). Every pane faces one of two intersecting canals, both of them blessed with the sounds of gondoliers singingly plying their trade. For us, it's pure romance. For Venetians, it's probably the equivalent of a bus route passing your house.

Soon enough we're off to explore the city, winding through laneways that always seem crowded, but only because they were never intended to accommodate more than two abreast at a time. By 6pm, we are at a no-name canalside bar, where I'm briefing Mrs Smith on the joys of Italy's pre-dinner drinking ritual, the *aperitivo*. (My two-part lecture will conclude with a discourse on the *digestivo* – after a helping of seafood pasta.) Before heading back to I Qs, we make our grand entrance into

Piazza San Marco in all its night-time glory. Mrs Smith is smitten and I am humbled. This calls for a round of grappa.

The banging headaches we wake up with the next morning come compliments of our *digestivi*. Luckily, breakfast (and fresh coffee) is served in the room at I Qs. Between shopping, sightseeing, a dodgy concert and the best squid-ink risotto in a 100-kilometre radius, day two of our Venetian escapade seems to glide right by. The night, however, is just starting and I have the evening planned to perfection: At 11pm, we'll stroll down the backstreets finding our way to Venice's landmark casino, where I'll flex my betting muscles while Mrs Smith sips cocktails by my side. Once I've made enough money to pay for the trip 10 times over, we'll be whisked away 007-style on a luxury water taxi that drops us off at the hotel's private boat entrance; I'll sweep Mrs Smith (now tiddly) into my arms and lead her into our Venetian palazzo...

Imagining the sound of 'O Sole Mio' playing softly in the background? Here's the part where the needle scratches

across the record. Mrs Smith is wearing heels and most of Venice's alleyways are cobblestone; by the time we make it to the casino, she's in agony. The casino's security system then produces a much younger-looking picture of me (with a moustache – remnants of a former life and a prior visit), resulting in a further delay at check-in. My UK bank blocks my Italian cash withdrawals, and less than 45 minutes after I've finally negotiated some seed money from the ATM, I am wiped clean by the house. At the €5 blackjack table. By an 18-year-old card dealer. A 3am walk home awaits.

Anyone who has walked through Venice in the wee small hours can attest to a silver lining in this story. If you want the city to yourself with a glimpse of the days of the Doges, then retrace our steps. No tourists, no noise, no souvenir shops, no loud restaurants or gondoliers... just the sound of your feet on the cobblestones, the night sky reflecting on the water and the soft lapping of the canals. That walk home was one of the best experiences of our lives.

Taking Mrs Smith by the hand on our last day, we cross the Accademia Bridge and are soon strolling along the banks of the Giudecca Canal. Around us Venice is carrying on its daily grind: young boys are fishing, parents parade their infants, the sun beams in the sky and the crisp autumn air is generous enough to let you get away with shirtsleeves.

Eventually, we pull up to Marcello's waterside restaurant, where the menu is in Italian, our waiter happens to be Marcello and every patron looks like a film star. I grab a waterside table and order a bottle of prosecco. As we enjoy our last indulgent meal of the trip I turn to Mrs Smith and say, 'What are the odds that I'll be on the planning committee for your 32nd?' She replies: 'You do have a curious way of impressing a girl, Mr Smith. I wouldn't have it any other way.'

Reviewed by Mr & Mrs Smith

NEED TO KNOW

Rooms Four apartment-style rooms (one double studio, and three suites).

Rates €209–€790, including Continental breakfast.

Check-out 12 noon, although this may be flexible; earliest check-in, 3pm.

Facilities Private pier; library of books, music and films to borrow; free WiFi throughout; laundry. In rooms: fully equipped kitchen, computer, flatscreen TV, CD/DVD player, Nespresso machine, La Bottega dell'Albergo fig essence toiletries.

Children If you'd like to bring the nippers, cots and extra beds are available for €80 and the suites have sofa beds. Babysitting with staff can be arranged in advance, at €20 an hour.

Also Small pets are welcome. I Qs can arrange helicopter trips over Venice and water taxis to take you around the city from the hotel's private pier. In-room massages can also be arranged on request.

IN THE KNOW

Our favourite rooms Each apartment has been designed in a different modern style, but all preserve a twinkle of their Gothic architecture. Larger suites Q3 and Q4 overlook the canal: Q4's seven windows and fireplace make it the lighter of the two, but we like the tatami flooring in Q3 – a thoughtful Oriental touch that dovetails nicely with the bright white hues and high-gloss Corian bathroom. Q1, the studio, can be annexed to Q2 to form a bigger two-bedroom suite.

Hotel bar There's isn't one in the hotel, but you can stash drinks in the fridge in your room, and staff will bring ice if you ask. Ask the concierge to point you towards the nicest nearest watering holes.

Hotel restaurant This is more like staying in a serviced apartment than a hotel: every room is equipped with a kitchen containing an oven and all the pots, pans and plates needed to whip up a meal. If you don't 'do' cooking on holiday, the area around the hotel is blessed with plenty of eating-out options (see below).

Top table There are no communal areas – stick to your apartment's dining table and listen to the water lapping outside.

Room service Staff bring milk, croissants and bread to your room every morning, and you can have groceries delivered.

Dress code Clean-cut Armani with a touch of Venetian exoticism.

Local knowledge I Qs' suites have views of the Palazzo Querini Stampalia, whose 16th-century exterior gives way to a striking and celebrated modern interior by 1960s architect Carlo Scarpa. In the art gallery upstairs, you'll find *vedutista* cityscapes, paintings by Tiepolo, Pietro Longhi and other members of the Venetian school, as well as drawings by Titian and Tintoretto and a selection of 19th-century furniture. The café's not bad, either.

LOCAL EATING AND DRINKING

Close by, in the eponymous square, **L'Osteria di Santa Marina** is a locally beloved joint with a penchant for delicate seafood and a spectacular tasting menu (+39 041 528 5239; closed Sundays and Mondays). Closer still – next door, in fact – **Alle Testiere** serves excellent fish dishes to just nine tables, so booking is vital (+39 041 522 7220). For a low-key lunch, **Osteria Da Carla** has a fantastic location just behind the Piazza San Marco (+39 041 523 7855). Try anything from the short menu, or eat little tapas-style tartines (such as toast with melted cheese and walnuts) at the bar. For a rambunctious and rustic evening of great pasta and better wine, head to **La Mascareta** (+39 041 523 0744), a largely untouristy slice of authentic Venetian nightlife, just a few moments from the hotel. Feel free to confuse it with **Al Mascaron** nearby, another low-key local fave (+39 041 522 5995).

GET A ROOM!

Hotel details Campiello Querini Stampalia, 4425 Castello, 30122 Venice (+39 041 241 0062; thecharminghouse.com).

To book Ring our expert Travel Team (you'll find all our numbers with your membership card on page 5) or go to mrandmrssmith.com/i-qs.

 Tickets for two to a local exhibition or gallery, such as the Palazzo Grassi.

Palazzina Grassi

STYLE Through the looking glass
SETTING A stroll from San Marco

'The clandestine mood of reception has been swapped for a white brilliance that rivals a set from *2001: Space Odyssey*. Our boudoir is like a heavenly mirage'

Venice: the land of elaborate masks, crimson coats, gilded gondolas, and most importantly, love. Mask? Check. Red mac? Sure. Gondola? Yessir. Love? Pass. I've got a 6'2", baseball-capped, bearded, tattooed friend called Gabriel along for the ride.

Adventure is clearly on its way: we catch the auspicious sight of Fabio Capello swaggering onto our plane, flaunting the kind of grace and nonchalance Italian men have finely tuned over the past two millennia. We, meanwhile, display the kind of hungover, sleepless, dirty-trousered allure the British have so faultlessly perfected.

From Venice airport, our senses are bombarded: the heat (despite predictions of rain from the BBC's weather website), the smell (that of sea that's graduated from finishing school) and the boats (which hook themselves into your memory banks, labelled 'Lucky little blighters'). We approach the gondoliers as they smoke and chat, each plying their trade in signature style, and we pick one. We follow our man as he walks past a succession of marvellously crafted wooden boats until stopping at his vessel: what a beaut. Sitting on the seats in the back instantly gives us – or indeed anyone in possession of a pair of sunglasses – the look of a Fellini star.

Such an introduction to this northern city is awesome. Venice is magnificent. The ages-old architecture inspires a feeling of being suspended in a lost time, as though you are travelling through thousands of photographs of somewhere incomprehensible. A city built in the sea! There is no 'popping across the road' here, or 'Let's quickly jump on the back of the bike', or even 'Just wait for the green man' – this is a watery city for the wanderer and the drifter. Which suits these flâneurs just fine.

As we float up to the steps of the Palazzina Grassi, towards a black-glass entrance crowned with a bull and a golden mask, it clicks that our adventure has only just begun. The doors pull back and we are met by an incredibly courteous and well-dressed man who magics away our bags and gently gestures us into the glossy reception of this Philippe Starck stay. The mask lives up to its symbolism, conjuring an atmosphere of secrecy yet warmth, like the burrow of a kleptomaniac rabbit. We shuffle through to Krug lounge for a glass of champagne and find a low-lit, alluring room full of objets d'art all laced with mysticism and charm. We sit back and soak it in.

Bubbles sipped, we follow the concierge to a mirrored lift, to be escorted to our room. He opens the door to 623, where another surprise awaits. The clandestine mood of the reception area has been swapped for a white brilliance that rivals a set from Kubrick's *Space Odyssey*. Our boudoir is seemingly a heavenly mirage: bed, carpets and walls are all white, the table, cupboards and television mirrored and the windows tinted a warm, light pink. There is a powerful sense of calm.

We turn to each other and laugh. We open cabinets, switch on the TV and marvel at its disappearance when we turn it back off; we listen to music through invisible speakers hidden throughout. Finally, we pull up the blinds to find our own balcony, with tables, deckchairs and huge chess pawns, as well as a fantastic view of Venice's windows and rooftops. After an hour of circling our room and picture-taking, we decide, reluctantly, it is time to roam.

The hotel is positioned on a distinctly Venetian passageway that leads onto a cobbled main street. From here you can easily trail signs to all the main sights. We are never further than a 10-minute walk from the tick-off-the-list landmarks. Our first ramble through the city quickly deposits us at the Peggy Guggenheim Museum, where our breath is stolen by works by Duchamp, Picasso and Mondrian. Then we amble to St Mark's Square, which is just how I had visualised it. *Correttos* sipped at Caffè Florian, live renditions of Italian folk songs listened to, and spaghetti slurped on the Grand Canal, we settle back to watch boats of the glitterati and Cincinnati persuasion pass by.

Over the weekend, our hotel becomes our home, and a wonderful place to pitstop for a shot or two of absinthe before heading back out again into what we've dubbed 'the land of the Minotaur'. At night, we head to PG's, the hotel's restaurant, for dinner and find it transformed from its daytime serenity into an exciting, bustling, sceney spot.

Surveying the Venetians and tourists happily drinking and eating within PG's sultry nightclubby clutches, it is easy to see why Johnny Depp took such a liking to this special place. After incredible Mediterranean cooking delivered with Asian precision, care of Luigi Frascella, we while away our evenings drinking in the bar.

Waking up on the morning of our departure, there is a feeling of disbelief that this Venetian weekend has even happened at all. As we close the door on our white wonderland and tiptoe into the ornate splendour of Palazzina Grassi's lobby for the last time, I know we are saying farewell to an extraordinary hotel in a unique city. Gabriel and I agreed we'll be back – next time with our Mrs Smiths.

Reviewed by **Jack Peñate**, singer-songwriter

NEED TO KNOW

Rooms 22, including one suite and six suite apartments.

Rates €352–€1,991, excluding breakfast (€38.50 a person). Apartments, €2,500–€12,000 a night.

Check-out 12 noon, but flexible until 3pm if the room's available. Earliest check-in, 2pm.

Facilities Library, members- and residents-only Krug champagne lounge; 1962 mahogany Celli boat; private landing pier; roof terrace; free WiFi throughout. In rooms: Starck fixtures and fittings, backlit mirror walls, programmable lighting, in-mirror LCD TV, iPod dock, minibar (with decent-sized bottles). There's a giant chess set outside, by the canal.

Children Cots are free for under-threes, but extra beds for older kids cannot be provided. A local nanny can be called upon for babysitting services (€25 an hour).

Also Well-behaved dogs are welcome for €50 a night. Check-in can be on-boat, in your room or in the bar. Staff can arrange a host of authentic Venetian experiences – from insider city tours to cooking classes from a countess.

IN THE KNOW

Our favourite rooms Junior Suite 220 has a mirrored bedhead and pink Perspex door that leads out onto a terrace overlooking the city's rooftops. There's an exclusive feel to the third-floor Suite: you can only get there by private elevator. Its terrace has sweeping Venice vistas, and you can get an eyeful of cityscape from the bed. Grassi's smallest rooms, the Superiors, aren't spacious, but the hall-of-mirrors effect gives the impression of size.

Hotel bar PG's is a mood-lit mahogany cocktail den of exposed brick, velvet and leather. Lamps resemble gorgon heads; 15th-century pillars prop up the bars, and candles flicker in glimmering Murano-glass holders. Suite Apartment guests also get access to the Krug Lounge, a sultry, scarlet-carpeted 'champagnerie' with animal-shaped leather stools.

Hotel restaurant Meals are served pretty much anywhere, but the main dining area is in PG's, where there's an open kitchen. Luigi Frascella is the man behind the menu: a contemporary reinvention of traditional Venetian *cicchetti*, with an Oriental flourish, using ingredients fresh from the Rialto.

Top table People-watch from a perch at the bar, or sit at the long table by the show kitchen to watch the chefs at work.

Room service Anything the hotel's kitchens can produce is available until midnight, after which a smaller, night menu kicks in. You can have food and drink brought to you anywhere you wish.

Dress code Rich, ducal fabrics: velvet, cashmere and damask.

Local knowledge Next door to the hotel, the neoclassical Palazzo Grassi has been transformed into a contemporary exhibition space by Gucci/Christie's billionaire François Pinault (palazzograssi.it). His own extraordinary collection is housed here and in the Punta della Dogana on the opposite bank.

LOCAL EATING AND DRINKING

Three minutes away, Bacaro da Fiore (+39 041 523 5310) is a traditional trattoria that doubles as a *cicchetteria*, serving up snack-size portions of fried fish and veg. It's a 15-minute walk to low-key-but-lovely Osteria di Santa Marina (+39 041 528 5239). Try the turbot ravioli in shellfish broth, scallop risotto and ice-cream macaroons. Take a boat out to Mazzorbo to dine on the freshest seasonal produce at Venissa Ristorante Ostello (+39 041 527 2281). The estate makes wine for its well-stocked cellar. For excellent Venetian food off the tourist-trodden path, try Osteria l'Orto dei Mori (+39 041 524 3677). Head next door to the Palazzo Grassi Café (+39 041 240 1337) for lunch by the canal.

GET A ROOM!

Hotel details 3247 San Marco, 30124 Venice (+39 041 528 4644; palazzinagrassi.com).

To book Ring our expert Travel Team (you'll find all our numbers with your membership card on page 5) or go to mrandmrssmith.com/palazzina-grassi.

 A bottle of prosecco and a selection of *cicchetti* (Venetian appetisers) made by the chef.

HOW TO... identify Renaissance art

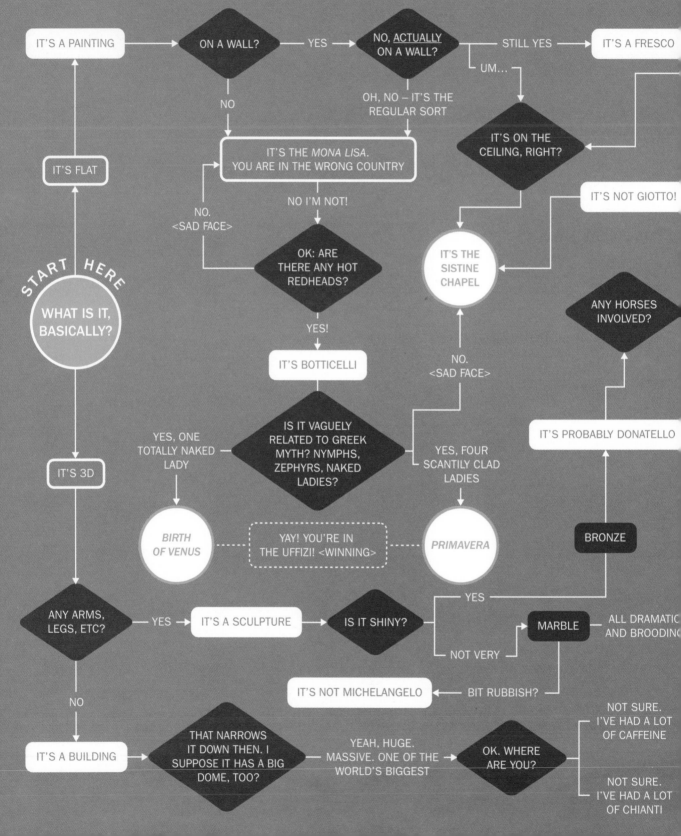

IT'S A PAINTING → **ON A WALL?** — YES → **NO, <u>ACTUALLY</u> ON A WALL?** — STILL YES → **IT'S A FRESCO**

ON A WALL? — NO ↓

NO, ACTUALLY ON A WALL? — OH, NO – IT'S THE REGULAR SORT ↓

NO, ACTUALLY ON A WALL? — UM... ↓ **IT'S ON THE CEILING, RIGHT?**

IT'S FLAT

IT'S THE *MONA LISA*. YOU ARE IN THE WRONG COUNTRY

NO. <SAD FACE>

NO I'M NOT! ↓

START HERE

WHAT IS IT, BASICALLY?

OK: ARE THERE ANY HOT REDHEADS?

YES! ↓

IT'S BOTTICELLI

IT'S NOT GIOTTO!

IT'S THE SISTINE CHAPEL

NO. <SAD FACE>

ANY HORSES INVOLVED?

IS IT VAGUELY RELATED TO GREEK MYTH? NYMPHS, ZEPHYRS, NAKED LADIES?

YES, ONE TOTALLY NAKED LADY

YES, FOUR SCANTILY CLAD LADIES ↓

IT'S PROBABLY DONATELLO

IT'S 3D

BIRTH OF VENUS ····· **YAY! YOU'RE IN THE UFFIZI! <WINNING>** ····· *PRIMAVERA*

BRONZE

ANY ARMS, LEGS, ETC? — YES → **IT'S A SCULPTURE** → **IS IT SHINY?** — YES

IS IT SHINY? — NOT VERY → **MARBLE** — ALL DRAMATIC AND BROODING

ANY ARMS, LEGS, ETC? — NO ↓

IT'S NOT MICHELANGELO ← BIT RUBBISH?

IT'S A BUILDING → **THAT NARROWS IT DOWN THEN. I SUPPOSE IT HAS A BIG DOME, TOO?** — YEAH, HUGE. MASSIVE. ONE OF THE WORLD'S BIGGEST → **OK. WHERE ARE YOU?**

OK. WHERE ARE YOU? — NOT SURE. I'VE HAD A LOT OF CAFFEINE

OK. WHERE ARE YOU? — NOT SURE. I'VE HAD A LOT OF CHIANTI

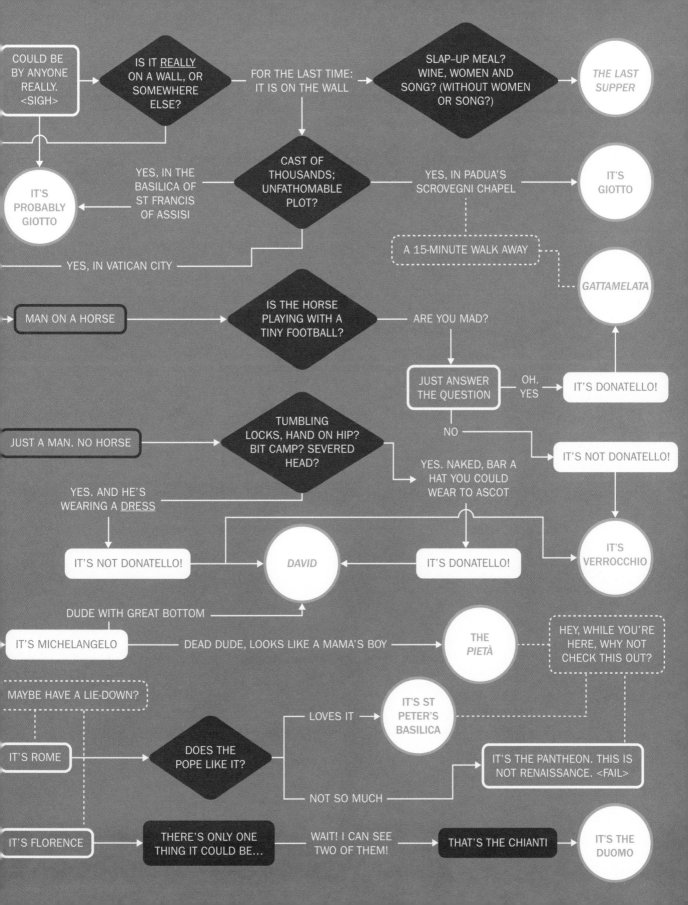

CENTRAL

SARDINIA

VENETO

EMILIA-ROMAGNA

Bologna

8

1

Florence 2

3

TUSCANY

7

6

Siena 5

4

Perugia

9

UMBRIA

10

CENTRAL

Ancona

LE MARCHE

LATIUM

ABRUZZO

11

12

Rome

13

L'Aquila

MOLISE

Campobasso

CAMPANIA

Naples

FLORENCE

CITYSCAPE Rich Renaissance tapestry
CITY LIFE Shopping and strolling

A love affair between culture, commerce and good living, this fine city has long been fêted as the most aesthetically pleasing in all Italy. Notching up more past glories than the average continent, Tuscany's capital still leads from the front: between its fairy-tale squares, centuries-old churches and sprawling palaces run streets alive with energy, style and irresistible shopping. It's luxury goods galore on Via Tornabuoni, artisan jewellers on the mediaeval Ponte Vecchio and delectable deli fare everywhere – the riches on offer are enough to get the most ardent anti-capitalists scrabbling for the plastic. The city centre is architecturally breathtaking, and compact enough to stroll in an afternoon; follow heart-stirring glimpses of the gingerbread-hued Duomo and its frosting-pale Campanile down narrow streets, and eat Italian soul food in a simple trattoria.

GETTING THERE

Planes Florence airport (www.aeroporto.firenze.it) is a 20-minute drive from the city centre; an official taxi into town should cost no more than €25. You can also fly into Pisa airport, from where a direct train takes just shy of an hour and costs €5.80 (trenitalia.com).

Trains The main station (Firenze SMN) is behind Piazza Santa Maria Novella, with high-speed connections to other cities in Italy and Europe.

Automobiles Having a car in Florence can be a hindrance – in fact, it's next to pointless – but a vehicle is essential if you want to explore the surrounding Tuscan countryside.

LOCAL KNOWLEDGE

Taxis You can't hail the metered white taxis in the street; go to a designated *fermata di taxi*. The major ones are manned 24/7; most operate 7am–1am. Socota is one of the biggest cab firms (+39 055 4242; radiotaxifirenze.it).

Siesta and fiesta Florentines are early risers. The main museums open at 8.15am (presumably the extra quarter of an hour allows everyone to enjoy a civilised espresso en route) and close at 7pm or just before; some shut on Mondays, so plan your cultural forays accordingly.

Do go/don't go Florence is packed throughout the summer, when it's also very humid; go in early spring or autumn.

Packing tips Aside from a sketchbook, a sunhat and sensible shoes, pack light: this is a shopper's paradise. You may even need a new bag to put all your acquisitions in (luckily there are plenty of leather-goods shops).

Recommended reads Even the title of EM Forster's *A Room with a View* conjures up piazza-perfect imagery; Giovanni Boccaccio spins 100 mediaeval yarns in *The Decameron*; and anyone who fancies themselves as a Renaissance muse should read Sarah Dunant's *The Birth of Venus*.

Local specialities If Florentines have a mantra, it's 'Give us this day our daily bread': they are fanatical about their *filone*, a salt-free loaf so beloved that its stale remnants are used to pad out dishes from *ribollita* (a hearty bean, veg and black cabbage soup) to *pappa al pomodoro* (bread and tomato soup). If you like your bread salty, go for *schiacciata*, an oil-drizzled crusty focaccia; Pugi is name-checked with reverence among residents for its version – you'll find one of these hallowed *focaccerie* at 10 Piazza San Marco (+39 055 280981). Other Florentine favourites include thick grilled Chianina steaks, *pasta e fagioli* (pasta with beans), cold cuts and game, all washed down with generous glasses of typically Tuscan Chianti.

WORTH GETTING OUT OF BED FOR

Viewpoint Climb the 414 steps to the top of Giotto's Campanile, or up Brunelleschi's Duomo itself for 360-degree city views (duomofirenze.it). Alternatively, drive up to Fiesole and look down across the entire town; if you have time to linger, gaze across those iconic terracotta-tiled rooftops while you lunch at Il Salviatino's La Terrazza restaurant (+39 055 904 1111).

Arts and culture Sixty per cent of the world's most important works of art are housed in Italy – half of them are in Florence. You'd have to try very hard to have a bad time just following your feet, but there are a few things you won't want to miss. The Cathedral of Santa Maria del Fiore, aka the Duomo, was completed in 1436, and its dome is a celebrated feat of engineering. The castellated Bargello palace contains an unrivalled collection of Renaissance sculpture. The famous Uffizi Gallery houses breathtaking Botticellis, Michelangelos and Leonardos. Book tickets in advance (+39 055 294 883; polomuseale.firenze.it).

Activities Overwhelmed by the number of sights to see? Hire an expert: art historian Camilla Baines arranges private viewings (info@thetuscanconcierge.com); Florence Guides (+39 335 807 1180; florenceguides.com) are knowledgeable and entertaining. See it all from the water as you're punted down the Arno in a vintage *barchetto*, with Florence River (florenceriver.it); romantic night cruises for two can also be arranged. Exercise-hungry desperados could jog in Cascine Park (also lovely for a riverside stroll, hack, cycle or swim). Speed freaks head to Mugello (mugellocircuit.it), an hour away, to watch Ducatis, Aprilias and Ferraris scream round the track.

Perfect picnic The historic *centro* is more blessed with piazzas than parks: find yourself a little enoteca (not Enoteca Pinchiorri, though, unless you're in the mood to splash out €12,500 on Pétrus), and linger alfresco over a glass of good wine and a snacking plate of antipasti. Alternatively, take your pasta-à-porter to Cascine Park, or Piazzale Michelangelo for a heart-stirring view of the city.

Daytripper Rent a vintage car and head for the hills (+39 0578 263298; zephyrus.it): spend a day in San Gimignano, famed for its fortified towers, cobbled streets and grand views; or Siena, a perfectly preserved mediaeval city. Pisa, home to the improbably leaning tower, is only 86km away.

Walks Behind the Palazzo Pitti, the beautiful Boboli Gardens offer meandering walkways, shady arbours and statue-littered lawns – and provide the template for almost every noteworthy formal garden in Europe.

Shopping The Mercato Centrale in San Lorenzo is a huge covered food market crammed with every local speciality. The market on Sundays around Piazza San Lorenzo can be disappointing; try hunting for antiques among bric-à-brac at the daily Piazza dei Ciompi flea market instead. There's also a huge market at Cascine Park on Tuesday mornings. Elio Ferraro is a vintage legend – his carefully curated couture collection is beautifully displayed among mid-century marvels on Via del Parione (+39 055 290425; elioferraro.com). Via Tornabuoni is luxury-label heaven; for cutting-edge designer clothes, Luisa Via Roma (+39 055 217826) is a high-fashion multi-designer boutique. Poke your nose into Farmacia Santa Maria Novella (+39 055 216276) on Via della Scala for the finest handmade fragrances: this amazing perfumery has been producing sensational scents since the 13th century.

Something for nothing Stroll across the Ponte Vecchio and spend a morning on the Oltrarno (the other side of the river): browse Via Maggio's antiques shops; peek at 16th-century altarpieces in Brunelleschi's Santo Spirito church; and hang out in the shady piazza afterwards.

Don't go home without... deciding which piece of Renaissance art you'd like to sneak back home in your suitcase. No cheating – you can only pick one!

FABULOUSLY FLORENCE

Michelangelo's pert-bottomed *David* has symbolised Florentine civic pride for 500 years, but the five-metre-high nude hasn't always had an easy ride: he's been struck by lightning, had his toes hammered off, and his left arm was smashed by an airborne bench. Moves are afoot to shift the attention-seeking statue away from the city centre – the real version, housed in the Accademia, is visited by a crush of 1.3 million adoring tourists every year.

DIARY

March/April Blowing up a wooden ox cart (*scoppio del carro*) outside the Duomo is the explosive way Florentines celebrate Easter. **May–June** Maggio Musicale Fiorentino (maggio fiorentino.com) is one of Europe's oldest music festivals and spans opera, ballet, classical and jazz. **Late June** Festa di San Giovanni around the 24th honours the city's patron saint; highlights include a regatta near Ponte Vecchio, a fashion show, and fireworks in Piazzale Michelangelo. **Early September** Children, lanterns, processions, street performances and parties: it's all going on for Rificolona on the 7th. **November** Documentary-makers gather for the mid-month international Festival dei Popoli (festivaldeipopoli.org). Later in the month, it's high-speed sightseeing in shorts at the Firenze Marathon (firenzemarathon.it).

Il Salviatino

STYLE Hip historic villa
SETTING Lush, leafy hillside

'The grand mansion rears into view
at the top of the hill – all strong, angular
and imposing, and standing among
beautiful floral gardens'

Given that some of the world's most exquisite and momentous cultural offerings hail from *bell'Italia*, I have high hopes for Il Salviatino. My own job is to sell beautiful fantasy and spectacle on stage; Walt Disney had it right when he said: 'Fantasy and reality often overlap'. So as I decant my biggest, most fabulous gold jewellery and my finest Italian shoes into my modest leopardskin-print weekend case, I hope that after a brief flight I'll soon be feeling like Gina Lollobrigida dating Michelangelo on the set of a Fellini film. With the Ferrero Rocher ambassador waiting on me as I savour my Barolo.

As our driver pulls into the grounds of Il Salviatino, passing through towering gates, the grand mansion rears into view at the top of the hill – all strong, angular and imposing, standing among beautiful floral gardens: my vision wasn't *so* far off. Imagine my delight as I emerge from the car to be greeted immediately by two handsome, immaculately groomed men in matching beige Italian tailoring, introducing themselves as my ambassadors for the duration of my stay. No gold-foil chocolates, though;

instead, a much more fitting glass of rosé champagne is offered to welcome us Smiths while our bags are whisked away to our awaiting suite. As there is no reception or formal check-in to mar the intimate feel of the house, all we have to do is call our ambassador with any whims.

The design feel of Il Salviatino is masculine, elegantly executed, and not overbearing. It's for grown-ups, make no mistake, with dark heavy woods contrasting against white walls adorned with Renaissance paintings, padded red velvet doors and vast, high ceilings. Anything girlish or floral is kept to the stunningly manicured gardens. Our suite has a beautiful view of the terrace, and the skyline of Florence twinkles beyond.

Then I realise my bathroom has no bath, only a shower. This is a deal-breaker for me: Miss Blaize and her bubble baths are not easily parted (a very British trait, I'm told). It is time to test my ambassador. My damsel-in-distress call is rewarded with a message flashing back on my phone: 'Il Magnifico has been alerted.' Within 15 minutes

I am given a new room with a Jacuzzi bath, a 20-foot bathroom and an even more beautiful view of the gardens. Il Magnifico is on my Christmas card list for ever.

Mr Smith books for us to dine on the terrace overlooking the gardens, despite my wariness due to the heavy rain earlier. Yet warm evening sunshine prevails (these ambassadors really can work miracles) and our alfresco experience is superb, accompanied by soft melodies wafting over from the pianist. The classic Italian cuisine is of course flawless: we sample everything from tuna tartare to meatballs and even wild pork; the penne with squid is a showstopper.

At the first sign of a goosebump, an ambassador appears at my side with an array of cashmere blankets to drape over my shoulders. A Hennessy nightcap in the well-stocked library completes a beautiful and romantic evening. Vintage books are to be found all over the mansion, not just the library – even in my room. There, nestled next to GB Shaw's plays, I find an unlikely source

of romantic advice in the form of the slim 1908 volume 'Modern Cement Sidewalk Construction'. Headings include 'Don't work for a rich cheap man and lose your reputation' and 'A lesson in the use of the expansion joint'. Wise words, indeed.

The next day, after a blissful breakfast of eggs Florentine (well, when in Florence), I fancy some retail therapy. The luxury shuttle service deposits us in the town centre, on – to Mr Smith's dismay – the equivalent of Bond Street, albeit infinitely more picturesque. Like a homing pigeon, I bypass labels I can buy in London and snap up some fabulous vintage, including an adorable Moschino jacket.

What I really came for is the famous perfumery, the Officina Profumo-Farmaceutica di Santa Maria Novella. Occupying a former church, it is full of herbal potions, spicy syrups and exotic tonics in pretty apothecary bottles: the stuff of dreams. It is the most sensual shopping experience I've ever known. Scents spill out into the street and, eventually, Mr Smith has to drag

away the person dressed in a Lagerfeld cape, turban and shades, madly sniffing at the windowsills. At least I have my own fragrance to remember this trip by.

In the hills overlooking Florence, Il Salviatino is perfectly located so that you can dip in and out of its compact city centre, retreating back to the mansion for sanctuary. So, after a day of shopping and sights, we seek out the spa. I select their signature treatment to revive myself: a rose-petal bath, scrub and massage. (I wince at the thought of recommending the 'grape-crushing' treatment to Mr Smith.) Two and a half hours of pure heaven later, I emerge scrubbed, polished and smelling of roses. So much so that, when I return to my room, Mr Smith remarks that I am 'glowing'; he checks to see if my feet are actually touching the floor.

The *aperitivo* hour is my favourite time of the day, and I couldn't leave Il Salviatino without sampling their service. The hotel's signature cocktail proves my favourite: a classic dry martini, done perfectly – just like all that they do. Nothing here is nouveau; even the light fittings are discreetly concealed to retain a classic feel. But more than that, although this isn't somewhere to experience on a budget, neither is it the place to have other people watch you spend your money; if that's your wont, head for St Tropez. Il Salviatino is about discretion and stealth wealth. Every detail, from the fragrant rose jam at breakfast to the fresh white roses in the rooms, screams (or rather, delicately murmurs) elegance. I really was Gina Lollobrigida for the weekend, and I won't lie, it was wonderful.

Reviewed by **Immodesty Blaize**, burlesque artist

NEED TO KNOW

Rooms 45 rooms, including 14 suites.

Rates €444–€2,900, including American-style à la carte breakfast.

Check-out 12 noon, but flexible, subject to availability; after 4pm, you'll be charged an extra night. Earliest check-in, 2pm.

Facilities Spa, gym, library, 12 acres of landscaped parkland, free WiFi throughout. In rooms: flatscreen TV, minibar, iPod docks available on request. Every bathroom has LED-lit rain showers with seats, and some have a Jacuzzi or antique bath tub. All guests are assigned a dedicated 'ambassador' to look after them during their stay.

Poolside The terraced pool area showcases a twin-tiered infinity pool filled with mineral-rich water: pairs of sunloungers overlook a green valley and are surrounded by the garden's scented roses and lavender.

Children Welcome, with free cots provided for three-year-olds and under. Extra beds are €75–€150. Babysitting costs around €70 an hour (book two days in advance). The restaurant has a kids' menu, and there are floats at the pool.

Also Diminutive dogs can come, too. The Devarana Spa's Thai therapists conduct treatments designed around guests' probable pursuits, including reflexology for sightseers' weary feet, and detox wraps to remedy any wine-tasting woes.

IN THE KNOW

Our favourite rooms The spacious Salviati De Luxe rooms in the main villa feature exposed brickwork and striking half-moon windows. The Melodia, Tegliacci and Affresco Suites are grand and opulent, with restored fresco ceilings, imposing fireplaces and plump chesterfields. The Ojetti Suite has a dramatic sun room, the floor of which is the glass ceiling of the hotel's tremendous main staircase, a private roof terrace and a Jacuzzi bath with a spectacular view.

Hotel bar The bar is a long, smart space on the ground floor, manned by baristas as beautiful as the surroundings. Patio doors lead out on to the balustraded balcony, which has wonderful vistas.

Hotel restaurant Two: Le Serre has a formal feel, with just a cluster of candlelit tables and impressive portraits; or there's relaxed La Terrazza, where you can sit outside – and at night, count the stars as you dine. The food at both is a reinvented take on traditional Tuscan fare. Crowd-pleasers include ricotta and spinach *gnudi* with sage butter, and almond tartlets with pecorino and pear sorbet.

Top table La Terrazza has tables overlooking the Italian Gardens – you can even spy Florence's Duomo in the distance.

Room service The 24-hour room service includes a selection of light snacks and dishes from both restaurants.

Dress code Honour local heroes, with Gucci, Pucci, Cavalli or Ferragamo threads.

Local knowledge Il Salviatino can arrange one-off experiences for guests, such as a visit to one of Florence's skilled craftsmen to have shoes or a shirt made to measure.

LOCAL EATING AND DRINKING

Vinandro, a cosy wine bar, is five minutes' drive away in Piazza Mino (+39 055 59121), and serves delicacies such as *tagliata* (Chianina beef steak with rocket and parmesan); the menu is brief but authentic (remember to book). North, on the outskirts of Montebeni, Ristorante Tullio on Via Ontignano (+39 055 697354) is worth visiting for hearty steak and *peposo* (spiced beef stew). Tullio has a deli, so stock up on picnic provisions, too. Sit among the bottles and hanging hams at Olio & Convivium (+39 055 265 8198), an elegant little eatery on Via di Santo Spirito that specialises in wine and olive oil. Sweet-tooths should stop for ice-cream at Gelateria Badiani (+39 055 578682) on Viale dei Mille.

GET A ROOM!

Hotel details 21 via del Salviatino, 50137 Florence (+39 055 904 1111; salviatino.com).

To book Ring our expert Travel Team (you'll find all our numbers with your membership card on page 5) or go to mrandmrssmith.com/il-salviatino.

 A half-hour wine or olive-oil tasting session.

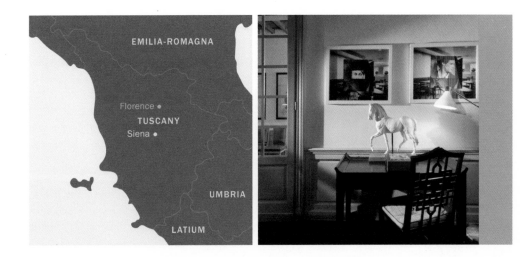

JK Place Firenze

STYLE Private perfection
SETTING Poised on a piazza

'African headdresses surmount a Charles X fireplace; 1960s paintings share space with 18th-century sculptures and deco furniture – clashing eras edited together beautifully'

Discreet as an opium den, the entrance to JK Place Firenze is on a low-key corner of Piazza Santa Maria Novella. And here we are, after a small hop from Paris, pressing a magic button to enter a secretly sumptuous 20-room bolthole. Once inside, this musk-infused former mansion doesn't even seem like a hotel – it's for this kind of hideaway that such clichés as 'island of tranquillity' and 'haven of peace' were invented. African headdresses surmount a sombre and imposing Charles X fireplace, and 1960s paintings share space with 18th-century sculptures and art deco furniture… Everything here is cream, grey or black; marble, wood and geometric – clashing eras all edited together beautifully. I sense Mrs Smith's pupils dilating.

Etchings, drawings and a Regency-era fireplace furnish JK Place's take on a reception, a snug space in the property's former library. Staff are elegant, friendly, well-groomed and as gracious as can be – and this coming from someone who knows what it takes to be a world-class concierge. Next to us, there's a tiny little glass-roofed former courtyard, where we'll eat breakfast communally at an impressive walnut table from the 1800s. Just beyond is a lounge where we plan to relax with a glass of chilled prosecco – on offer gratis at cocktail hour – under the cool glow of a huge Bang & Olufsen TV. It's funny how, in Italy, it's ubiquitous in bars to have a giant screen playing glossy fashion and music shows on a loop – even when you're already somewhere so glamorous.

Our high-ceilinged room is a junior suite, and it riffs on the same chic monochrome theme. Cream and black architectural drawings line the walls, stacks of his and hers fashion magazines sit bedside a hi-tech telephone, and there are even two marble bathrooms treating us to a separate shower and bath. As if that doesn't underline luxe living strongly enough, there's thick grey carpet all around, fresh white roses, and an inviting plate of fresh fruit with cold Acqua Panna and Pellegrino at our disposal. We are entirely enamoured. We want to live here. Forever.

After a quick glass of the delicious Tuscan white Vernaccia di San Gimignano in the lounge, we head out to explore this city, the crucible of the Renaissance. In 10 minutes flat, we're at the La Bottega grocery store at the corner of Via dei Neri. I confess we've sidestepped the many cultural offerings of this diminutive but distinguished city – the way to this pair's hearts is through our *stomaci*. Soon we're laden with charcuterie, pecorino, and a cheap bottle of Lambrusco opened for us on the premises. We set out across the river for a wander along vertiginous and winding streets, to find an ideal evening picnic spot.

Up the road past Galileo's house, we end up at the Forte di Belvedere. The riverside grounds of this fortification in the Oltrarno district have wonderful views over the city. Eating, drinking and merriment ensues, interrupted only by a peculiar puss intent on sampling our ham and the occasional Asian and Russian tourist asking directions. As our bottle of wine is down to the dregs, we start to saunter back downhill and are caught off-guard by a

downpour. Darting in and out of 16th-century porticoes – the vestiges of former noble residences – we end up at the artisan-packed mediaeval Ponte Vecchio and stroll over one of Italy's most celebrated landmarks.

Rainclouds disperse, and we head back to JK Place, where a kindly night watchman sneaks us a bottle of 'clandi' prosecco and shows us the way to the hotel's rooftop terrace. Empty, and cushion-festooned, it's a heavensent spot for a pair of romancing weekend-awayers like us two.

A word on the concierge credentials of JK Place: being one myself lends a different perspective when visiting other establishments – and to encounter such intuitive service is a delight. Coming back weary from a day's walking, eating and drinking, unable to think for ourselves, being steered up here with a bottle on ice and glasses and given a view of the nearby Duomo lit up in all its magnificence has created an unexpectedly memorable end to our evening. The bubbly goes down

well under the bright Florentine moonlight, and Marvin Gaye on my iPhone completes a night that has been filled with an antipasti picnic, mirth, and a little too much of the local vino.

Day two of our all-too-short weekend treats us to a more formal feast, care of the closest Michelin stars. La Tenda Rossa is a half-hour taxi ride away in the village of Cerbaia. Mrs Smith suggests this family-run affair was last decorated when nouvelle cuisine was at the height of fashion. (I ponder whether the menu is also somewhat trapped in the same timewarp, but we both agree the food shines thanks to the use of superb produce.) After a tasting of locally produced olive oil, we dine on langoustine ravioli with white beans and orange marmalade, a light and delicious version of *fritto misto*, all the while quaffing a splendiferous local chardonnay named Batàr. How does the rest of our evening play out? Ahem. It in fact continues well into the next morning, care of pints in the neighbouring Irish Pub – well, it is St Patrick's Day…

Finally we retire to our room for more music and wine. Cosseted in this corner of paradise, we realise what makes this hip hotel so special. A place that can make you feel so at home, seemingly without too much effort, yet enveloping you in chic luxury, must surely be prized. We salute you, JK.

Reviewed by **Adrian Moore**, concierge

NEED TO KNOW

Rooms 20, including five suites.

Rates €310–€1,000, including Continental or American buffet breakfast, welcome drinks and minibar soft drinks.

Check-out 12 noon, but may be flexible on request; earliest check-in, 2pm.

Facilities Library with books, CDs and DVDs; roof terrace; free WiFi throughout. In rooms: flatscreen TV, DVD/CD player, minibar. In-room spa treatments can be arranged and guests have access to the Olimpo Spa on nearby Via Tornabuoni.

Children Cots for babies and extra beds for under-12s are free and, with a day's notice, nannies can be arranged to babysit for €40 an hour. Monitors are available from the concierge. The restaurant has a stash of highchairs.

Also Small pets are welcome. There are a few designated smoking rooms.

IN THE KNOW

Our favourite rooms For a 360° view of Florence, check into the two-level Penthouse at the top of the hotel and admire the Duomo from your bath tub or the private terrace. The other headline boudoir is the Master Room – a chandeliered sanctuary of clean lines and cream drapes, with great views over the main square. Classic Room 9 has a four-poster queen-sized bed, high ceilings and a staircase up to the bathroom.

Hotel bar JK Lounge, with its teak terrace opening onto the piazza, is a see-and-be-seen setting for an *aperitivo*, a glass of wine or a cappuccino. There's an honesty bar for guests in the main lounge available until 11pm, with free home-made cakes, snacks and soft drinks, and a rooftop terrace open in summer. The Pink Room downstairs is a decidedly sexy club-like space for cocktails and conversation.

Hotel restaurant JK Lounge also serves light lunches, afternoon tea and dinner, with a strongly seasonal menu of Tuscan specialities, and brunch on Sundays. Styled by Michele Bonan, the room's decor combines classic Fifties seduction with ironic 1970s references.

Top table The sofa by the fireplace in the JK Lounge is most romantic; but you simply *have* to hit the terrace in summer.

Room service Breakfast can be brought to you, and JK Lounge's restaurant menu can be served in rooms until 11pm.

Dress code Fashionably relaxed.

Local knowledge In Piazza della Signoria, Café Rivoire (+39 055 214412) serves superb hot chocolate, cocktails and *aperitivi* and is great spot for watching the world bustle by – with a magnificent view of Michelangelo's domineering *David*.

LOCAL EATING AND DRINKING

Cantina Barbagianni on Via Sant'Egidio is in an ancient cellar; it is ideal for dinner à deux, or a great-value two-course lunch (+39 055 248 0508). Near the Duomo on Via dell'Oche, Coquinarius is a charming, intimate place; its salads and pastas are popular with ladies who lunch (+39 055 230 2153). Formal and glamorous, Cibrèo on Via de'Macci (+39 055 234 1100) is possibly the most famous trattoria in Italy. Try your luck at I Latini on Via Palchetti (+39 055 210916). The kitchen decides what you'll be eating – you just name the colour of wine you prefer, and whether you want fish or meat. Thrice Michelin-starred jacket-and-tie joint Enoteca Pinchiorri on Via Ghibellina is set in a Renaissance palace, where Giorgio Pinchiorri himself helps you choose from his 150,000-bottle cellar (+39 055 242757). In a side street behind the Uffizi, Ora d'Aria is masterminded by rising star Marco Stabile, who applies cutting-edge culinary techniques to trad Tuscan dishes. Showstoppers include suckling pig with garlic and lavender cream (+39 055 200 1699).

GET A ROOM!

Hotel details 7 piazza Santa Maria Novella, 50123 Florence (+39 055 264 5181; jkplace.com)

To book Ring our expert Travel Team (you'll find all our numbers with your membership card on page 5) or go to mrandmrssmith.com/jk-place-firenze.

 A bottle of spumante and a surprise gift from JK Place.

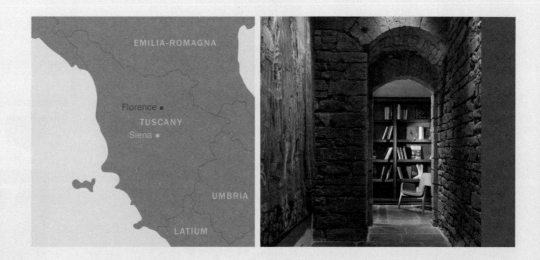

Palazzo Vecchietti

STYLE Discreetly decadent townhouse
SETTING Strozzi shopping streets

'Our suite had an English drawing-room
air, its 15-foot ceilings embellished with
cornices, mirrored lunettes over the door,
and an abundance of wainscoting'

It is a truth universally acknowledged, that a single man in possession of a good Florentine pied-à-terre, must be in want of a Mrs Smith, for weekending in Medici-shire. 'That,' said Mrs Smith, getting out of the taxi, 'is the finest his 'n' hers entrance to a hotel that I have ever seen.' Indeed, the slim entrance to the Palazzo Vecchietti certainly exemplified Conrad Hilton's adage regarding location, location, location: to the right was the Ferrari store; to the left, an outpost of that oh-so-seductive luxury label Dolce & Gabbana. Testosterone-fuelled on both sides – a good omen for the weekend.

The two-year-old Vecchietti, which occupies one of the best preserved 16th-century buildings in the *centro storico*, is perched between the Piazza Repubblica and the Palazzo Strozzi, my favourite building in Florence. The hotel lobby is in a graceful, arcaded courtyard, converted into a four-storey atrium with a skylight when the building was renovated. The Vecchietti offers something rare in Florence: suites and apartments with a residential feel, but with hotel services – concierge, laundry, housekeeping.

Our junior suite had an English drawing-room air, its 15-foot ceilings embellished with cornices, mirrored lunettes over the bedroom door, and an abundance of wainscoting. But it wasn't all Regency chasteness: the windows, tall enough to stand up in, had thick floor-to-ceiling aubergine curtains (the sort you see in the background of a Titian), and there was a couch upholstered in the same colour and with snazzy ivory piping. The bed was a real double, not two singles yoked together, as you so often get in Italy. This was definitely 'a pad'.

'But what's that scent?' asked Mrs Smith, sceptically eyeing a plug-in air freshener – a personal bugbear of hers. 'I know a better solution…' Since the first thing on Mrs Smith's Florence to-do list was a visit to the historic apothecary of Santa Maria Novella – famous for its concoctions of potpourri, soaps and scents based on ancient recipes – we went straight there. She scooped up sachets of the house potpourri and when we got back, distributed a few of them about the suite with immense satisfaction. 'Now,' she said, 'where are you taking me to dinner?'

What the Vecchietti lacks in restaurants and bars, it makes up for in detail and decadence. Rooms have kitchenettes, so it's not as though you can't rustle up a snack in situ. We were happy, though, to forgo Palazzo Vecchietti's intimacy and seclusion in the middle of the city for a sociable Florentine supper. The hotel recommended Trattoria il Parione, a warm gleam in a stoic, grey street near the Arno. The pasta was excellent, but what I remember most is the waiter, who asked if we wanted our main course right away or if we'd prefer to wait five minutes while enjoying the wine. That has never happened to me before in Italy.

You need earplugs at the ready if you want to keep out the sounds of a Saturday morning in central Florence. Roused by the motorbike buzz and clanking of glass bottles being flumed into a

recycling bin, we called the butler and ordered up *due cappuccini* and a light breakfast of pastries – it was a real luxury not having to go out.

Then, while Mrs Smith descended into Dolce & Gabbana to riffle its rails of siren-style fashion, I walked over the Ponte Amerigo Vespucci to visit my shoemaker, Stefano Bemer, who has a tiny workshop on Via di Camaldoli. Around 11am, we met up at Santa Maria del Carmine to savour Masaccio's famous friezes in the Brancacci Chapel.

In the afternoon, I dragged Mrs Smith to my custom shirt-maker Leonardo Bugelli for a fitting (well, when in Florence…). The half-chest piece he sews inside shapes the shirt beautifully (and compensates for my ever-longer hiatuses from the gym). We concluded the day with a visit to the Palazzo Medici Ricciardi to see the Chapel of the Magi, a sublime comic-strip of frescoes by Benozzo Gozzoli on the subject of the three kings.

'The Vecchietti offers something rare in Florence: suites and apartments with a residential feel, but hotel service'

'It's time for a glass of wine,' I asserted when we left, and swept Mrs Smith into a taxi, telling the driver to take us to one of my Florentine secrets. Fuori Porta – a crostini bar with a wine list as thick as a small-city phonebook – is across the Arno, just outside the old city wall. Once there, I went for it, ordering a bottle of Fattoria di Felsina Fontalloro 1995. The afternoon segued through more pasta and a stroll through Boboli Gardens.

We capped off the day watching Gigi d'Alessio's big-band musical variety show with surprise guest Liza Minnelli, and we slept in the next morning. We just had time to dash off for a quick visit to the Marino Marini Museum, a deconsecrated church in Piazza San Pancrazio dedicated to the polymath Futurist artist, just five minutes on foot from Palazzo Vecchietti. The finale was lunch nearby at Buca Mario, a little chapel of food a few steps down from the street in Piazza Ottaviani. We ordered in a kind of call-and-response, with each dish we ordered occasioning an approving 'Va bene' or 'Bellissimo!' from the waiter. Which was exactly how our Italian weekend had turned out.

Reviewed by **Gary Walther,** travel editor

NEED TO KNOW

Rooms 14, including three suites and two one-bedroom apartments.
Rates €249–€1,200, including American buffet breakfast.
Check-out 12 noon, but flexible if there's availability. Earliest check-in, 2pm.
Facilities Free WiFi throughout. In rooms: flatscreen TV, iPod dock, Nespresso machine and minibar.
Children Welcome: cots for babies are free, and under-fives can stay at no charge in their parents' bed; extra beds can be added for €70 a night. Suites, Junior Suites and apartments have sofa beds. A nanny can be brought in to babysit (€25 an hour) – just give a day's notice.
Also Small pets are welcome. In-room beauty treatments available on request.

IN THE KNOW

Our favourite rooms For the most space, go for Donatello (Room 207), which has high ceilings, rich, velvety fabrics and sky-high bookshelves next to the vast expanse of window in the sitting room. Even the sofa bed looks inviting. For the best views, it's got to be Machiavelli (Room 302), where you can see Palazzo Strozzi and Piazza della Repubblica from the terrace. As far as the two apartments go, Leonardo da Vinci gets our vote: bold carpets, plush sofas, two living rooms and a massive terrace.
Hotel bar Alas not, but there's a well-stocked minibar in rooms.
Hotel restaurant None, just a banquet-fit breakfast room on the top floor, with a grand table, heavy curtains, leather seats and oil paintings aplenty. As well as a feast of fruits, croissants and cakes, guests have a choice of cooked items. Private dinners can be organised on request.
Top table The best seat in the house: head of the breakfast table. There's also a small lounge area on the second floor, ideal for a quick drink before dinner.
Room service Breakfast can be served in rooms if required, between 7.30am and 10.30am.
Dress code Portrait-worthy perfection; some velvet wouldn't go amiss.
Local knowledge Learn your way around an Italian kitchen, courtesy of a private chef and a trip to the owners' villa, 35 kilometres out of the city in the Tuscan countryside (€250 each). After a trip to the local market to pick out produce and plan a menu, you'll head back to the villa to fashion your dishes and taste-test your talent.

LOCAL EATING AND DRINKING

In a 14th-century building around the corner on Via del Parione, **Taverna Parione** is famed for its innovative Tuscan dishes (+39 055 214005). Also nearby, on Piazza degli Antinori, **Cantinetta Antinori** has a noble tradition (quite literally) of serving regional favourites, made with fresh produce from the aristocratic Antinori estates (+39 055 292234). At the other end of the scale, **Mario's** on Via Rosina is a lunch-only, local-packed pasta place serving spectacularly cheap but totally delicious dishes (+39 055 218550). Get there early and be prepared to squeeze in – it's a short walk from the hotel. A 10-minute stroll away on the Oltrarno, gastronomic enoteca cum trattoria **Il Santo Bevitore** on Via di Santo Spirito is a simple room with dark wood panelling and rows of wine bottles (+39 055 211264). For seafood, take a cab to **Fuor d'Acqua** on Via Pisana (+39 055 222299).

GET A ROOM!

Hotel details 4 via degli Strozzi, 50123 Florence (+39 055 230 2802; palazzovecchietti.com).
To book Ring our expert Travel Team (you'll find all our numbers with your membership card on page 5) or go to mrandmrssmith.com/luxury-hotels/palazzo-vecchietti.

A bottle of wine and a basket of *biscotti di Prato* (almond biscuits). Guests staying three nights or more also get two tickets to the Uffizi or Accademia, or an afternoon with a personal shopper.

TUSCANY

COUNTRYSIDE Fields of dreams
COUNTRY LIFE Pleasure by the plateful

Everybody knows Tuscany's USPs: cypress-dotted slopes, vines lined up neatly on a green and gold patchwork of fields and olive groves… when Mother Nature planned this idyllic patch of Italy, it was picture-postcard perfection she had in mind. Perfectly preserved Renaissance treasures in ancient cities vie for attention with the flavours of the farmlands, and, edged by auburn hills and fragrant pine forests, the pristine beaches of the Versilian Riviera lure the Italian glitterati (and any oligarchs who happen to be yachting by). But don't let the crowds convince you there's no getting away from it all here; sure, this beloved province will treat you to the gamut of holiday activities, but whether you want to tour the Chianti trail, café-hop in Siena or flop onto a lounger for a sun-kissed snooze, Tuscany's temptations can be enjoyed at every pace.

GETTING THERE

Planes Access wine country and southern Tuscany via Florence (aeroporto.firenze.it), which is an hour's drive from Siena or Arezzo. For Versilia, Pisa's Galileo Galilei airport (pisa-airport.com) is an easy 30 minutes away.
Trains International routes serve Florence's Santa Maria Novella station; from there, regional services to Lucca, Pisa or Siena take around 90 minutes each (trenitalia.com).
Automobiles Tuscany's cities are best explored on foot; relish the region's vine terraces by driving cross-country with the roof down; for extra romance, rent a classic car from CLM Viaggi (+39 057 728 7415; clmviaggi.net).

LOCAL KNOWLEDGE

Taxis In larger cities, there will be ranks around town and at train stations. In Lucca, try Taxi Piazzale Ricasoli (+39 0583 494989). Hailing cabs isn't an option in the hills; but Alessandro Pierangioli in Montalcino runs a taxi service – and a wine shop (+39 0577 849113).
Siesta and fiesta Many shops close between 1pm and 5pm. Restaurants will get especially busy from 8pm to 9pm, but In Versilia, summer nights only start to look lively around 11.30pm, and bars don't close before 3am.
Do go/don't go Tuscany is a tourist magnet throughout the summer, but once you've escaped to your retreat, you won't notice. Pisa and Siena are best enjoyed off-season.
Packing tips Bring tress-taming headgear for open-top touring; designer beach togs for the Riviera; a corkscrew for on-location cork-popping in Chianti and Montepulciano.
Recommended reads Frances Mayes restores a villa and lives the rural dream in Under the Tuscan Sun; John Mortimer's Chiantishire comedy thriller Summer's Lease is set in Mondano; sculptor Matthew Spender (son of poet Stephen) portrays farm life near Siena in Within Tuscany.
Local specialities Peasant fare is king, with fagioli-filled tasty soups and stews often the headline acts. Supporting roles are played by beautiful green cold-pressed olive oil, pecorino cheese, spinach, truffles and mushrooms. You'll certainly appreciate a hearty meal, to help you soak up the area's irresistible liquid enticements – those hills aren't lined with vines for nothing. Castiglion del Bosco is the go-to winery for Brunellos (castigliondelbosco.it). The sweet-toothed should sample panforte di Siena: a spicy, chewy calorie bomb of almonds, honey, cocoa and

candied peel. Head to Nannini's pasticceria in Siena at Conca d'Oro on Banchi di Sopra for the best panforte, cantucci and orange-infused *riciarelli* biscuits (+39 0577 236009; grupponannini.it).

WORTH GETTING OUT OF BED FOR

Viewpoint Hilltop towns and rolling vineyards give Tuscany enough visually arresting vistas to fill a book; you'll soon find your own favourite. To the south, spectacular views are found atop Montepulciano's Duomo, and from Montalcino's fortress, where you can see across rooftops to the Val d'Orcia. In Versilia, ramble up the west path to the chapel of Azzano near Seravezza for a glorious coastal panorama.

Arts and culture It's not just about Florence; Renaissance riches gild the entire region. Siena has a wealth of Gothic gems, including the humbug-striped Duomo, as well as works by Donatello (in the baptistery), Duccio (in the Museo dell'Opera del Duomo) and Lorenzetti (in the Palazzo Pubblico). In summer, book tickets for open-air opera in the remains of San Galgano abbey near Siena (sangalgano.org). Arezzo boasts Piero della Francesca frescoes in the basilica of San Francesco; on the coast, Pietrasanta's museum has a hoard of maquettes by the sculptural greats (museodeibozzetti.it), and outside Viareggio, you'll find Museo Villa Puccini (giacomopuccini.it), elegant former home of the eponymous opera maestro.

Activities Admire the San Antimo abbey in Montalcino, a magnificent 12th-century Benedictine monastery; time it right and you'll catch the monks' Gregorian chanting (7pm; 6.30pm on Sunday; antimo.it). From vespers to Vespas: there's a lot of countryside to get through, so take to the highway – hire wheels from tuscanyscooterrental.com (+39 055 912 1976) in Gaiole in Chianti, which arranges guided or solo tours, too. The Bagno Vignoni is home to natural hot springs and historic Roman baths – book day passes and treatments in advance at Hotel Adler Thermae in San Quirico d'Orcia (+39 0577 889000).

Best beach The Versilian Riviera is all about beach clubs – the most exclusive are in Forte dei Marmi. Viareggio's beach is more Lacoste than Lanvin, and Marina di Pietrasanta's is a lovely wide stretch, as yet uncolonised by the yachtie brigade. Our favourite sandy spot is the elegant Il Cavallone beach club and restaurant on Lido di Camaiore (bagnocavallone.it). If untamed rocky coves are more your (beach) bag, head to Maremma's craggy coast.

Daytripper Famed for its Leaning Tower, Pisa's other marvels – the cathedral and baptistery in the beautiful Campo dei Miracoli – are no less spectacular... and a lot more stable. If you like your architecture unsullied by spandex-clad happy snappers, the ancient Etruscan village of Volterra is a hands-down winner.

Walks The car-free, tower-topped town of San Gimignano is on the Via Francigena, the eighth-century pilgrims' route from Canterbury to Rome (viafrancigena.com). If you don't fancy the full 1,056-mile schlep, try the eight-mile chunk between Gambassi Terme and San Gimignano, which takes in vineyards, farms, forests and pretty villages.

Shopping The Prada outlet in Montevarchi, Arezzo offers discounts of up to 70 per cent (+39 055 91901) – go early in the day to snare the best bargains. The Mall in Leccio Regello outside Florence is home to labels from Bottega Veneta and Balenciaga to Marni and McQueen (+39 055 865 7775). If you prefer browsing to buying, try a local market – Montepulciano's is every Thursday; Montalcino's, every Friday. We love Siena's Wednesday-morning food market at La Lizza; and, on the third Sunday of every month, its antiques market on the Piazza del Mercato.

Something for nothing Siena's Palio horse race is contested twice a year by the city's 17 *contrade* (districts), each with their own loyalty-stirring symbol, including the eagle, the panther and, um, the snail. Enjoy a haphazard tour of the city by trying to find the statues or plaques for all 17.

Don't go home without... visiting the Poggio Antico winery (poggioantico.com) in Montalcino, high in the Brunello range. Dine in its excellent restaurant while you're there.

TOTALLY TUSCANY

Wend your way through 'Chiantishire', between Siena and Florence; there are hundreds of estates, so visit chianticlassico.com to plot your route, or give wine expert Lawrence d'Almeida a call: he'll guide you around the grapes and arrange a table for lunch (+39 055 642828). Further south, Montepulciano and Montalcino are the places to hit: Valdipiatta produces some delicious Vino Nobile di Montepulciano (valdipiatta.it).

DIARY

February/March Join Viareggio's colourful street parades for the liveliest Carnevale in Italy (ilcarnevale.com). March Pisa marks New Year on the 25th (the day of the annunciation). The year officially begins at noon, when sunlight streaming into the Duomo hits a marble egg above the altar. June The San Donato Joust in Arezzo – mediaeval mayhem and lance waving; there's another event in early September (portacrucifera.it). July/August Siena's two Palio events see bareback horsemen fight tooth and hoof to win the race round the Campo (ilpalio.org). Early September Where better to get stuck into a wine fair than at Greve, for the Chianti Classico festival? (greve-in-chianti.com). October The refreshingly informal Lucca Film Festival rejoices in international cinema (vistanova.it).

Borgo Santo Pietro

STYLE Flagstones and fireplaces
SETTING Cypress hill gardens

'We wandered out, falling upon an Eden of secrets – a herb garden here, a fountain there; divans scattered under pergolas; peacocks appearing and disappearing'

Candles burned from every end, we'd been mixing hard work and benders. Our break in an elegant villa with spa in the middle of the Val di Merse was perhaps undeserved, but certainly needed. Moments after arrival, Mrs Smith and I are ushered onto a scenic terrace blushing with lemon trees and offered our first Negronis. It's like an injection of pure, instant relaxation.

Borgo Santo Pietro is an ancient building dating back to the 12th century, carefully restored by the energetic Jeanette Thottrup and her husband Claus, an elegant, understated Danish gentleman. The renovation of the building must have been a hell of a job, but it has been worth the effort: the villa and its estate is perfectly restored and fully functional – with well-stocked frigobars.

The Borgo has just eight suites – large, inviting bedrooms that overlook manicured grounds mazed with long hedges and gravelled paths. Once we were installed in ours, a plate of fresh fruit arrived along with delectable squares of white coconut ice and an excellent bottle of Franciacorta.

Suitably refreshed, and it being sundown, we wandered out, falling upon an Eden of secrets – a herb garden here, a fountain there; pergolas under which divans were scattered; peacocks appearing and disappearing. Further along, there were prepared courts for outdoor diversions such as pétanque and lawn tennis. We strolled under a portico, beside a rockery and swimming pool. A pervasive feeling of peace and warmth accompanied the fading day.

Our first night, we dined at the hotel, and had an excellent meal. Friendly and attentive service is helped along by the high ratio of attendants per guest. The cellar is looked after by the young sommelier Mirko Favalli, equipped with knowledge and a desire to please, as well as chutzpah in choosing some obscure and pleasantly challenging wines. We had much to discuss. It is hard to recall the number of courses (well, they were numerous), but I will never forget the 1995 Faccoli sparkling wine; Mrs Smith, meanwhile, took great interest in the prized Manni olive oil and triple choice of salts on the table: a black variety from Hawaii, pink from a river in Australia, and white from Trapani.

After a meal like that, we needed a bit of a lie-down. Thankfully, good-sized, classy rooms are further enhanced by an impeccable choice of mattress – a line specially flown in from Denmark. The following day, after a reviving slumber and an energising breakfast in the garden, we hit the area's less-beaten tracks, steering clear of Siena and San Gimignano, where lightning-bursts of flash photography could be seen from afar.

We embarked on a round trip from the mediaeval village of Chiusdino – the first part on a panoramic road on the top of hills, passing ancient settlements and alpine forests. Next, Radicondoli, another mediaeval village; a few miles further is Mensano. This picturesque town's 12th-century church has 14 column capitals and a Romanesque sculpture cycle by Pisan master sculptor Bonamico, and Mrs Smith is intrigued by a labyrinthine pattern set into the diminutive piazza outside its main entrance. A small family trattoria in the ancient centre here – Osteria del Borgo – serves honest, inexpensive Tuscan food at tables outside. *Perfetto*.

Casole d'Elsa, the livelier of the small towns we saw, holds communal barbecues on Sundays in the summer. It is also home of the excellent Osteria del Caffè Casolani, which has a pleasant rustic space inside and tables outdoors. There is no written menu, and the verbal offering is limited, but impeccable. Home-made pasta with wild pig ragu and a selection of local cheeses and charcuterie together with pulses made a perfect alfresco lunch. After two glasses of vernaccia, when we asked for a refill they casually gave us the rest of the bottle. 'It is nearly finished – have it.' A quick reminder that we were a thousand miles away from our home city of London.

From here, the old blue Lancia (driven by our guide Alfonso) crossed the valley and segued into gentle hills and isolated old farms, and we headed to Scorgiano. This settlement of just a few huts is the only point of sale for the Montagnola farm, which has 1,500 acres of land and forest, mostly dedicated to the organic raising of Cinta Senese. These pigs are cured in a similar way to Iberico ham. Great for us – not so mouthwatering a fate for them.

'It's hard to remember the number of courses (well, they were numerous), but I will not forget the 1995 Faccoli wine'

Back at base, a pianist playing West Coast jazz on a 19th-century rosewood Steinway eased us into our evening while we, in considerate undertones, discussed the inscrutable selection of art. What seemed the bust of a stern schoolmistress we deduce in fact to be someone's elderly aunt. Another portrait of an old dame had these Smiths agreeing that there was something teasingly exciting about it: perhaps a reminder that brains plus money is always sexy.

On our last day, before lunch, Mrs Smith paid a visit to the spa for a one-hour massage that ended up being two; then she disappeared to the nearby river for a skinny-dip. I opted for a seat by the pool, plunging in occasionally – a preliminary ritual before the next Negroni. Too quickly, though, our driver's car wheels were crunching their way down the gravel drive. As we glided through the Borgo's gates, we looked up at the two enigmatic sphinxes guarding the entrance. Unlike them, we were grinning from ear to ear.

Reviewed by **Giuseppe Mascoli**, restaurateur

NEED TO KNOW

Rooms 11, including eight suites.

Rates €335–€1,760, including à la carte breakfast, and a bottle of prosecco, selection of fruit and flowers in your room on arrival. You can also rent the villa in its entirety, fully staffed, for €54,000 a week (excludes food and drink).

Check-out 12 noon, but flexible, depending on availability. Earliest check-in, 3pm.

Facilities Spa; hot tub; 13 acres of grounds; tennis, badminton and basketball courts; bocce pitch; small playground, bikes to borrow; free WiFi throughout. In rooms: plasma TV, DVD player, iPod, minibar. Most rooms have fireplaces.

Poolside The organic lines of the heated freshwater infinity pool help it blend in with the landscaped grounds. Wicker and wood sunloungers, canvas parasols and a pool bar demand sun-soaked lazing.

Children Warmly welcomed: extra beds (€90) and cots (€30) can be supplied to suites. Babysitting (€18 an hour) can be arranged with advance notice, and little ones even have a secluded playground to romp around in.

Also Small pets can check in with you (€30 a night). The bespoke Santa Maria Novella toiletries are exclusive to the hotel.

IN THE KNOW

Our favourite rooms Honeymooners love the lavish Santo Pietro Suite – French doors open out onto a vast private balcony, and there's a Roman steam bath and shower as well as a roll-top soaking tub in the ensuite. We also fell for the feminine bathroom of the Via del Pellegrino junior suite, with its white and silver claw-foot tub and glass chandelier.

Hotel bar Take drinks at the poolside bar, or anywhere in the hotel grounds until 11pm: you'll be given a mobile so you can summon something to sip wherever you are. Try a Borgo cocktail of champagne and white rum over granita.

Hotel restaurant Breakfast is served in the open-plan kitchen, with a cosy crackling fire in winter. Later, the chef whips up an Italianate storm of Mediterranean seafood and handmade pasta in the elegant dining room, Valle Serena.

Top table For lunch, a spot overlooking the Lemon Tree garden; for dinner, a candlelit table in the Rose Garden.

Room service Breakfast can be brought to your bedside 8am–11am; a lighter snacking menu of antipasti, salads and snacks is available from midday to midnight. Dishes can be ordered from the restaurant menu (for 25 per cent extra).

Dress code Loose linens (nipped-in waists + Italian cuisine = lengthy spell on the fainting couch).

Local knowledge Watch out for open-air opera in the roofless remains of the Cistercian abbey of San Galgano (sangalgano.org). There are many legends associated with the building; there's even a stone-embedded sword in the neo-Etruscan hermitage, where you find a wonderful fresco cycle by Sienese master Ambrogio Lorenzetti.

LOCAL EATING AND DRINKING

The village of Palazzetto is only a five-minute walk away; there, you'll find a local pizzeria with a wood-burning oven at the Albergo Ristorante il Palazzetto (+39 0577 751160). On the outskirts of Chiusdino, Bistro Dai Galli is every mother/daughter-run country trattoria cliché you can imagine – and all the better for it (+39 0577 750206). Otherwise, your best bet is probably Siena, a half-hour drive away, where there are some fantastic restaurants, including Osteria Le Logge, home to local gastro hero Gianni Brunelli, who has brought his twin passions of cookery and pig-breeding to a mutually rewarding conclusion (+39 0577 48013). Not far from here, Tre Cristi is a great option for fish, seafood and gigantic steak and occupies three rooms of a 15th-century palazzo (+39 0577 280608). On the walking route between San Galgano and Monticiano is Salendo Wine Bar, serving cold Tuscan treats and wine – perfect for a lingering lunch.

GET A ROOM!

Hotel details Località Palazzetto, 53012 Chiusdino (+39 0577 751222; borgosantopietro.com).

To book Ring our expert Travel Team (you'll find all our numbers with your membership card on page 5) or go to mrandmrssmith.com/borgo-santo-pietro.

 A free massage each.

Castiglion del Bosco

STYLE Grape estate
SETTING Verdant Val d'Orcia

'There are nearly 4,500 verdant acres to explore; we tackle just one tiny corner, passing a 12th-century church with spectacular Lorenzetti frescoes'

As an Italian man living in London, Italy is never far from my thoughts. So strong are the memories in my head of summer holidays spent on the Ligurian coast that, when I land, I can tell I'm in Italy even with my eyes closed – maybe because of the background noise, our disorganised way of joining queues, or the yelled invitations from the illegal taxi drivers as soon as you step out of Arrivals.

Surrounded by green in all its colour-chart graduations, our two-hour drive from Florence airport takes us to the emerald lawns of Castiglion del Bosco through a slideshow of what Italy is today: rural farmhouses, vineyards, warehouses at the side of the motorway, railway crossings – and the magnificent and eternal hills of Tuscany. Castiglion del Bosco appears at the end of a dirt track; not just a hotel, but an ancient village. An entire *borgo* has been transformed into a luxury resort and golf course.

'So, who's the owner?' I ask. I'm answered in a hushed voice, their way of respecting someone who doesn't want to show off: 'Il Signor Ferragamo.' They're referring to Massimo – the son of Salvatore Ferragamo. Soon I see how obvious this is, from the injection of luxurious leather throughout: on the furniture, finely moulded onto edges of plasma screens, on the phone in reception, inserted into the wardrobe's panels – precise, sophisticated, tailor-made by the same hands that had created bespoke shoes for stars from all over the world. Every detail, such as the impossibly soft bedlinen, or the beautiful stone in the bathrooms, is an expression of respect of traditional crafts and lifestyles, but also a refinement of modern luxury – as the Italians do best. I can't help but be patriotic sometimes.

We start our tour of the estate, and as they speak to me in their central-Italian accent, it's as though I have Roberto Benigni at my side; every 'k' endearingly becomes an 'h', and kindness is never a formality. There are nearly 4,500 verdant acres to explore; we tackle just one tiny corner, passing by a small 12th-century church with spectacular Lorenzetti frescoes reminiscent of the works of Giotto. As for the infinity pool, it has a view of the Tuscan hills overlooking Montalcino that's worthy of a masterpiece. I cannot resist taking a picture. The lifeguard coaxes me to dive right in: 'You must try it! It's heated at 28 degrees.' We add swimming and horse-riding in these hills to a fast-lengthening to-do list with 'spa time' right at the top.

The Daniela Stainer Spa is located in a dedicated building and after a short walk from our room, we are left in the hands of its superb and professional staff. A magically peaceful place, the spa offers unique therapies based on organic and exotic ingredients. We start with a steam sauna before treating ourselves to a 'luxury couples massage', during which a melted mixture of natural oils is drizzled on the skin and combined with a relaxing and unwinding full body rub. I don't think there is anyone in the world who wouldn't love this spa.

And now to our suite, which is in a centuries-old building, formerly the stables. It is furnished and decorated in

perfect harmony with the style of the rest of the property: ochre-yellow walls blend perfectly with pale, rich fabrics, and the vermilion-red leather mirrors the majolica tiles in the bathroom. The interiors throughout are shot with mouthwatering seasonal hues: cream, khaki, apricot, tomato and grass green. Though this hotel is beautiful enough to justify doing absolutely *niente* during a stay here, there are plenty of lures to get even the laziest sybarites out of bed and espresso- or Brunello-sipping. Castiglion del Bosco is also a members' club; to keep its VIPs happy, the estate comes with a cookery school, spa, golf course and dedicated concierge service, which can arrange activities from Jeep jaunts to bike rides.

This hotel is not just a feast for the eyes, though, and our minds soon drift to dinnertime… for this, there are two restaurants awaiting. For high gastronomy, there's Ristorante del Drago, but we're in a more relaxed mood. Ambling through the butter-toned buildings into a tiny piazza we seek out what was once a priest's house and is now Osteria la Canonica. We start – of course – with a

'Deliciously rounded by the barriques, our powerful Brunello is the perfect match for superb *pici con ragù di manzo*'

Brunello di Montalcino, produced by their own vineyard; the estate is one of the five biggest producers of this stand-out Italian red. Deliciously rounded by the barriques, our powerful tipple is the perfect match for simple but superb *pici con ragù di manzo* and vegetables plucked from the hotel's own organic garden.

On our last afternoon we visit the mediaeval village of Montalcino, just 10km away. Here, I stare at the faces of the inhabitants, their Etruscan noses, the deep wrinkles etched in by cold winters and torrid summers. Another glass of Brunello warms our souls. A herd of fawns crosses our path. Are they real? Or is that Brunello playing a trick on me? At the airport, awaiting our flight back, I turn to Mrs Smith and say. 'Let's buy it.' She raises an eyebrow. 'Let's buy what?' she asks. My answer: 'A return ticket, so we can come back again. Soon.' Castiglion del Bosco is not only a hotel to recommend, it is a quantum leap, and an experience for all your senses.

Reviewed by **Matteo Torre**, Ferrari

NEED TO KNOW
Rooms 23, including 18 suites.
Rates From €350, including breakfast (an American or Tuscan spread).
Check-out Noon, but flexible, subject to availability (a charge may apply). Earliest check-in, 3pm.
Facilities Golf course, organic *orto* (kitchen garden), church, cookery school, winery, spa, gym, library, cigar room, free WiFi (in suites and communal areas) and a boutique. In rooms: flatscreen TV, CD/DVD player, iPod dock, minibar.
Poolside The heated infinity pool is set on the crest of a hill carpeted with lavender and bluebells, with rolling fields and the hilltop town of Montalcino in the distance. Expect beautiful views: the Val d'Orcia is Unesco-protected.
Children Free cots and extra beds can be added to larger rooms. Babysitting with a local nanny is available from €30 an hour (book a day in advance). There's a Kids Club area to keep little ones entertained (but they'll need supervision).
Also Pint-sized dogs can come too. The Care Suite Spa develops a special treatment menu each season, inspired by the vegetables sprouting in the gardens. All manner of activities – from horse-riding to hot-air ballooning – can be arranged.

IN THE KNOW
Our favourite rooms The Terrace Suites are bestsellers – beloved for their vast terraces and elegant styling: antique furniture, olive-and-gold *Mona Lisa* hues. Junior Suite della Torre is set in the centre of Il Borgo (the heart of the estate), with views of the *piazzetta* (little square) and countryside. Characterful details include the beamed ceiling, grape-coloured furnishings (both white-green and dusky purple), and rural Tuscan landscapes on the walls.
Hotel bar The snug CdB bar has a wonderful terrace overlooking the woods, lakes and Montalcino. Snack on *stuzzichini* (appetisers) and sample the estate's award-winning wine.
Hotel restaurant There are two: Osteria la Canonica, set in the old priest's house, is the relaxed option, serving light Italian staples – pasta, cheese, cured meats and the ilk. The more formal Ristorante del Drago excels in rich Tuscan classics such as Chianina steak in Brunello sauce; menus are seasonal, highlighting produce from the kitchen garden.
Top table Each restaurant has its own terrace, so soak up the sunshine over glasses of local red, and stargaze by night.
Room service You can choose from the restaurant menus between 7.30am and 11pm; light snacks from the hotel bar can be ordered between 4.30pm and 1am. There's also a night menu (lighter still), to take you through till 7.30am.
Dress code Feudal chic: olive, corn-gold and russet hues; luxurious fabrics.
Local knowledge Go truffle hunting with a local expert and his dogs (a translator or two will join you). Different kinds of truffle are sought out across the year: *marzolo* from January to April, *scorzone* from June to September, and the prized *tartufo bianco* from October to December. After the tour, guests can take part in a tasting or a funghi-themed meal.

LOCAL EATING AND DRINKING
Try the delicious handmade pasta at Osteria la Via di Mezzo, on Via Soccini (+39 0577 806320), in the charming little town of Buonconvento. Dishes are authentic, flavoursome, and fairly priced. Osteria Porta al Cassero (+39 0577 847196) on Via Ricasoli in Montalcino has a relaxed feel and a meaty menu (try the stewed boar or spiced chicken). The dining room's walls are peppered with black-and-white photographs, and there's a father-daughter team at the helm. For tiny portions and big flavours, head to the Michelin-starred Arnolfo Ristorante on Via XX Settembre in Colle Val d'Elsa (+39 0577 920549).

GET A ROOM!
Hotel details Località Castiglion del Bosco, 53024 Tuscany (+39 0577 191 3001; castigliondelbosco.com).
To book Ring our expert Travel Team (you'll find all our numbers with your membership card on page 5) or go to mrandmrssmith.com/castiglion-del-bosco.

 A wine-tasting tour for two.

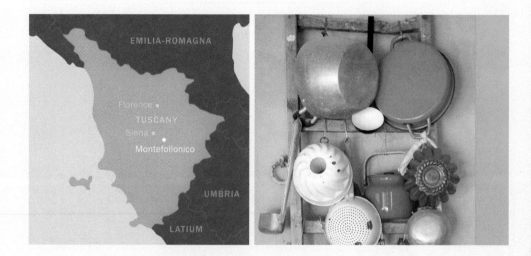

Follonico

STYLE Fairy-tale farmhouse
SETTING Valley of vines

'A vintage dress hangs beside an antique day-bed; there's an ancient wooden chest for our belongings, and walls are adorned with photos of the stars of *La Dolce Vita*'

It's good to suffer hardships: they make rewards feel more deserved. If someone had uttered those words to me, as I sat in the hospital waiting room in Florence, I would have told them to rot in hell, in all the languages at my command. So, in one language.

Mrs Smith and I were on a run of bad luck. While running for a train, that morning, in oh-so-glamorous central Hackney, Mrs Smith had leapt down the stairs, knee-first. The cracking noise as she landed had made the station master turn pale. Only adrenalin carried Mrs Smith, limping, on to our flight, and by the time we'd landed, her leg had expanded to resemble a joint of prosciutto. She couldn't walk. Of our two-day holiday, we spent most of the first day in L'Ospedale di Firenze, getting X-rays. In other news, I'd lost my wallet and my driving licence, but that didn't matter that much, since there were no hire cars left anyway.

Like I said, it's good to suffer hardships. Well, it's good, as long as your reward is getting to spend time at

Follonico: a beautifully restored 200-year-old farmhouse hidden away in a Tuscan valley with panoramic views of astonishing countryside. Hobbling out of our taxi, we were greeted by the warm welcome of Follonico's lovely owners – Suzanne and Fabio.

They considerately offered us the ground-floor Alba Chiara suite – a delightful double room and bathroom separated by an adjoining gallery or *loggia* with stone floors and exposed beams. The suite is decorated sparely and elegantly, in keeping with all the rooms in the house. A vintage dress and hat hang beside an antique day-bed, there's an ancient wooden chest for our belongings, and walls and surfaces are adorned with photos of the stars of Fellini's *La Dolce Vita*, a film we'd watched for the first time – and loved – just a few days before.

With Mrs Smith's leg iced and propped up on two plump cushions, we relaxed into a stupendous night's sleep. The bedlinen is apparently hand-woven by a family one village over, and the mattress and pillows were made not of feathers, nor foam, but of an unknown material that we were too busy peacefully sleeping on to bother accurately identifying. (Later, we're told the mattress is a 'spring-independent' one, though we're none the wiser.)

Pushing open our French windows in the morning, we saw Follonico in full daylight for the first time. In every direction were vineyards and olive groves dotted with bushy cypresses. The picturesque hilltop villages of Montefollonico and Montepulciano perched alluringly on the horizon.

Follonico, as Suzanne was careful to point out, is a home, not a hotel. There are just six guest rooms, and all visitors eat a simple breakfast together in the family dining room with Suzanne, Fabio and their three adorable children. There was wildlife everywhere. That morning, the family cat had brought in a tiny baby bunny rabbit. Several guests had brought their dogs with them, and the polite breakfast conversation was matched with the strange gurglings of the frogs in the pond just outside.

It is also apparently not uncommon to see deer, wild boar and porcupines roaming freely.

After breakfast, as we contemplated our immobility, basking in the deck chairs on the terrace outside our room, we were approached by two thoughtful visitors from NYC who took pity on Mrs Smith and offered to take us on a day of adventure in their hire car.

We drove through hills so green and skies so blue that it brought to mind – for any person who has spent too long in front of their laptop – the Windows XP screen saver. When we stopped in Pienza, a sweet eighth-century town, groups of Italian teenagers took time out from snogging sessions to gawp at Mrs Smith's 'ham leg'. In Bagno Vignoni – a tiny spa town – the highlight of our exceptional lunch was a dish of warm figs, covered in thinly sliced *lardo* (that's ham fat, in Italian) and drizzled in honey.

Getting lost a few times along the way was, as Suzanne correctly pointed out, a joy in itself. We ended the

afternoon in the enchanting company of Katya, an expat Londoner who had settled in Tuscany to make wine: the prestigious Brunello di Montalcino. As she took us around her organic farm, San Polino, her passion and charm were enough to convince us each to buy several bottles of the 2006 vintage.

That evening, on Fabio's recommendation, we ate at another Montefollonico establishment – Ristorante 13 Gobbi. In the middle of the restaurant was an immense, open-topped wheel of pecorino cheese with a glass dome suspended above it. Should you order the tagliatelle with pecorino (and you'd be foolish not to), the waiter brings out a serving of steaming home-made pasta and tosses it directly in the round of cheese before serving it to you. At the end of the night, the glass cloche is gently lowered. It was so simple yet so ingenious; much the same appeal at Follonico. There is flair and imagination everywhere, but nothing is overdone. It was perfect. Indeed, if you have any hardships that need rewarding – a paper cut, say, or a slightly delayed bus – then I wholeheartedly recommend you spend a curative stay in the care of Suzanne and Fabio.

Reviewed by **Joe Dunthorne**, writer

NEED TO KNOW

Rooms Six, including four suites.

Rates €150–€170, including Continental breakfast.

Check-out 10.30am. Earliest check-in, 4pm.

Facilities Don't expect much by way of hi-tech entertainment: Follonico's all about living it Tuscan and loving it simple. There are gardens all around, free WiFi throughout, Ortigia organic bath products, and little else to distract you.

Children Little Smiths are welcome and cots are free. The owners have three children, so there is a stash of books, DVDs, toys and games at the hotel.

Also Keen to bring your dog? Speak to the owners in advance to arrange.

IN THE KNOW

Our favourite rooms The beautiful frocks that hang on rails to complement rooms' colour schemes were hand-picked by owner Suzanne. Stake out petite suite Rosso Tramonto, flooded with natural light through its three windows, and made sugar-sweet with pops of lilac and pink in the furnishings and theatrical hanging garments, which double as decorations. If you crave space, spread yourselves across Verde Intenso's suite of three rooms, each on a separate level, connected by a stone staircase. Shots of dazzling aquamarine on bedlinen and cushions pep up a neutral palette.

Hotel bar There's an honesty bar with soft drinks and local wines – take a bottle of Brunello to enjoy in your room.

Hotel restaurant Tasting plates of pecorino and cured meats can be rustled up if you're feeling peckish, but breakfast is the only meal that Follonico serves. It's pretty special, though; all the treats are sourced within 15km of here, and a selection of freshly baked breads are delivered daily from a bakery in Pienza. Owners Suzanne and Fabio are happy to help arrange impromptu picnics in the grounds, and will provide cutlery and crockery.

Top table Given the wonderful views (a green sweep of Tuscan landscape), you'll be enjoying breakfast outside in summer; at a table by the patio windows in the breakfast room come winter.

Room service None, so raid the delis in Montefollonico and Montepulciano for panforte, cantucci and orange-infused riciarelli biscuits or local cheeses and cured meats.

Dress code Channel your inner prince and princess with oversized shirts and romantic vintage dresses.

Local knowledge Visit some local wineries: favourites include Icario (icario.it), a family-run estate in Montepulciano; and San Polino (sanpolino.it), an organic producer of Brunello di Montalcino, in Montalcino.

LOCAL EATING AND DRINKING

La Chiusa (+39 0577 669668) in Montefollonico, is another picturesque Tuscan farmhouse, serving local specialities in its rustic restaurant. Try traditional dishes such as duck with wild fennel, and marinated goose. Sample home-made pasta at Osteria del Conte (+39 0578 756062) in Montepulciano. Pici – a sort of fat spaghetti – is the area's most renowned variety; team your *pici con ragu* or *tagliata con rosmarino* with a glass of Rosso di Montepulciano. Renowned Ristorante 13 Gobbi (+39 0577 669755) at 5 Via Lando di Duccio has perfected pici in duck sauce. Food is the focus; decor and service are casual and frill-free. Osteria La Botte Piena (+39 0577 669481; labottepiena.com) on Piazza Dionisa Cinughi, Montefollonico, is popular for its pecorino-laden cuisine. Even the *bruschette* are impressive: toppings include pecorino with spicy pear jam, or with anchovies. You'll be vying with the locals to eat here, so be sure to book.

GET A ROOM!

Hotel details 2 Località Casale, 53049 Montefollonico (+39 0577 669773; follonico.com).

To book Ring our expert Travel Team (you'll find all our numbers with your membership card on page 5) or go to mrandmrssmith.com/follonico.

 A bottle of Icario Rosso.

Fontelunga

STYLE Terracotta temptation
SETTING Val di Chiana gardens

'Ivy-festooned villa on the outside, modern
interior design magazine on the inside,
this boutique B&B makes the houses
on those flashy property shows seem dull'

Swaying there in the olive groves, the Tuscan sun is beating down on us. A juicy, just-picked fig is melting in my mouth. It's not your average Friday afternoon. Mrs Smith puts her hands in mine and we consider how long we could get away with staying at Villa Fontelunga before work notes our absence…

We've been beaming non-stop since we arrived. Our first sight of this bright sienna-coloured *padronale* near Cortona inspired our highest-watt smiles, and a smidgen of smugness. Traditional ivy-festooned blue-shuttered villa on the outside, modern interior design magazine on the inside, this boutique B&B makes houses on those flashy property TV shows seem positively dull. Greeted as though we're old friends of the owners Simon, Philip and Paolo, we soon have a welcoming glass of local red wine in our hands.

Philip whisked us on a personal tour of the property; Fontelunga unfolded as somewhere wonderfully elegant and undeniably Italian. Between massive terracotta plant pots on the gravelled courtyard are old-fashioned tables and chairs. From here, there are views across a faultlessly landscaped garden to valleys that an artist could make thousands from.

A hidden nook is full of Tuscan elements combined with an exclusive LA rooftop feel. If there's a spot better suited to lounging in the shade, I'd like to know of it. OK, perhaps where I then saw a swing for two… Further snooping reveals a tennis court, and now there's fresh-fig-eating. A quick game of hiding behind olive trees later (it's never *not* funny to jump out and shout 'Boo!' at Mrs Smith), we seek out our suite. After grabbing another fruit from the tree and a glass of Chianti from the honesty bar.

A converted dovecote houses our junior suite, and glass bricks transform nest holes into windows that throw magical shapes into our cosy double-sinked, deep-tubbed blue and white bathroom. White-washed walls and farmhousey flooring frame charming lived-in touches from one-time film-set designer Philip. Above the bed hang tiny glass orbs, lighting up the room as they catch the sun. Our bed peers through French doors onto our private terrace, steps from the pool, hills beyond. Taking advantage of free WiFi, we hop onto Spotify and load up some suitable music (think *Il Trovatore* or the Intermezzo *Cavalleria Rusticana*. Not ringing any bells? Try imagining a slickly shot ad for olive oil or pasta sauce).

Newly revived, we're back in the main villa following the lead of the cute resident Scottie dogs. This involves flopping on the comfy Barber Osgerby sofa, in an exposed-brickwork sitting room, where design flourishes and coffee-table books remind us we're in Tuscany. (Meanwhile Mrs Smith sniffs out a few trashy mags hidden in the corner, perfect for poolside reading.)

Soon enough, Philip appears and asks our desires for dinner; quick as a flash he's made reservations at Osteria del Teatro, a favourite of Anthony Hopkins. We jump in the car and head over the hills to Cortona, just

one of the staggeringly beautiful mediaeval town an olive stone's spit away. Duck breast and courgette-flower gnocchi devoured in a 16th-century dining room, we return home, close our shutters and lower the shades…

Morning arrives and sightseeing calls. We're barely an hour from Florence and Siena, and even closer to Arezzo, so after a quick dip in the pool, some fruit and fresh pastries and another cup of world-class coffee on our terrace, we head to this most Italian of towns. Arezzo is where Oscar-winning *Life is Beautiful* was shot. 'It is beautiful, pigeons fly, women fall from the sky – I'm moving here,' says its hero Guido. If only we could too. (Although, disappointingly, it doesn't *actually* rain Mrs Smiths. Not on the day we visit, anyway.)

After a day pretending to be movie stars – eating gelati, attempting the world's hammiest Italian accents – it's wonderful to retreat to rustic Villa Fontelunga. On Tuesday and Friday nights they host a four-course supper, and tonight it's just us and some Australians.

As Mrs Smith can attest, I get bored with stuffy hotel restaurants and this communal set-up is the ideal antidote. Less maître d', more *Come Dine With Me*. Minus the badly made meals and ridiculing voiceover, obviously. We drink and make merry, adding our new friends on Facebook (gotta love that WiFi), eating humble, home-cooked food prepared with fresh ingredients.

Post-prosecco and canapés (oh, those zucchini fries!), we settle onto a long table in the open-plan kitchen for a parade of delights. Ravioli, local pork and veg, then a rich chocolate torte. I don't think I've ever enjoyed a dinner party this much – Mrs Smith and I almost forget that this is a hotel. Never has the cliché 'home from home' been a more accurate description – it's like staying with distant relatives. Savvy ones armed with every secret on where to eat to parking your car without paying.

Too quickly our Tuscan adventure is over, and Mrs Smith's suitcase is closed for the final time. Or maybe not? A final insider tip from our NBFs is that en route to the airport there are fashion outlets for Prada, Gucci, D&G and Armani. The only time I've seen Mrs Smith happier than when she finds a skull-patterned Alexander McQueen scarf at 70 per cent off was when she first set eyes on Villa Fontelunga.

Case crammed with designer steals, we head home, fantasising about being back in that king-size bed overlooking olive groves and Val di Chiana vineyards. Jolting me from that daydream is the harsh beep of an airport metal detector. I delve into my pockets to find the keys to our suite. Now really, wouldn't it be rude not to return them in person?

Reviewed by **Chris Cox**, magician

NEED TO KNOW

Rooms Eight rooms and a junior suite.

Rates €160–€395, including Continental buffet breakfast.

Check-out 11am, but may be flexible, depending on availability. Earliest check-in, 3pm. Reception closes at 8pm, so let the hotel know if you're arriving later than that.

Facilities Gardens, tennis courts, mountain bikes to borrow, library of books, DVDs and CDS, free WiFi in all rooms and communal areas. In rooms: iPod dock, CD player, bottled water. Every room has double-aspect views and the junior suite has a TV and DVD player, too.

Poolside A sun-warmed saltwater pool amid the olive groves overlooks the valley and nearby Cortona.

Children Welcome: there's a cot and extra bed available for €40 a night, a children's menu is on offer in the restaurant, and a local nanny can be summoned to babysit for €25 an hour.

Also There's usually a minimum two-night stay. Well-behaved little dogs are welcome. Be schooled in *la cucina povera* (peasant cooking) with a class at the villa – book your session at least a day in advance.

IN THE KNOW

Our favourite rooms The Oro room (a Superior) has wonderful views of the secret garden. Flashed with silver tones, the Junior Suite, Diamante, is in its own separate cottage with a private terrace that looks out across the Val di Chiana.

Hotel bar There is a 24-hour honesty bar and the staff have a nifty way with a cocktail shaker. You can also sit in the dining area with a tipple or two.

Hotel restaurant The dining room serves up Continental breakfast, and light lunches and dinners can be prepared if you book them at first thing. Twice a week, on Tuesdays and Fridays, owners Paolo and Phillip host a four-course dinner party, including prosecco with crostini and a bottle of wine per couple. The kitchen's closed on Saturdays.

Top table Ask to eat outside in the gardens, and catch the sun setting, resplendent, over the Tuscan countryside. The twice-weekly dinner party is served at a communal table – outside, if the weather permits (and it usually does).

Dress code Country-appropriate casual, with a flamboyant frisson.

Local knowledge Amble among the 14th-century homes and ancient olive-tree woodland of Isola Maggiore, the only inhabited island on Lake Trasimeno, half an hour away. The 10-acre patch of land was the site of Francis of Assisi's hermitage in 1211 and the setting for the saint's legendary encounter with an over-affectionate fish.

LOCAL EATING AND DRINKING

In pretty Cortona, Pane e Vino on Piazza Signorelli serves hearty dishes and has an extensive wine list (+39 05 7563 1010; closed Mondays). Head to Il Teatro round the corner on Via Maffei for pasta and rich ragus (+39 0575 630556; closed Wednesdays). In Marciano, book a table under the painted ceiling at Hosteria la Vecchia Rota, which bakes excellent pizzas (+39 0575 845362). Antico Osteria l'Agania on Via Mazzini in Arezzo dishes up delicious home-made pasta (+39 0575 295381; closed Mondays). Try the tagliatelle, and creamy polenta with the classic regional sauces. Il Goccino in Lucignano is a restaurant and brick-vaulted wine bar with a cosy roof terrace (+39 0575 836707). In Siena, Pizzeria di Nonno Mede on Via Camporegio has great pizza and views of the black and white Duomo (+39 0577 247966).

GET A ROOM!

Hotel details 5 via Cunicchio, Pozzo della Chiana, 52045 Arezzo (+39 0575 660410; fontelunga.com).

To book Ring our expert Travel Team (you'll find all our numbers with your membership card on page 5) or go to mrandmrssmith.com/fontelunga.

 Welcome drinks for two and a bottle of cold-pressed extra-virgin olive oil.

Locanda al Colle

STYLE A classic vintage
SETTING Camaiore hill-crest lookout

'Riccardo has a great eye, and an exquisite and eclectic collection of furniture. He's filled the Locanda with these treasures, each piece beautiful in its own right'

When I was 17, I had a fantasy about how I wanted my life to be. I wanted to go to Florence and paint, draw, and sketch. And be very, very romantic. Alas, an overprotective uncle saw how distracted I was by English schoolboys, thought that I would never be able to cope with Italian men, and dashed my dreams of heading off to the atelier schools with the long-haired Chelsea girls and dreadlocked ex-Etonians. Now, a decade later, Locanda al Colle has reinvigorated my lust for Tuscany. These days I am greedier than that schoolgirl: why settle for the hustle and bustle of the city when you can have rolling hills and rural romance, too?

Locanda al Colle combines the best parts of a home and a hotel: there's no reception desk or uniforms or paid bars, and the owner, Riccardo, has created an atmosphere of luxurious informality that never compromises the level of professionalism. He has cleverly arranged the nine bedrooms, giving each of them individual features so you can stay in one that seems tailor-made for you. Mr Smith and I were checked into a top-floor room that has a slanted chestnut-beam ceiling, stone floors, elegant antiques, a state-of-the-art shower and a bath (so we were both happy). Our favourite bit though (on this we agree) is a private roof terrace complete with a day-bed for lounging on when the sun is too hot, and a fireplace to keep you warm once it has gone down. Other rooms are suitable for families or larger groups, with private gardens or kitchens, but with our secluded room and long stints alone by the swimming pool, there was nothing more we needed.

Riccardo has a great eye, and was buying up Grayson Perrys and Mark Francis pieces before the big gallerists. Over two decades spent travelling around Europe working in fashion, he has accumulated an exquisite and eclectic collection of furniture, re-upholstering chairs owned by Mussolini's son-in-law to make them 'less Fascist, more funky'. He's filled the Locanda with these treasures, each piece beautiful in its own right, combining them seamlessly with the traditional Tuscan architecture to create a guesthouse that feels immaculate, every detail considered, but not so precious that you can't run around trying out every armchair for size.

Locanda's location makes for plenty of adventures. On our four-wheeled excursions, Mr Smith pointed out that my yelping at the Italian drivers was probably more dangerous than anything they were doing. Half an hour away was the walled city of Lucca, where we hired bicycles and rode the 30-minute loop; it's amazing how much guilt it relieved when we tucked into our daily pizza. In under an hour, we were in the middle of Florence, climbing over the side of the Ponte Santa Trinità to picnic on one of its buttresses. Hidden from passing tourists, with a beer, a gelato and an unopened sketchbook, there was lots of snogging – making up for that unromantic all-girls art-history school trip all those years ago.

Versilia's long stretches of sandy beach were within a 10-minute grasp; Pisa's famously leaning tower only a bit more. When we got lazy, Pietrasanta was just 5km away.

This compact, unspoiled, pedestrianised town has impressive churches, galleries, antique shops and a bell tower that the padre allows you to climb up, even if you are wearing a short skirt. There is also Paul Smith's favourite dining room, Enoteca Marcucci, which has one of the best wine lists in Italy, and which, incidentally, selected all the house vintages for the Locanda. After a quick hit of culture, some sightseeing, and a splash of good old Catholic guilt, we could be back at the hotel before the bubbles fizzled out of our remaining prosecco.

The meals at the house are worth staying in for. Like in all great Italian homes, the main kitchen is at its heart, and there is always someone in it squeezing fresh blood oranges or filling the building with appetising aromas. We ate on the patio when it was warm enough and in the kitchen when it wasn't. There is no menu – Riccardo and his friends just create delicious unpredictable yet classic dishes, such as slippery mushrooms in filo pastry for breakfast. Riccardo has a knack of anticipating exactly what you desire, before the

'Someone is always in the kitchen, squeezing fresh oranges, filling the building with appetising aromas'

thought even crosses your mind. 'Yes, of course I want a glass of pink prosecco with my tiramisu.' Grateful sigh. 'Yes, of course I want raspberry cheesecake for my breakfast.'

Once, while watching *The Godfather*, an Italian friend interrupted a kitchen scene to tell me – with no trace of irony – 'People think that in Italy we eat spaghetti and meatballs all the time, but we don't! Only, like, three times a week.' When it came to our very last meal, as I hadn't been able to find the classic dish on any menu during our escapades, Locanda's kitchen rustled some up with what they had in their cupboards. As greedy as my demands were, as ever, they did everything they, or we, could think of to make our stay as perfect as possible. Locanda al Colle – thanks for making a schoolgirl's dreams come true.

Reviewed by **Martha Freud**, designer

NEED TO KNOW

Rooms Nine, including two suites.

Rates €150–€300, including breakfast and tax.

Check-out 10am, but flexible (by half an hour) subject to availability. Earliest check-in, 12 noon.

Facilities Leafy gardens, access to the nearby Cavallone beach club, and free WiFi throughout. In rooms: iPod dock, complimentary bottled water and Erbario Toscano bath products.

Poolside The slender rectangular pool is heated, and flanked by a stone patio dotted with sun-loungers and parasols.

Children Smith Jrs are welcome; cots (free) and extra beds (€60–€80, depending on the season) can be provided. Babysitting is €20 an hour (book 24 hours ahead).

Also Canine companions can come too. Ask owner Riccardo to arrange a poolside massage or an Italian or cookery class (for you, not the canines). He can also organise scooter rental or bicycle hire.

IN THE KNOW

Our favourite rooms Deluxe room Aurora's panoramic terrace has an outdoor chiminea beside a day-bed; inside, it's elegant and luxurious, with a green and gold palette and black and white photos of nudes adorning the walls. If you crave space, opt for the taupe-toned Colle suite, which has a fireplace in the sitting room, 1950s animal-print armchairs, elegant Tiffany lamps and a stately four-poster bed. Plus, it's an easy sneak to the pool from the terrace.

Hotel bar Help yourself to drinks from the honesty bar, and enjoy them on the terrace, in the gardens, by the pool, or in one of the cosy sitting rooms.

Hotel restaurant There's no formal restaurant, but lunch is served every day, and twice a week (on Wednesdays and Saturdays) guests are invited to a sociable dinner hosted by Riccardo and his friends. Candlelit tables on the terrace set the scene for a memorable meal (washed down with plenty of vino). Typical dishes include sesame tuna and farro wheat with pesto.

Top table On the terrace in clement weather, naturally; at the communal kitchen table if it gets too chilly (unlikely).

Room service None, but in any case, it's wise to save your appetite for the three main meals.

Dress code One of the hotel's signature colours: chartreuse, olive, dusky grey or pearl pink.

Local knowledge The town of Pietrasanta, 10 minutes away by car, is a hub of artistic industry: visit one of the studios (Riccardo can arrange a tour) and look out for exhibitions in the Piazza del Duomo or the church of Sant'Agostino.

LOCAL EATING AND DRINKING

Most wining and/or dining destinations are a short drive away in the neighbouring towns and villages. Trattoria Il Marzocco on Via Marzocco in Pietrasanta serves delicious dishes that nod to Sicily, Morocco and India (+39 0584 71446). Sample Tuscan specialities at Trattoria Gatto Nero in Piazza Carducci, Pietrasanta (+39 0584 70135). Dishes are hearty and flavour-packed: pasta with broccoli and pine nuts, and rabbit with rosemary. For faultless fish, head to Trattoria Buonamico on Via Sant'Andrea in Viareggio (+39 0584 943266). Antipasti are generous; seafood, succulent. Set in an old farmhouse, Osteria il Vignaccio delivers on dazzling views and Tuscan cuisine cooked to ancient recipes (+39 0584 914200). The restaurant is tucked away on Via della Chiesa, in Località Santa Lucia di Camaiore. Sample local wines at Enoteca Marcucci in Pietrasanta (+39 0584 791962).

GET A ROOM!

Hotel details 231 via la Stretta, Località Capezzano Pianore, 55041 Camaiore (+39 0584 915195; locandaalcolle.it).

To book Ring our expert Travel Team (you'll find all our numbers with your membership card on page 5) or go to mrandmrssmith.com/locanda-al-colle.

 A bottle of prosecco or wine. In addition, SilverSmith members receive a gift of Erbario Toscano products; GoldSmith members receive a box of Erbario Toscano scented oils.

UMBRIA

Dead centre between Florence and Rome, Italy's landlocked heart spreads out as a bucolic blanket of hills, peaks and plains. Populous Perugia is the region's centre, industrious Terni its southern hub. But away from the larger towns, Umbria comes into its own: terracotta-topped villages line up like a pageant of fortified beauties, abundant in churches and castles. Cultural heritage is not Umbria's only rich vein – the Slow Food movement is strong in this produce-laden province. If it's not the wild boar and woodland truffles supplying your plate, it could just as easily be lamb from the mountains, trout from the rivers, or a tipple from one of many local wineries. Too long has Umbria lived in Tuscany's shade – the region's diverse attractions make it as well-rounded as the vowels in its melodious name.

GETTING THERE

Planes The region's main airport is Perugia-Sant'Egidio (airport.umbria.it) – 40km from Montefalco; 90km from Norcia. International flights are limited to Frankfurt, London and Tirana, but you can also connect via Milan.
Trains Foligno (for Montefalco) and Spoleta (for Norcia) stations are on the train line between Florence and Rome.
Automobiles The SS75 is the arterial road into the region, north and south. Driving to Spoleto and Foligno is relatively straightforward, but if you're going as far as Norcia, make sure your car is up to the mountain roads. Hire wheels at Perugia airport.

LOCAL KNOWLEDGE

Taxis Few and far between; get your hotel to book. For cabs around Norcia, try Taxi Spoleto on Piazzale Giovanni Polvani (+39 0743 220489). For Montefalco taxis, try Foligno-based Sebastiani Sabatino (+39 330 522679).
Siesta and fiesta Lie low between 1pm and 5pm; shops close around 8pm. The long soirées of the south don't reach Umbria, so don't expect much nightlife past 11pm.
Do go/don't go June onwards brings a festival spree to the region, adding extra colour to your visit. For a balance of crowds versus weather, spring months March to May are favourable, beating September and October by a whisker. If you don't mind cooler temperatures, you can have Umbria all to yourself, December to February.
Packing tips A penknife for picnic cheese and ciabatte, and uncorking the Orvieto; binoculars to help you pick out the bird life and wild boar around the Monti Sibillini.
Recommended reads *The Road to Assisi* by Paul Sabatier, biography of local hero St Francis; Barry Unsworth's *After Hannibal*, a tragi-comedy about an international hotchpotch of characters who are Umbrian neighbours; a book of saints to flesh out your tour of the region's many churches.
Local specialities Umbrian olive oil is more peppery and fruity, less acidic than other Italian varieties; pick up a first-press oil from one of the small *frantoi* (olive mills) near Spoleto, such as Frantoio Feliziani (+39 0743 260488; feliziani.it). Wild boar, mountain lamb and game are typical meats of the region. Umbria's ricotta is salted and rolled in bran – perfect for crumbling over pasta. Castelluccio lentils di Norcia – IGP regulated – are from the high-altitude plains of the Monti Sibillini and, like puy,

make a toothsome, nutty soup. This is a major wineland, with stars such as Orvieto Classico and Montefalco reds. And... Perugia is home to the famous Baci ('kisses') chocolates – well, it's more thoughtful than Toblerone...

WORTH GETTING OUT OF BED FOR

Viewpoint The Marmore waterfalls – 165m high – will have you marvelling at the power of nature, but don't be fooled: Romans engineered their path many centuries ago. Four trails guide visitors around the torrent. Climb the Specola tower for a *bella vista* over the countryside.

Arts and culture The region's historic hubs are cultural attractions in themselves – the walled hilltop town of Todi, mediaeval Cesi di Terni, and the Roman ruins at Spello among them. Orvieto's Gothic cathedral has a magnificent façade and fabulous frescoes inside. Tour the town's underground city, a huge cave system dug out some 3,000 years ago (orvietounderground.it). The Roman ruins at Carsulae near Terni include an amphitheatre, gateway and tombs; see archaeological treats ex situ at the National Archaeological Museum (archeopg.arti. beniculturali.it). The Burri collection is a contemporary-art marvel in Città di Castello (fondazioneburri.org). In Perugia, there are 30 roomfuls of Umbrian art, including frescoes, at the Galleria Nazionale (gallerianazionaleumbria.it). For modern pieces, the Palazzo della Penna houses works from the 18th century onwards (perugiacittamuseo.it).

Activities Saddle up to trek the Castelluccio plain with Riding Bianconi in Norcia (March to November; bianconi. com). Rafting Umbria (raftingumbria.it) or Sibillini Rafting Center (raftingcorno.it) can take you downstream on the Corno with duck's-eye views of the Frasassi gorge. In winter, try snowshoeing at Forca Canapine (forcacanapine. com), which also has short, intermediate ski runs.

Perfect picnic Pick up a bottle of Montefalco, the freshest bread you can find, truffle paste, olives, prosciutto and a hunk of caciotta cheese from Antica Enoteca di Benozzo Norcineria in Montefalco (+39 0742 378804), and head to Monte Subasio. Here you can spread your rug on the huge hump of heathland above Spello and Assisi, with views back to Montefalco and Bevagna.

Daytripper Gubbio, a two-hour drive from Norcia (90 minutes from Montefalco), is an incredibly well-preserved mediaeval town on the lower slopes of Mount Ingino. Unravel its coil of shaded narrow streets, admire its historic architecture, and crane your neck at its crenellated castles. For lunch, Taverna del Lupo, at 21 Via Ansidei, is an attractive, arch-ceilinged, stone-walled trattoria. Order something with truffles, a speciality of the house (+39 075 927 4368; tavernadellupo.it).

Walks There's no shortage of trails – mountain, lakeside or woodland – in this scenic area. Find routes among the peaks online for Monte Subasio (parks.it/parco.monte. subasio), and Monti Sibillini (sibillini.net). Above Norcia, follow the path from Forca d'Ancarano and seek out the abbey of Sant'Eutizio. The trail runs along the Castoriana valley, and passes through picturesque, semi-abandoned villages. Take a picnic and sit outside the church at Ospedaletti, which has a loggia for shelter if it's raining.

Shopping For colourful, handpainted majolica ceramics, head to the workshops of Deruta, south of Perugia. Pick up a kitsch stitch or two in Perugia, famed for its embroidery: try the Bottega d'Arte Ceccucci on Strada di Prepo, for tablecloths and miniature tapestries known as *arazzetti* (bottegadartececcucci.com).

Something for nothing It won't set you back a cent to see Assisi of St Francis fame, which has a pleasing café-lined piazza and lovely boutiques to browse. This Unesco-listed site is second only to Rome for its religious significance, its sprawling basilica a lure both for cure-seeking pilgrims and art fans: the frescoes are amazing (assisionline.com).

Don't go home without... a bottle of Sagrantino di Montefalco, Umbria's flagship wine. Excellent boutique winery Paolo Bea in Montefalco can give you a tour of vintages, tips and tastings (paolobea.com).

UNIQUELY UMBRIA

Truffles are an Umbrian delicacy: these pricey, earthy-tasting tubers can be found in patés, pastes and shaved on pretty much everything. *Scorzone* (summer truffles) are the most abundant; hard-to-find black or white truffles are their rarer cousins. You might be tempted to take home a bottle of truffle oil – but these are mostly synthetic; you're better off tasting the real thing with just a drizzle of extra virgin olive oil and some salt.

DIARY

February Norcia fêtes the end of the winter truffle harvest. **May** Costumed processions, archery and banner throwing in Assisi (calendimaggiodiassisi.it). **May/June** Orvieto re-enacts a knightly contest on horseback in the main square with the Palio dell'Oca. **June** The Festival dei Due Mondi in Spoleto: two weeks of opera, theatre and ballet (festivaldispoleto.com). **July** Umbria Jazz is a festival of blue notes, big bands and improv around Perugia (umbriajazz.com). **August** The family-friendly Montefalco Festival sees street performance, dance and oenogastronomy come to town (montefalcodoc.it). **October** Perugia celebrates the mighty bean with its Chocolate Festival (eurochocolate. com). **December** Orvieto's Umbria Jazz Winter takes place over New Year (umbriajazz.com).

Palazzo Bontadosi

STYLE Cardinal's inn
SETTING Panoramic piazza perch

'One look at Cardinal Bontadosi's former home in Montefalco is enough to infer that men of the cloth had a pretty good time in 15th-century Italy'

Nicknamed ringhiera dell'Umbria (the balcony of Umbria), Montefalco is a pretty hilltop mediaeval town – among Italy's best preserved. All around is the kind of flawless Italian landscape that postcards were created for: endless views of olive groves and manicured vines. And as newly minted Mr and Mrs Smiths, we can't wait to get to our hotel, Palazzo Bontadosi, located in its central Piazza del Comune…

Palazzo Bontadosi's façade – all bright glass and white walls – stands out among weathered, faded-grandeur hues of its grey and ochre neighbours. It injects a zippy modern freshness while managing an air of restraint. Inside are more light white walls, and sleek designer furniture. Mirco Cingolani, the manager, greets us smiling – clearly the one who sets the tone for all the staff to have such friendly and helpful dispositions. The gallery-like ground-floor level is a modern art space; before we've even checked in, Mrs Smith is admiring the sought-after terracotta pieces by Graziano Carotti. It's not just visitors here who get to enjoy Bontadosi's curation: working with international galleries, the hotel sponsors exhibits to be shown in Paris, Berlin and LA.

One look at Cardinal Bontadosi's former home in Montefalco is enough to infer that men of the cloth had a pretty good time in 15th-century Italy: domed ceilings and ancient art are part of the palace's restoration back to full Renaissance glory. The count's study is now a bedroom with decorated doors, frescoes and a bathroom set in an alcove once used to entertain his *ragazze*. The beds, meanwhile, are entirely modern-day with their profusion of pillows, and our room, one of only 10, has redcurrant and plum walls and dark oak floors.

Freshened up, we head for *aperitivi* in the small but sexy Art Lounge bar before dinner at Aurum. Taking decorative cues from its name ('gold' in Latin), the hotel restaurant is low-key but refined, and packed with locals and visitors. Mediterranean cuisine is light and precise; incongruous ingredients and bonsai-sized portions are eschewed, and locally sourced vegetables and meats have their provenance noted on the menu – a nice touch.

As a wine writer, I visit Montefalco several times a year, and am delighted once again to be in the home of the full-bodied sagrantino red. Enthusiastic as always, staff navigate the well-thought-out wine list as deftly as the food menu, and Mrs Smith soon has a glass of this inky tannic vintage in hand. One glug and she suggests we return in the summer so that we can enjoy supper outdoors on the pretty square or in the garden.

Since this luxury hotel is also a spa, we reserve part of the next day for some supine pampering. After a breakfast feast that would suggest we had more energetic plans – cappuccino, muesli, warm croissants, home-made jam tartlets and chocolate muffins, not to mention eggs and bacon – we head to the cellar for 12th-century tranquillity and 21st-century treatments, including wine therapies featuring that beloved local grape, sagrantino.

Robed and slippered, we drift down to the small, romantic saltwater pool, built into the ancient cisterns. Available by reservation only, the pool and Turkish baths are off-limits to outsiders. Next, Mrs Smith happily surrenders to an expert smearing of citrus-accented

'We return to the hotel for *aperitivi*. Dusk begins to settle, and the beauty of the setting strikes us once more'

mask during her facial, conducted in a candlelit therapy room, while I succumb to a hot-stone massage. Soon, I'm drifting off to a New Age soundtrack, dreaming I'm swimming with mermaids. No doubt the dark interior and soft lighting nudge Mrs Smith into sleep mode, too; perhaps she's fantasising she's been transported back to the Middle Ages...

So soothed, it's hard to picture us pounding pavements next, but local attractions beckon: the offer of local Montefalco Rosso and Montefalco sagrantino wines is dizzying, as is that of honey, salumi, cheeses and olive oil. A swift stroll reveals the wonderful staples of this artistic centre of Italy. Umbria is famous for its high-quality meats, especially pork, and we pass butcher shops, *enoteche* and the town's main bar where locals gather to chat and gossip.

After pausing at L'Alchimista in the main square, for traditional fare at its inexpensive best, we make the short drive to nearby Bevagna – considered by many to be one of Umbria's prettiest towns. Having admired its castles and churches, we return to the hotel in time for pre-dinner drinks. Dusk begins to settle, and the beauty of the setting strikes us once more. Navy blue, the starlit night is accented by the piazza's soft lighting and the hotel's brightly glowing entrance: it's the kind of magical moment that makes you wish you never had to leave...

Reviewed by **Ian D'Agata**, wine expert

NEED TO KNOW

Rooms 10, including four suites.
Rates €160–€240, including Continental breakfast and tax.
Check-out 12 noon, at the latest. Earliest check-in, 2pm.
Facilities Spa, art gallery, gardens, free WiFi in communal areas and some rooms. In rooms: flatscreen TV and minibar.
Poolside There's a small, heated saltwater pool in the underground spa, housed in a 12th-century cellar. The ancient stone walls are moodily lit by a sparkle of suspended lights.
Children Cots for babies are €10 a day; extra beds will set you back €40. Hotel staff can babysit for €20 an hour.
Also In its two treatment rooms and atmospheric hammam, the spa offers a locally inspired health and beauty menu, including extra-virgin olive oil massages, honey facials and wine therapies such as sagrantino Jacuzzis and grape-seed rubs. Artists, guests and locals mingle over a bottle or two in the hotel's gallery, which hosts regular exhibitions of sculpture, pottery and painting. See an artwork you like? Make an offer.

IN THE KNOW

Our favourite rooms Fine-art fans should request Room 1, Cardinal Bontadosi's former study, which has frescoes covering the walls and concave ceiling. The bathroom is in the alcove, and the scene of many a clandestine meeting between the cardinal and his girlfriends, 500 years ago. Room 9, a Superior, is an altogether more modern composition in red and white, with a beamed ceiling and a scarlet branch adorning the headboard. Junior Suite 7 has a four-poster and is the only room with a terrace, which looks out over the valley.
Hotel bar Bontadosi has a bar attached to its art gallery, which mixes mean mojitos and serves an extensive selection of big-hitting regional reds.
Hotel restaurant Aurum suits its former-palace setting: dripping in gold, with white Verner Panton chairs, wine-stocked shelves, vaulted ceilings and gilded domes. The menu changes with the seasons, but expect a contemporary spin on traditional dishes such as gnocchi with wild boar ragù.
Top table Sit out on the piazza and soak up the sun, or people-watch at a table by the arched window.
Room service The restaurant menu is on offer in rooms during Aurum's opening hours, until 10.30pm.
Dress code Cardinal scarlet, with a touch of gold.
Local knowledge Ask to arrange a car to take you to Arnaldo Caprai (+39 0742 378802; arnaldocaprai.it) or Paolo Bea (+39 0742 378128; paolobea.com): both wineries produce some of Umbria's finest Sagrantino di Montefalco.

LOCAL EATING AND DRINKING

L'Alchimista overlooks the hotel from the other side of the piazza (+39 0742 378558); tuck into simple but tasty Umbrian fare in the outdoor area, wrapped up in one of the loaner blankets if the mountain air's a bit chilly. On Piazza Mustafà, try Spirito di Vino and its 700-strong wine list (+39 0742 379048). This mediaeval inn offers light lunches and hefty dinners, with lots of local specialities on the menu, including bruschetta, salami and regional cheese. For classic Umbrian dishes, head to Il Coccorone on Largo Tempestivi (+39 0742 379535), and don't go home without trying the home-made pasta – look for the words *fatta in casa* on the menu. The walls of Castel Petroso on Corso Mameli are lined with wine bottles, most of which won't have travelled further than the local vineyard (+39 0742 379817).

GET A ROOM!

Hotel details 19 piazza del Commune, 06036 Montefalco (+39 0742 379357; hotelbontadosi.com).
To book Ring our expert Travel Team (you'll find all our numbers with your membership card on page 5) or go to mrandmrssmith.com/palazzo-bontadosi.

 Two tickets to the Museum of Montefalco, an art collection in a 14th-century church; a tour and tasting at Colle Ciocco Winery; and 20 per cent off at Umbrian linen and interiors boutique Tessitura Pardi.

Palazzo Seneca

STYLE Aristocrat's peaceful palace
SETTING Truffle-hunting town

'The Bianconis are the royal family of hospitality in Norcia, having run a clutch of hostelries in town for more than 150 years. The experience has clearly paid off'

Mrs Smith and I are staggering across the moonlit Piazza San Benedetto in Norcia's mediaeval centre, heaving in crisp mountain air, a thick sheen of pork-truffle after-sweat across our rookie brows – damning evidence of Granaro del Monte's seven-course *menù gastronomica*, ordered three hours earlier in a moment of foolish, first-night bravado. But what else were we supposed to have ordered? Everything we had read proclaimed Norcia Italy's ultimate foodie town, one of the country's black truffle centres, and the home of *norcineria* – the alchemic method of magicking pig into melt-in-the-mouth salami-type sausages and cured hams.

In a bid to escape the disapproving glare of stern old St Benedict, we scurry down one of the side streets and turn the corner into what we at first believe to be a truffle-induced Shakespearean hallucination: Romeo, in a fur-lined glossy puffa jacket, stands at the top of a rickety old ladder with a single red rose in his hand. The ladder's balanced at one end against the wooden shutter of a crumbling first-floor bedroom and anchored in place

at the other end by the foot of the young suitor's best man – similarly attired, and lifting a saxophone to his lips. Two more shiny puffas are leaning against the crumbly old wall underneath the window. One begins to tap out a gentle bossa nova on a makeshift bongo, while the other joins in softly on guitar, picking out the chords of Antonio Carlos Jobim's 'Corcovado'. Sax-puffa slides in with a smooth, melty solo that brings a light to the room, and a Juliet to the window. Mrs Smith digs her nails into my arm. Suddenly, a crescent of puffas step out of the shadows, singing the seductive, woozy Astrud Gilberto vocal part. Juliet looks down, smiling.

Back in the cool, airy room, we discard clothes and flop onto the huge four-poster, motionless. Sweet woodsmoke floats in from the street and we conk out to the soothing tones of the Italian answer to Chris Tarrant on Rai.

Something magical has happened overnight: we're somehow no longer full. Mrs Smith is languishing in the deep, moonstone marble bath. In a bid to hasten our descent on the breakfast table, I decide to enhance her experience by perching cross-legged on the Philippe Starck stool and talking knowledgeably on the subject of truffling (the French use pigs for snuffling; Italians seem to favour dogs; the Russians use bear cubs), local lentil and spelt crops (the most prized in the world), the surgeons of nearby Preci (world-beaters in the Middle Ages, with a lucrative sideline in helping talented young male singers hit the very highest notes) and St Benedict's less-celebrated younger sister, St Scholastica (would we consider the name for our first female child?). Before I can get on to the local mules' testicles, she is grabbing her shoes and suggesting a drive into the mountains (after rye toast, smoked boar, local cheese and pears, of course).

A nerve-wrackingly narrow, winding road takes us out of Norcia, higher and higher up into the mountains. The snow piled on either side of the pass grows thicker and higher with every passing kilometre, we lose radio reception completely and start encountering warning signs for mountain rams. The road levels, dips and drops us suddenly into the vast basin prairie of the Piano Grande, a gargantuan, flat expanse that, in spring, blooms with wildflowers – a different colour each week.

We stop for a beer and a vista across Piano Grande from Castelluccio, a tiny mountain-top village, famous for those lentils and for the white graffiti daubed on its walls – it allegedly serves as a means of social documentation or a means of spreading scurrilous local family gossip, depending on which book you read.

As we drive back into Norcia, a wedding is taking place in the piazza – we later discover this was the big day of our hotel's head chef. Perhaps he was the midnight serenader? Among the guests, we spot our hostess Mama Bianconi, who last night gave us a friendly guided tour of the Grotta Azzurra property across the street (also the scene of our super seven-courser), as well as the reading rooms, tea salon, sun terrace and spa of Palazzo Seneca itself. The Bianconis are the royal family

'The head waiter presents an astonishing grappa, aged in seven different types of wood'

of hospitality in Norcia, having run a clutch of hostelries in the town for more than 150 years. The experience has clearly paid off.

At dinner in the Palazzo's Vespasia restaurant that night, Mama is back on duty, as are her sons, Vincenzo and Federico. All three are natural, genial hosts, and visit our table to quality-check each aspect of our stay and to talk proudly of the region's food, people and scenery. Vespasia's menu offers a modern take on traditional local produce, light compared with the hearty fare of the Grotta Azzurra, and we're thankful for the mere five courses on the tasting menu.

Less modest is our approach to the local Montefalco (a rich, earthy and full red) and the astonishing grappa presented to us by head waiter Paolo. He tells us it's been aged in seven different types of wood and we make a valiant effort at distinguishing each of the seven, before admitting defeat and curling up in our wing-back chairs. As the acoustic guitar duo opens their set with 'Corcovado', we close our eyes and mull over which items of luggage to sacrifice for some take-home Norcian bounty…

Reviewed by **Adam McDougall**, the Lexi Cinema

NEED TO KNOW

Rooms 24, including five suites.

Rates €140–€800, including buffet breakfast and use of the spa.

Check-out 11am, but flexible if the room's available. Earliest check-in, 2pm.

Facilities Spa, gym, courtyard garden, library, DVDs and free WiFi throughout. In rooms: flatscreen TV, DVD player, minibar and free bottled water.

Children Little Smiths are welcome: cots are free, extra beds are €40, and babysitting with a local nanny is €15 an hour (book a week in advance). The restaurant has a menu for young 'uns.

Poolside No pool, but the spa has a Turkish bath, sauna and Jacuzzi. Guests can use the indoor and outdoor pools (and gym) 350 metres away at Hotel Salicone (the top-notch facilities are popular with professional football players).

Also Petite pooches can come along too, at no extra cost.

IN THE KNOW

Our favourite rooms Abhor packing light? Book Superior Room 107 for its enormous dressing area; it also has a wrought-iron bed with a brown leather sofa at its foot. The bathroom only has a bath, however. Room 210 has a wet room shower (the whole ceiling rains on you), and a private terrace with sun loungers.

Hotel bar No bar as such, but staff will fetch you drinks. Sup them in the library, or ensconced in one of the peat-brown armchairs by the fire in the drawing room.

Hotel restaurant Vespasia is elegant and airy, with linen-dressed tables, white walls, comfortable leather armchairs (straight-backed for Mr Smith, curvy for Mrs) and fresh, flavour-packed cooking. Treats such as *tagliolini* (noodles) with Norcian black truffles, and split rib-eye with pecorino and breaded vegetables showcase the local produce.

Top table By a window so you can admire the elegant landscaped garden; in warm weather, stake out a courtyard spot.

Room service 24 hours, including drinks, snacks and light meals, as well as dishes from the restaurant.

Dress code Relaxed European finery: spruce up casual threads with an Hermès scarf, knotted insouciantly.

Local knowledge Wander into Norcia and admire the *castellina* (a fortress built in the 16th century), the Gothic church of Sant'Agostino, and the main basilica, dedicated to St Benedict. Pick up picnic supplies from the delis – cured ham, salty pecorino or mild *cacciota* cheese will stand you in good stead – and the bakery on the main drag sells moreish salt-encrusted rolls.

LOCAL EATING AND DRINKING

If you're into truffles or cured ham, welcome to heaven. Palazzo Seneca's owners are also behind the mighty Granaro del Monte, a minute away in Hotel Grotta Azzurra on Via Alfieri (+39 0743 816513). At 150, it's one of Umbria's oldest eateries; sit by the fire and order the charcuterie-heavy tasting menu. Norcian locals flock to Dal Francese for their funghi fix; it's modest, traditional, two minutes' walk from the hotel and specialises in improbably good value *tartufo* dishes (+39 0743 816290). Outside Norcia, in Castelluccio, Taverna Castelluccio on Via Dietro la Torre is worth the 45-minute drive for its *cucina povera* – try the *coratina di agnello* (+39 0743 821158). If you make it out to Spoleto, Ristorante Apollinare is squirrelled away below the Aurora Hotel on Via Sant'Agata (+39 0743 223256). It has a cosy outside terrace, an irreverent approach to Umbrian cooking, and a knack of attracting Italian celebrities.

GET A ROOM!

Hotel details 12 via Cesare Battista, 06046 Norcia (+39 0743 817434; palazzoseneca.com).

To book Ring our expert Travel Team (you'll find all our numbers with your membership card on page 5) or go to mrandmrssmith.com/palazzo-seneca.

 A bottle of Umbrian red; late check-out (if available). Stay three nights or more and get a three-course lunch (including wine and water) at Granaro del Monte; book a suite, and you'll get a spa treatment each.

ABRUZZO

COUNTRYSIDE Protected peaks, historic hamlets
COUNTRY LIFE Ancient arts and crafts

Spanning countryside and coast, Abruzzo is rustic, rural, romantic Italy at its undiscovered finest. The way of life in this mid-calf patch of the country has changed little over the years: residents still farm the land in fresh Apennine air; artisans use age-old techniques to craft ironwork, ceramics, lace and gold jewellery. Though many of this remote region's hilltop settlements were built in the Middle Ages, their towns and castles astonish today's visitors; the rest is taken care of by the mountains, where the wild terrain is unspoilt, its ancient sheep-droving routes intact, and a seasonally changing carpet of colour sees high plateaux clad in snow, crocuses, orchids or poppies. If the coast calls, get back down to sea level and hit the long, sandy shores of the Adriatic, an hour's land-cruise from Abruzzo's rugged centre.

GETTING THERE

Planes Abruzzo Airport is three kilometres outside of coastal Pescara (abruzzoairport.com). On the other side of the Apennines, Rome's airports are easier main gateways to the province: Ciampino is two hours away, and Fiumicino is two and a half hours away (adr.it). **Trains** L'Aquila station is half an hour by car from Santo Stefano di Sessanio in the east; Trenitalia (trenitalia.com) provides routes to the rest of Italy, usually via Terni. From Rome, the journey will take just over three hours. **Automobiles** This remote mountainous region will be much easier to navigate with a sturdy set of wheels, as everything is a drive away. All three airports have assorted car-hire outposts.

LOCAL KNOWLEDGE

Taxis You're more likely to find a mule pulling a cart than a cab in these peaceful parts: ask your hotel for advice. **Siesta and fiesta** As is usual in the Italian countryside, shops tend to close for most of the afternoon. Dinner at 8pm is about as wild as the local nightlife gets. **Do go/don't go** The slopes will be snow-covered from December until early April, with the warmest temperatures in June and July. Evenings in the mountains are chilly. **Packing tips** A shepherd's crook to move roving animals out of your way; something cosy to wrap up in on cold mountain nights; wildlife-enlarging binoculars. **Recommended reads** The Miracle of Castel di Sangro is Joe McGinniss' account of two years following a local team's journey from sub-division to Serie B; for romance in wartime Abruzzo, read Christopher Castellani's A Kiss from Maddalena; and Robert Forczyk's Rescuing Mussolini – Gran Sasso 1943 recounts how German troops liberated the Italian dictator from his hilltop hideout. **Local specialities** Abruzzese cuisine is fond of the humble lentil: the region's own iron-rich variety is an old and rare species that thrives only in mountain climes. Munch on milk-fed mountain lamb from the plains: it will either be roasted (abbacchio), cubed and on skewers (arrosticini), grilled on charcoal, or braised in a casserole. Maccheroni alla chitarra is named after the 'guitar' strings that form the pasta strips; look out for a kick of chilli, another stalwart of the region's food. Best wine? The fruity, dry red, Montepulciano d'Abruzzo, produced throughout the region (montepulciano is the grape, and not the Tuscan town). Head to the Cerulli Irelli Spinozzi winery in Teramo to try some (+39 0861 243290; cerullispinozzi.it).

And... the women of Scanno still sport the traditional cloaked-in-black costume: a full-length pleated skirt, headdress and apron. The ensemble weighs around 12kg.

WORTH GETTING OUT OF BED FOR

Viewpoint Stare out at the green expanse of the Majella massif from Passo San Leonardo (sanleonardo.com), the high point of the mountain road, just along from Pacentro.

Arts and culture You may wish to bypass L'Aquila, as many of its galleries and museums are still being restored after the 2009 earthquake. Instead, visit historic Sulmona: Piazza Garibaldi has a Baroque fountain and Piazza XX Settembre hosts a brooding statue of classics hero Ovid, born in the town. Wander Castelli's pottery workshops to see brightly coloured majolica being made; take some home from Ceramiche Simonetti on Villagio Artigiano (+39 0861 979493). More majolica can be seen at the tile-decorated tomb of local war hero Andrea Bafile, hidden in a cave at the end of Bocca di Valle. Guardiagrele is a smith town in the truest sense: it's famed for its intricate gold, copper and wrought-iron works, displayed in the shops dotted along the old town wall. Don't miss Santa Maria Maggiore, with its asymmetrical Majella-stone façade, Baroque interior, ancient bell tower and one of master goldsmith Nicola da Guardiagrele's famed crosses.

Activities Roccaraso (roccaraso.net) is one of the country's largest ski resorts (and Abruzzo's best). National parks constitute a third of Abruzzo's territory: go on miniature safari in the Majella National Park (parcomajella.it) to spot the freely roaming wolves and bears, and keep an eye on the sky for soaring birds of prey; this limestone massif encompasses gorges, caves, rivers and peaks, 30 of which reach 2,000 metres or higher. The Gran Sasso National Park (parconazionalegransasso.it), favoured backdrop of dashing heroes (George Clooney in *The American* at least), has lots of horse-riding and walking routes through its remote terrain, with hidden hermitages, waterfalls and castles along the way.

Perfect picnic Pack your hamper with breads and cheeses from the daily market in Santo Stefano di Sessanio's main square for a lakeside picnic on Lago di Scanno. The breathtaking scenery takes in a church as well as the water. In summer, boats and pedalos can be hired.

Daytripper The seaside city of Pescara on the Adriatic Coast has 20 kilometres of uninterrupted sandy shores. While you're there, peek in the home of poet and political pest Gabriele d'Annunzio (casadannunzio.beniculturali.it), and the Museo delle Genti d'Abruzzo (gentidabruzzo.it), which charts the history of the region's people.

Walks Hike up to Rocca Calascio, the oldest and highest mountain fort in Italy; it dates back to the 10th century. If reaching the 1,460-metres-above-sea-level peak is a bit of an uphill struggle, stop in Calascio village for some lunch; try Rifugio della Rocca for some nourishing local fare (+39 338 805 9430; rifugiodellarocca.it).

Shopping Abruzzo has plenty of open-air produce markets, including a twice-weekly one in Sulmona's Piazza Garibaldi (Saturdays and Wednesdays). Sulmona is also famed for its many gold shops, as is Scanno: take the scenic drive along rocky gorges and hair-raising bends to glean some Orient-inspired filigree jewellery at Di Rienzo Armando at 1 via de Angelis (+39 0864 74329). In summer, Castelli has an alfresco ceramic market, with artisans at work.

Something for nothing Drive up to Campo Imperatore, a peak-encircled plain filled with wild flowers. It's a scenic drive that's been captured in countless TV ads for German cars (and *Ladyhawke*). The remote refuge hotel here was where Mussolini was imprisoned until his escape in 1943.

Don't go home without... stocking up on confetti at Confetti Pelino on Via Stazione Introdacqua in Sulmona (+39 0864 210047). No, not the stuff you throw at newlyweds: the sugar-coated almonds have been made here for centuries.

ABSOLUTELY ABRUZZO

Abruzzo is where luxury spice saffron made its Italian home, after a priest brought it back from Spain 450 years ago. The crocus it grows in flourishes on the Navelli Plain, and is arduously farmed, hence the hefty price tag – it takes 100,000 flowers, and a whole lot of labour, to produce 1kg. The result is worth it: Abruzzese saffron is widely considered the best in the world, lending its deep colour and rich aroma to risottos the land over.

DIARY

17 January Festa di Sant'Antonio Abate celebrates an Egyptian saint and lasagne all at once (scanno.org). **May** On the first Thursday of the month, residents of Cocullo celebrate their patron saint, St Dominic, by toting his statue through town. So far, so Catholic. But this procession includes live snakes, brought by pilgrims to honour the serpent-loving saint. After conventional festival staples – fireworks, banqueting – the party ends with a breakfast picnic at the foot of the town's hill. We don't know what happens to the snakes… (comune.cocullo.aq.it/festa.asp). **September** Santo Stefano di Sessanio hails the lentil harvest by cooking lots of them outside the city hall. **October** Villa Santa Maria's Festa dei Cuochi brings Abruzzese dishes to the masses (rassegnacuochi.com).

Sextantio Albergo Diffuso

STYLE Fortress conversion
SETTING Mediaeval Apennine mountain

'Our repast induces a glow that is further fanned by our bedroom, a 12th-century stone grotto with heated floorboards and a luxurious Philippe Starck bath'

Two or three times a month I create a romantic meal for Mrs Smith – a few candles, a more-than-decent bottle of wine, and the best I can muster in the kitchen. It's a way of shrugging off our day-to-day familiarity – but it has never worked this well before. As I arrange the *culatello di Zibello* on a platter, Mrs Smith stands close, clutching her glass with a mischievous grin. 'Now, tell me,' she says, once we're seated and clinking glasses to our impending trip. 'What's this Tantric sex hotel you're taking me to?'

'Oh, it's a surprise darling,' I mutter. Taking a long sip of wine, I begin rummaging through my mind – in much the same way one tears up a hotel room when a passport goes missing – trying to work out where she might have got this idea. Ah, it's the name: Sextantio Albergo Diffuso. The hotel is in Santo Stefano di Sessanio, a 16th-century village some 4,000 feet up in the mountains of Abruzzo. (Sextantio is in fact the Latin name for Sessanio.) This eyrie is only 65 miles or so from Rome, but having departed the city late in the afternoon – just in time to get caught up in rush hour – we arrive well after 10pm, and we despair of finding a bite to eat. The only sign of life in the village – a tight cluster of mediaeval houses crowned with a chess-rook tower – is a candlelit window. Peering in, we find ourselves greeted by a waiter, the very charismatic Massimo, who has stayed up to welcome us with open arms.

Using my feeble Italian, I order a snack. Next thing, a seemingly never-ending procession of dishes is coming our way from the kitchen – seven courses in all. We weren't *that* hungry, but how can I tactfully stem this flood of food? Remember the Monty Python sketch where John Cleese is a chef so offended he whips out a machete while the maître d' impales himself on the client's fork? Clearly the smartest thing to do is to keep on eating: why ruin dinner?

As for Mrs Smith, so far, so good. She is transported by the mediaeval dining room, which has stout timbers crisscrossing the ceiling, thick, half-wagon-wheel arches, and a fireplace a man could stand in. (These, I think, are the missing ingredients back home.) The wine is from a vineyard dating back to Roman times, and the food is so fresh it is practically still growing on our plates. The repast induces a glow that is further fanned by our bedroom, a 12th-century stone grotto with a few mod cons, among them heated floorboards and a luxurious Philippe Starck bath. 'And there's not even a TV to break the spell,' says Mrs Smith.

In Italian, *albergo diffuso* means a hotel that is scattered among a number of buildings. In Sextantio's case, the hotel rooms are individual houses, but there's more to it than that: the owner of the hotel, the Sextantio Company, has more or less adopted Santo Stefano di Sessanio as an archaeological project.

At one time, Santo Stefano was so prosperous from the wool trade that it provided a quarter of the revenue of the Kingdom of the Two Sicilies. But when entrepreneur turned hotelier Daniele Kihlgren first came here, the

village's population was down to 70, its infrastructure crumbling fast. Kihlgren's motto is 'development without construction', which means turning traditional houses into accommodation without tarting them up, but also avoiding the sort of reverence for the past that would turn them into period sets. No luxury hotel guest really wants to go back to the 16th century, hence the Starck tub – an inspired touch. Kihlgren has also restored some of the public buildings and furnished them in period style, and has concluded an agreement with the local council to preserve the surrounding countryside against villa construction – which he calls an Italian first.

Breakfast is served in the erstwhile house of the shepherd master, where we find a table laid as though for a royal banquet: fresh ricotta and pecorino cheese, prosciutto, chorizo, homebaked cakes and frittata, with a roaring fireplace the perfect backdrop. Our days are happily spent getting lost in the village's maze of alleys and walking through the *Campo Imperatore* (alpine meadows), where the only thing that breaks the silence is

'Our days are happily
spent getting lost in the
maze of alleys; the only
sound is a cowbell or two'

a cowbell or two. There are a few small shops
that sell local products: mountain cheese, massive
loaves, salami, little jars of wild saffron, jam,
honey and local liqueurs of plums and berries. At
the *tisaneria* we sample infusions of blueberry
and saffron and nibble on lacy biscuits made in a
waffle iron.

Dinner the second evening is at the inexpensive,
family-run Tra le Braccia di Morfeo, where you can't
go wrong. The bruschetta in particular is in a league
of its own. Ever tried mincing garlic and celery with
olive oil, then spreading it on toast? I hate celery
but this dish changed my mind – a definite
contender for the menu back at Casa Smith. Mrs
Smith is so enchanted with the atmosphere that
she forgets about the Tantra. Instead, she adopts a
new mantra: 'When are we going back?'

Reviewed by **Daniel Vernon**, documentary director

NEED TO KNOW

Rooms 27, including seven suites.
Rates €220–€450, including Continental breakfast.
Check-out 11am, but flexible if there's availability. Earliest check-in, 3pm.
Facilities Library, free WiFi throughout, mountain bikes and snowshoes to borrow. In rooms: minibar, underfloor heating and artisan bath products.
Children Cots and extra beds are provided free. Babysitting with a local nanny costs €15 an hour (give a day's notice).
Also Pets are allowed. The hotel can recommend local guides for tours of the mountains.

IN THE KNOW

Our favourite rooms Palazzo delle Logge overlooks the village square and the Medici gate. For views out to the Apennines from the lounge and balcony, pick Casa sulle Botteghe. All the dimly lit and atmospheric rooms at Sextantio are minimalist and mediaeval, with working fireplaces, stone walls and wooden doors. The beds are high enough to fit a chamber pot beneath (although there are real flushing toilets in each bedroom these days) and have hand-stuffed woollen mattresses.
Hotel bar Head to La Cantinone in the cosy wine cellar for *aperitivi* and antipasti. If the local red doesn't take your fancy, the *digestivi* will: try the bitter, herby genziana, or the sweet cherry ratafia. There's also the Liquorificio, where a selection of local liqueurs is on offer, as well as tipple-lined benches dotted around the communal areas.
Hotel restaurant Locanda Sotto gli Archi serves Abruzzese cuisine on softly worn wooden tables; the plates are handmade by local craftsmen. Try traditional antipasti such as pork liver salami, prosciutto and the freshest ricotta. Maccheroni alla chitarra – the speciality pasta of the area – is also rustled up in the kitchens here, and served with lamb ragù. A breakfast spread of home-made pastries, tarts and cakes is laid out in the bar every morning.
Top table Close to the huge fireplace – especially when the mountain temperature drops.
Room service None.
Dress code Humble hemp and cotton to match the ancient earthen surroundings.
Local knowledge The hotel's bread-making classes teach participants how to use a wood-burning oven from the 16th century to make crisp pizza bases. Guests can also enrol for Abruzzese cookery courses that take in both the method and the history of mountain cuisine. Weaving is also on offer.

LOCAL EATING AND DRINKING

Try Tra le Braccia di Morfeo (+39 0862 899110) on Via Nazario Sauro for traditional dishes made with regional ingredients in a setting that's half restaurant, half gallery (with local craftwork for sale). On Via del Lago, Locanda sul Lago (+39 0862 899019) is a small inn at the bottom of the village, with views of the lake and Santo Stefano, and hearty mountain food, such as the region's classic zuppa di lenticchie, and lamb reared on a nearby plateau. The antipasti are what impresses at Ristorante Clemente (+39 0864 52284) on Vicolo Quercia in Sulmona, especially the cheese offerings: baked hunks of pecorino, warm, fresh ricotta and fried fromage-filled pastries. For ice-cream, you can't beat Gelateria la Rotonda on Corso Ovidio, also in Sulmona, right next to the San Francesco della Scarpa church.

GET A ROOM!

Hotel details Via Principe Umberto, 67020 Santo Stefano di Sassanio, L'Aquila (+39 0862 899112; sextantio.it).
To book Ring our expert Travel Team (you'll find all our numbers with your membership card on page 5) or go to mrandmrssmith.com/sextantio-albergo-diffuso.

 Wine tasting on arrival; a tour of the village; and free mountain-bike and snowshoe hire. Members staying three nights or more also get dinner for two: a four-course tasting menu, including wine, water and coffee.

HOLIDAY

ROME

CITYSCAPE Archaeological eye-candy
CITY LIFE Piazza people-watching

It's true: Rome wasn't built in a day – and almost every moment of its lengthy and splendid history is still visible in some form. Parts of the city are perfectly mediaeval; Renaissance and Baroque buildings soar skyward, and breathtaking sculpture sits on every corner. With the Vatican in town, Easter and Christmas are highlights on Rome's calendar, but pilgrims of an artistic persuasion flock to the tiny city state all year to adore Raphael and Michelangelo's Sistine Chapel frescoes. Rome is also about the art of life – food, fashion and fun are enjoyed with religious zeal in this most sensual of capitals. Live *la dolce vita* as the locals do: colonise a café in the Campo de' Fiori; linger longer over rustic pasta in a traditional trattoria; let your feet wander and your eyes roam.

GETTING THERE

Planes Rome is served by two airports: Fiumicino and Ciampino (adr.it). A fixed-fare cab from Fiumicino's official ranks costs €40. From Ciampino, the 15km taxi ride costs €30; or, for a couple of euros, take the bus to Anagnina metro station (30 minutes from central Rome).
Trains From Stazione Termini you'll get express connections to other Italian cities, including Florence. The Leonardo Express to Fiumicino airport departs every half an hour, takes 35 minutes and costs €14 (trenitalia.it).
Automobiles Don't. Seriously. Unless you want to venture further, a car will be more of a pain than a pleasure. Cars with foreign plates are not allowed in the historical centre. If you can find one, blue-zone spaces cost €1 an hour; the daily rate for carparks is about €30–€35.

LOCAL KNOWLEDGE

Taxis Official white cabs can be hailed anywhere, but it's quicker to go to a rank, where you'll also find numbers to call. Avoid unofficial, unlicensed taxis, especially for airport transfers – if in doubt, ask your hotel to book.
Siesta and fiesta Romans holiday in August, so some shops and restaurants will be closed; ring before you set off without reservations. Hotels in August can be great value though. Some businesses also close 1pm–3.30pm.
Do go/don't go In summer, the city gets sweaty; you may prefer spring or autumn, but winter is the quietest. Any time of year, dive off the busy tourist routes and explore Rome's countless lesser-known treasures at random – the museums are often surprisingly uncrowded.
Packing tips A pick and shovel to unearth artefacts lurking beneath the streets (the reason Rome's metro has never been completed); flat shoes; blister plasters.
Recommended reads *Decline and Fall of the Roman Empire* by Edward Gibbon is *the* history book; Patricia Highsmith's *The Talented Mr Ripley* is set partly in Rome; HV Morton's 1950s memoir *A Traveller in Rome* is evocative; Anthony Capella's lit-rom-com *The Food of Love* is peppered with mouthwatering culinary descriptions of life in the city.
Cuisine The foundation of Roman food is *cucina povera*; much of it focuses on offal and working-class staples, such as *trippa alla Romana* (tripe with tomato ragù) and *baccalà* (fried salt cod), but there are plenty of less challenging delicacies, such as *saltimbocca* (veal rolls

with sage) and *rigatoni all'amatriciana*. Testaccio, where the city's stockyards once were, is still the preserve of Rome's butchers, and there are dozens of trattorias and delis, including Volpetti (+39 06 574 2352; volpetti.com) at 47 via Marmorata. There's a vibrant café culture, but no self-respecting Roman would order a milky cappuccino after mid-morning; go for a high-octane ristretto instead.

WORTH GETTING OUT OF BED FOR

Viewpoint Piazza del Campidoglio by night, for panoramas over the Forum and the Palatine, or the top of the Spanish Steps, for a view over the Centro Storico to St Peter's – one Shelley and Keats doubtless swooned over.

Arts and culture Wherever you wander, Rome's importance to Western civilisation is marked in stone: the Colosseum, the Forum, St Peter's and the Vatican, the Sistine Chapel, and the Pantheon – its dramatic interior richly decorated in a multitude of marbles, all beneath a massive masonry dome. If you want to visit the Vatican, plan carefully: queues can be horrific and if you're only here for a few days, your time might be better spent elsewhere: Galleria Doria Pamphilj (doriapamphilj.it) is a palazzo groaning with 15th- to 18th-century treasures; Villa Borghese boasts spectacular grounds and a magnificent art collection (galleriaborghese.it). Rome's millefeuille of history is illustrated near the Colosseum by the Basilica di San Clemente (basilicasanclemente.com), a 12th-century church built on top of a 4th-century Christian basilica, founded on an older pagan temple.

Activities Attend a private wine-tasting class at the prestigious Rome International Wine School on Via della Croce near Piazza di Spagna (+39 331 999 5549). Row, row, row your boat gently across the lake at Villa Borghese (galleriaborghese.it). Saddle up and ride along the catacomb-lined Appian Way with private guiding company Nerone (nerone.cc). If swordplay in sandals lights your fire, train as a gladiator with the Gruppo Storico Romano re-enactment society (info@gsr-roma.com). There's an air of the Colosseum about the Stadio Olimpico, home to football teams AS Roma and Lazio. Buy weekend-game tickets at the stadium box office or the Orbis agency (+39 06 474 4776) in Piazza dell' Esquilino; bring ID.

Perfect picnic With so many trattorias to try, picnicking won't be top of your to-do list; that said, if portable snacks are your thing, there are few pleasures as great as licking a hazelnut ice while you stroll the sunny side of the streets.

Try Giolitti at 40 via Uffici del Vicario (+39 06 699 1243); or Il Gelato di San Crispino near the Trevi fountain at 42 via della Panetteria (+39 06 679 3924).

Daytripper Join the locals as they head for the cool waters of Lake Bracciano (lakebracciano.com), a picturesque reservoir about half an hour's drive outside Rome.

Walks A stroll at sunset in the lush Pincio Gardens, above Piazza del Popolo, is a pleasantly romantic way to wind down (and cool down) after a sunny day's sightseeing.

Shopping Via Condotti, starting at the foot of the Spanish Steps, is Rome's most prominent shopping street; running parallel, Via Frattina comes a close second. Via del Corso focuses on younger styles. If you prefer edgy and unusual, poke about near Piazza del Popolo; Via Sistina is good for small, stylish outlets; between these roads on Via Crispi, pop in on the Underground market, a four-floor collectibles emporium for vintage rummaging. On Via Nazionale, you'll find leather stores and a handful of boutiques. Alfresco Porta Portese flea market in Trastevere is the largest in Europe, held on Sundays from 7am until around 2pm.

Something for nothing An audience with the Pope is free (vatican.va). Or test the world's oldest lie detector in the portico of Santa Maria in Cosmedin, where you can play at being Hepburn and Peck in *Roman Holiday*. No fibbing, though: if you lie while your hand is in the carved-marble Bocca della Verità ('mouth of truth'), it will be bitten off.

Don't go home without... strolling the lively farmer's market in Campo de' Fiori near Piazza Navona: its colourful stalls of flowers, fruit and veg set up every morning but Sunday.

REMARKABLY ROME

Think of Rome and you'll picture Italy's gilded youth zipping around astride mopeds. Do as Fellini's dashing journalist Marcello did and scoot the sights aboard a vintage Vespa with Happy Rent (+39 06 4202 0675). Hire one and wobble wherever your wheels take you, or let their drivers ferry you on a city tour. If bikes just ain't your thing, you can also hire cute-as-a-button mini motors, including vintage Fiat 500s and Autobianchi.

DIARY

Mid-March Riff, an impressive independent film festival (riff.it). **March/April** On Good Friday, a torch-lit procession from the Colosseum up Monte Palatino re-enacts the 14 stations of the cross. On Easter Sunday, the Pope delivers his blessing from the balcony of St Peter's. **May** Primo Maggio (primomaggio.com), the May Day festival in Piazza San Giovanni, welcomes spring with a free gig. **29 June** The feast day of Rome's patron saints shuts the city down. **September** Big-hitting culture at the RomaEuropa Festival (romaeuropa.net). **October** The Rome Film Fest (romacinemafest.org). **November** The Roma Jazz Festival (romajazzfestival.it) brings bebop, swing and all things snazzy to the Eternal City. Teatro dell'Opera di Roma hogs the opera-season limelight (operaroma.it).

Babuino 181

STYLE Palace turned city pad
SETTING Steps from Piazza del Popolo

'The best bit is hidden behind shutters and drapes: a small but magnificent balcony, the perfect vantage point for people-, Vespa- and couple-spotting while sipping coffee'

'Tutt' a posto? Everything good?' our waiter asks, refilling our glasses with yet more perfectly chilled Frascati. Frankly, things couldn't be any more *a posto*. Mr Smith and I are on honeymoon in Rome – staying at luxurious hotel-meets-private-apartments Babuino 181 in the upmarket Tridente district – and dinner has been a lovely, post-nuptial reminiscing session. By the time dessert arrives, we've already dissected the wedding speeches, laughed at the awkwardness of the first dance and argued passionately about whose relatives were the most embarrassing.

Rome, we're finding, is a city very much to our tastes. So far, we've browsed the boutiques of Via Sistina (me) and gazed longingly at the football kits and flags on display in the AS Roma store on Piazza Colonna (Mr Smith). The romantic, foliage-festooned Otello alla Concordia, tucked away down a tiny cobbled sidestreet off Via della Croce, suits us both nicely, though. The fresh pasta is perfectly al dente; the saltimbocca meltingly tender; the service attentive and impeccable. We wander down the

linguine-thin Via del Babuino, which connects the bustle of Piazza di Spagna to the only marginally less bustling Piazza di Popolo, passing jewellers, fashion outlets and appointment-only antique dealerships en route.

Babuino 181 isn't the sort of hotel that has a doorman, bellboy and room-service menu; if that's what you're after, Rome has plenty of five-star *grande signore*. But if, like me, what you really want from a stylish stay is a luxury home from home in which you can relax in elegant surroundings without being pestered by over-zealous cleaning staff, and where you feel free to hang your clothes off the end of the bed and walk around in your underwear, this is the place for you.

A discreet entrance leads to a smart, marble-swathed lobby. Two friendly concierges at the desk direct us into a futuristic-looking glass lift that glides up a couple of floors to our room. With a wave of our keycard, the door clicks open and we're confronted with a wall-mounted iPod-style control panel, which glows eerily blue in the darkness, and allows us to adjust the temperature and lighting to our exact requirements. Mr Smith prods inexpertly at it for a minute (I hope this isn't a sign of how things will be now we're married), and our luxury suite is illuminated. Spread before us is a huge open space, decorated in a sophisticated mix of pristine caramels, creams and browns. Diaphanous drapes hang over floor-to-ceiling windows that overlook the boutique-browsing below; warm woods and beaten copper form contemporary artwork panels on the walls.

In one corner sits a circular walnut table and inviting-looking chairs – our dining area, should we wish to invite any Romans back for supper – and just to the right of this is the most enormous flatscreen TV I've seen outside of *MTV Cribs*. In the middle of the room is a Vatican-sized bed, mounted on a suede-covered base, and beyond this the honey-coloured, marble-and-mosaics bathroom – home to a giant bath tub, deep side-by-side sinks

and a shower that's big enough for four (should we wish to invite any more Romans back).

The best bit is hidden behind shutters and more drapes. A small but magnificent marble balcony is revealed, the centrepiece of the hotel and the perfect vantage point from which to people-, Vespa- and couple-watch while sipping a coffee from our in-room Nespresso machine – or, as Mr Smith and I do that very evening, finish off a bottle of chilled prosecco while we wait for our 10-month-old baby to do the decent thing and go to sleep.

Mr Smith has suggested a trip to the Museo d'Arte Contemporanea, so, next morning, we're in a gallery with a baby that has just learned to walk. Art-lovers' legs are roughly tugged, each new painting is responded to with a high-pitched scream and alarms are triggered every few minutes, as Miss Smith lurches towards priceless artworks. Thank God, then, for the Italians' innate love of *bambini*.

'Shopping is as much a part of life in Rome as blaring car horns in traffic and dodgy Europop'

Even the armed guards who rush in to thwart a would-be art thief end up clicking their fingers and waving indulgently at our gurgling offspring.

After all that, I need a break. As Mr Smith decamps with mini Smith to Villa Borghese in search of greenery and chaseable pigeons, I head for Via Condotti, home to the flagship stores of the most upmarket Italian ateliers. I've always known that shopping is as much a part of life here as blaring car horns and dodgy Europop, but I'm amazed at what a cross-generational experience it is. The *bella figura* is alive and well: 70-year-old women here sport the same manicured nails, glossy lips and designer jackets as their twentysomething counterparts. As I flit between Fendi, Gucci, Versace and Bulgari, I'm in the company of teenage girls and great-grandmothers. Fashion knows no age-limits in Italy and I leave, bag-laden, feeling truly inspired.

As I head back to Babuino 181 through a maze of cobbled side streets, in which stallholders hawk everything from fresh juice and cherries to magazines and jewellery, I pass a tiny *salumeria*. Inside is row upon row of the sort of items that, I know, will make Mr Smith very happy indeed – aged prosciutto, fine Parmigiano, snooker-ball-sized lumps of minced pork, studded with herbs and dusted with cheese – so I pop in to pick him up some pre-dinner delights. And for dessert? Well, he'll have to wait to see what I've got wrapped up in tissue paper inside the La Perla bag that's swinging from my arm… *Tutt' a posto*, indeed.

Reviewed by **Sarah Maber**, editor

NEED TO KNOW

Rooms 14, including six suites.
Rates €325–€750. Continental breakfast is sometimes included – check when booking – otherwise it's €20 each.
Check-out 12 noon, but you can check out later for €100 (subject to availability). Earliest check-in, 2pm.
Facilities Free WiFi throughout. In rooms: flatscreen TV, iPod dock, minibar, Nespresso machine, Comfort Zone toiletries.
Children Welcome. Cots can be added free; extra beds are €50. The hotel can organise babysitting for €25 an hour, with half a day's notice.
Also Close to the hotel is the eponymous *babuino* (baboon), one of Rome's 'talking statues'. The fountain is next to the Chiesa di Sant'Atanasio dei Greci, on Via del Babuino.

IN THE KNOW

Our favourite rooms Room 302, the Babuino Suite, has plenty of natural light and a private terrace. It's a perfect fit for families, with two rooms, a guest bath and a large lounge area with space for two extra beds. Rooms have a digital lighting system; fresh orchids and Diane Epstein prints provide the personality. A Deluxe Suite on the corner of the building, Room 105 comes with cobbled-street views of both Via Margutta and Via del Babuino. Each of the bathrooms has honey-coloured marble walls and countertops, with mosaic tiling in the shower.
Hotel bar None, but cocktails are occasionally served on the roof terrace, and there are options nearby – try the Art Studio Café (+39 06 326 09104) at 187 via dei Gracchi. Raid your minibar for wine and snacks if you want to stay in.
Hotel restaurant The roof terrace restaurant serves traditional Continental and Italian cuisine.
Top table Mingle in the modern communal lounge, or admire Rome's twinkling lights from a table on the terrace.
Room service Breakfast, snacks and other light bites can be brought to your room.
Dress code Euro-flash: cashmere and silks in cappuccino and chocolate hues.
Local knowledge Ask the hotel to book tickets for the Borghese Gallery, housed in the Villa Borghese at 5 piazzale del Museo Borghese (+39 06 841 4065; galleriaborghese.it). The paintings, sculptures and antiquities formed Cardinal Scipione Borghese's 17th-century collection, and deserve at least an afternoon's browsing. Also save time for the villa's family-friendly gardens, which give the art a run for its money.

LOCAL EATING AND DRINKING

Due Ladroni at 24 piazza Nicosia (+39 06 686 1013) is a glitzy affair – expect to paparazzi-dodge on your way in. Since its doors opened in 1945, a loyal crowd of well-connected diners has flocked here for the fresh fish, seafood and Neapolitan-inspired dishes. The restaurant is of a nocturnal bent, staying open until 1.30am. The Smith-approved **Hotel de Russie**, just a few doors down from Babuino 181, is perfect for an afternoon espresso – sit in its expansive courtyard (+39 06 328 881). At cocktail hour, locals love to perch on **Gusto**'s patio on Piazza Augusto Imperatore for appetisers and champagne before lingering over a late dinner (+39 06 322 6273). Seafood-centric **Pierluigi** (+39 06 686 1302) at 144 piazza de' Ricci is 15 minutes away, but well worth the cab fare. Try the *moscardini* – battered and fried octopus served with juicy lemon wedges – or paper-thin aubergine filled with prawns and creamy mozzarella.

GET A ROOM!

Hotel details 181 via Babuino, 00187 Rome (+39 06 6992 1907; romeluxurysuites.com).
To book Ring our expert Travel Team (you'll find all our numbers with your membership card on page 5) or go to mrandmrssmith.com/babuino-181.

 A bottle of Franciacorta (sparkling wine from Lombardy).

Residenza Napoleone III

STYLE Super-luxe palazzo
SETTING Fashionable Via Condotti

'Instead of notepads, there's a stack of wine-bottle labels from the family's own vineyard. A panama hat hangs on a hook, in case you forgot yours'

The only problem with tourism is the other tourists. In Rome, where tourism was more or less invented, they traipse around in huge groups in high season, with their backpacks and sneakers and shorts, swamping the Spanish Steps, gawping at the Trevi Fountain, dripping ice-cream onto the Colosseum. Worse is the horrible moment when you catch your reflection in a shop window and realise that, contrary to the mental image you've been entertaining all day, you are not in fact a chic Italian in handmade shoes and tailored linens, but a sweaty tourist fumbling with a camera and map. Shock! You are one of *them*, the great uncouth swarm, the one blot on this otherwise perfect city. Thankfully, there is a solution: stay at the Residenza Napoleone III and live out your fantasy of being a suave Italian for the weekend. For this is not a hotel – those are for tourists – but your own private palazzo on Rome's smartest street.

On our first morning, Mrs Smith and I return from a stroll along Via Condotti, past branches of Fendi and Ferragamo, to find a cluster of holidaymakers reading an official information panel outside the Residenza. It explains that the building dates from 1556 and that in the late 16th century it was transformed by its owner, a diplomat for the Medici family, into one of Rome's grandest residences. It goes on to note a ceiling inspired by the Sistine Chapel, the dozen busts of Roman Emperors that line the corridors, and the staircase with 100 marble steps ('regarded as one of the marvels of Roman civil architecture'), before regretfully telling readers that, though it sometimes hosts exhibitions, the building is not normally open to the public.

At this point, I draw from my pocket a small brass key attached to a green velvet rope. As the tourists look on, I step towards the huge wooden gates that fill the building's arched stone entrance, open the small door within a door, and go inside. Smug? *Noi*? The building is actually called the Palazzo Ruspoli, after the family who bought it in 1713. Today, the Ruspolis still live here, but along with running a chic riad in Marrakech, they rent out two apartments, calling them the

Residenza Napoleone III, after the French emperor, who used to stay here when visiting Rome.

Walking up the marble staircase, past the busts and the frescoes, then along the wide and high corridors, our steps echoing on the stone floor, it feels as though we've broken into a private museum. There's no reception desk, restaurant or bar – all of which helps if you're trying to forget you're a... well, you know. There's just a discreet butler to bring breakfast and make reservations for dinner (should you wish).

Our apartment, the Roof Garden Terrace Suite, is reached via a spiral staircase. There's a tiny bedroom, a bathroom (stocked with Bulgari products and pretty soap containing rose and lavender petals), and an upstairs sitting room. If you're seeking slick hotel minimalism, the latest gadgets and decor in a hundred tones of taupe, this is not your Holy Grail. If you're a bit bored of all that, and fancy somewhere with lots of character, you're at the right address. Staying here feels as though

we've borrowed the lived-in flat of a distant aristocratic relative. Surfaces are crowded with objets d'art, the walls are bookcase-lined, there are paintings and statuettes of racehorses and piles of auction catalogues. Instead of a notepad, there's a stack of wine-bottle labels from the family's own vineyard. A panama hat hangs on a hook, in case you forgot yours.

But the real draw is just beyond the sitting room: throw open the French windows and you are in a capacious private roof garden with the most incredible view over the Italian capital, among olive trees and bushes of mint, thyme and lavender. On our first day, it rains, but the second dawns warm and bright; we eat breakfast under a parasol outside, listening to the bells ring out from the city's churches and trying to work out which of the endless terracotta domes are the Vatican's.

Testament to how truly 'Roman' our Residenza Napoleone apartment already has us feeling, by the middle of day two, I've left an extra shirt button undone

'We eat breakfast under a parasol, listening to the bells ring out and trying to identify which domes are the Vatican's'

and I'm making expansive hand gestures. But if you want to pretend you're an 18th-century royal, you need to book the Napoleone Suite: it is jaw-droppingly lavish, with three vast, high-ceilinged rooms, full of golden chairs, antique mirrors, tapestries and huge oil paintings. In the breakfast room is a notable 18th-century painting by Giovanni Paulo Panini; in the living room, an oil masterpiece in an ornate frame swings off the wall to reveal a massive TV. The marble-lined bathroom hides behind another artwork, and a widescreen film projector is concealed in the drapes above the immense bed. Buckingham Palace isn't a patch on this.

Of course, Rome has the best sights of any city (not to mention world-class gelato), so we spend a happy couple of days pounding pavements and gawking alongside the tourists at the Pantheon, St Peter's and the Keats museum. But ultimately, nothing compares to the pleasure of retreating from the fray to the roof of our own palazzo, cracking open a bottle of prosecco and watching darkness settle over the city.

Reviewed by **Tom Robbins**, travel editor

NEED TO KNOW

Rooms Two suites.

Rates €730 for the Roof Garden Terrace Suite; €1,400/€1,930 for the Napoleone Suite (depending on whether you book the adjoining Blue Room, too). Prices include Continental breakfast.

Check-out 11.30am; earliest check-in, 12 noon. Both may be flexible.

Facilities Two reception rooms, library of DVDs and CDs, free WiFi throughout. In suites: plasma TV, film projector and screen, DVD/CD player, minibar, Bulgari bath products. In the Napoleone Suite, there's also a kitchenette, and an iPod with a Bose dock. A maid keeps the place spotless and a private tour guide and butler can be arranged.

Children Extra beds can be added for €100 a night. Cots are free. If you take the connecting Blue Room (which can have twin beds), you get an extra bathroom, too. Babysitting can be arranged.

Also Well-behaved pets allowed. Beauty treatments available on request. There are gyms, pools and saunas nearby.

IN THE KNOW

Our favourite rooms The opulent and luxurious Napoleone Suite is the apartment to book for the palatial, silk-draped, canopy-bed experience. If there are four of you, add on the connecting Blue Room, which is up a little wooden staircase. In the sitting room, a large painting is flung open to reveal a wall-mounted flatscreen hidden behind its frame – the bathroom and kitchen are similarly concealed. The Roof Garden Terrace Suite is much humbler, but it has a multilevel decked terrace with fabulous views of Rome. NB, though, the steep staircases are not for the faint of heart.

Hotel bar No actual bar space, but you can arrange for your minibar to be stocked up as you like it.

Hotel restaurant None, but the Napoleone Suite has a kitchenette with a hob and bookings can be made for you at local restaurants. Special-occasion catering can be arranged.

Top table Breakfast is laid on a grand Bulgari-silver spread in the Napoleone Suite's silk-papered dining room, lined with paintings of Roman monuments. From the Roof Garden Terrace Suite's alfresco table, you can see the real thing.

Room service Nothing's brought to you except breakfast, but staff are helpful and arrangements can be made for dinner.

Dress code Your own interpretation of palazzo pants.

Local knowledge Five minutes away, at the foot of the Spanish Steps, the Keats-Shelley House is a tiny museum where the tubercular poet came to convalesce (it didn't work out well). The house holds a collection of manuscripts, memorabilia and paintings, as well as a library of Romantic literature (+39 06 678 4235; keats-shelley-house.org).

LOCAL EATING AND DRINKING

La Rosetta on Via della Rosetta is a Michelin-starred fish (and only fish) restaurant next to the Pantheon; the menu is based on the day's catch (+39 06 686 1002). The tuna tagliatelle and fish carpaccio with olive oil are both excellent. Another fine seafood restaurant is Quinzi e Gabrieli on Via delle Coppelle serving delicious dishes in a series of rooms decorated with spectacular artwork (+39 06 687 9389). On Via Borgognona, Nino has been feeding the glitterati classic Italian dishes with a Tuscan accent for decades (+39 06 679 5676). Il Brillo Parlante on Via della Fontanella is the perfect low-key lunch stop, with a well-stocked wine bar upstairs (+39 06 324 3334). The eternally popular Café della Pace is the night-or-day spot where the stylish crowd go to be people-watched (+39 06 686 1216).

GET A ROOM!

Hotel details Palazzo Ruspoli, 56 via della Fontanella di Borghese, 00186 Rome (+39 347 733 7098; residenzanapoleone.com).

To book Ring our expert Travel Team (you'll find all our numbers with your membership card on page 5) or go to mrandmrssmith.com/residenza-napoleone.

 A bottle of Anagallis wine from the Ruspoli family's vineyard in Chianti, plus late check-out (when availability permits).

HOW TO... cheat at opera

THE MARRIAGE OF FIGARO (1786)
Music Mozart **Words** Lorenzo da Ponte

Mozart's fluffy, knockabout, dress-as-a-peasant-girl, hide-in-a-cupboard farce is the operatic equivalent of a *Carry On* film. Light-hearted and bawdy, with randy young pages, fake love-letter schemes and the odd 'hang on, so you're actually my mother? But I was going to marry you!' moment, *Figaro*'s a fitting follow-up to *The Barber of Seville*.

10-SECOND VERSION Wily valet comes dangerously close to marrying mother, but wins sensible, non-incesty wife despite randy count wanting to get in there first. Much cross-dressing. No one dies.

MORAL **The grass may be greener on other men's lawns, but try to stick to your own turf, eh?**

BIG NUMBER Figaro's teasing bass aria *'Non più andrai'* ('No more gallivanting') is the most fun, but the Countess' lament *'Porgi, amor, qualche ristoro'* ('Love, give me some comfort') is the classic soprano audition piece.

RIGOLETTO (1851)
Music Verdi **Words** Francesco Maria Piave

Based on a Victor Hugo novel, this grim tale of misogyny and murder is probably the second-best hunchback-based story in history (Hugo gets first place, too). It has everything a good opera should: rampant adultery, a dreadful curse, corrupted innocence, and one heck of a grisly ending.

10-SECOND VERSION Sarcastic, adultery-abetting hunchback gets his comeuppance in a sack of dead daughter. Some cross-dressing. A smidgen of untimely death.

MORAL **Lock up your daughters.**

BIG NUMBER The lusty duke's anti-feminist tenor anthem *'La donna è mobile'* ('Women, eh?').

DON GIOVANNI (1787)
Music Mozart **Words** Lorenzo da Ponte

Mozart categorised it as *opera buffa*, which is a bit like calling *Love Story* a 'knockabout romcom'. This dark and dramatic morality tale starts with attempted rape, segues quickly into murder, skips through adultery and ends on the hero being dragged to hell by a magic stone ghost and some demons. Wow.

THE 10-SECOND VERSION Don Giovanni, to be blunt, can't keep it in his pants. Surely one can't go through life seducing married women, callously casting them aside and occasionally killing their fathers? It turns out that, no, indeed one can't.

MORAL **Hands off the ladies, steer clear of the wine, go easy on the murder.**

BIG NUMBER In *'Madamina, il catalogo è questo'* (Sweetheart, here are the figures') Giovanni's servant Leporello catalogues, in aria form, the exact number of his master's conquests, broken down by country (if you must know: 640 in Italy, 231 in Germany, 1,003 in Spain, etc).

LA BOHÈME (1896)

Music Puccini **Words** Luigi Illica, Giuseppe Giacosa

This tale of poverty-stricken artists in 19th-century Paris is one of the most performed operas in the world, and required viewing for any struggling creatives. Not that it's in any way reassuring about such career choices, mind.

10-SECOND VERSION Poor but soulful poet bears a candle for flighty, flirty seamstress. Flighty, flirty seamstress develops TB and dies of the cold or pneumonia or poverty or something. The end. Poet is still poor. The actual end.

MORAL **Money may not buy you love; but it could buy you essential medical care.**

BIG NUMBER Soprano showstopper Musetta's waltz – '*Quando me'en vo*' ('When I walk') – in which she modestly celebrates precisely how hot she is; Rodolfo's '*Che gelida manina*' ('Your tiny hand is frozen') is one of opera's great chat-up lines. Not.

THE BARBER OF SEVILLE (1816)

Music Rossini **Words** Cesare Sterbini

The prequel to *The Marriage of Figaro* (written 30 years later by a different composer) is the classic *opera buffa* – a genre that can be distinguished from the heavyweight stuff by the fact it features more zippy songs and a lot less death. It's a fun, farcical hum-along romp – and who doesn't like those?

10-SECOND VERSION Sourpuss Doctor Bartolo's after his ward's money; the count's just after his ward. Helped by Figaro's borderline crackpot ideas ('I know! Disguise yourself as a drunken soldier!') and a well-stocked dressing-up box, the count wins a wife, the doctor keeps her money, and Figaro gets by without having to do much barbering.

MORAL **Money can't buy you love, but it can buy you a lot of outfits.**

BIG NUMBER Figaro's jaunty, rollicking entrance aria, '*Largo al factotum*' ('Make way for the factotum'). All together: 'Fi-i-i-garo! Fi-i-i-igaro! Figaro-figaro-figaro-figaro F-i-i-i-garo!'

MADAME BUTTERFLY (1904)

Music Puccini **Words** Luigi Illica, Giuseppe Giacosa

This Japan-set tale of devotion and betrayal doesn't tug on the heartstrings so much as yank them from your chest, soak them in puppies' tears and then use them to string the violins played at your granny's funeral.

10-SECOND VERSION Boy meets girl. Boy marries girl. Boy is not that fussed about girl. Girl feels otherwise. Boy goes back to America. Girl has child, waits three years. Boy comes back. With new wife. Girl kills self. Boy is complete bastard.

MORAL **Never trust a sailor.**

BIG NUMBER *Butterfly*'s haunting, swooping, lung-hammering tragic aria '*Un bel dì vedremo*' ('One good day, we will see').

SOUTH

Palermo •

ABRUZZO

MOLISE

Campobasso

CAMPANIA

Naples

SOUTH

PUGLIA

Bari

5　1　3

Capri

4　2

6

AMALFI COAST

Potenza

7

8

Brindisi

BASILICATA

AEOLIAN ISLANDS

CALABRIA

Catanzaro

AMALFI COAST

COASTLINE Winding roads, secret coves
COAST LIFE Sailors and sirens

Craggy, curvy and riddled with hidden beaches, the Amalfi Coast is one of the most spectacular stretches of shoreline in the world. Just south of Naples, this postcard-perfect promontory attracts landscape-seeking artists, glamour-thirsty film stars and seafood-hungry gourmands from around the globe. The serpentine coast road weaves around rocks and tunnels through the mountains, never losing sight of the sea. Crumpled-wedding-cake towns spill down to the shore, where weathered fishing skiffs dock to unload the catch of the day; alongside them, summer heat-seekers sip limoncello at the terraced bars of Positano or sample simple grills in pretty Praiano. This volcanic headland reaches out from the ankle of Italy towards the Tyrrhenian, its sheer mountainside plummeting into the darkly deep, sun-sparkled sea.

GETTING THERE

Planes Naples' Capodichino airport (gesac.it), around 40 miles from Sorrento, is the most convenient entry point for Campania's coast, with frequent international flights.
Trains Naples has three main rail stations: Mergellina, Campi Flegrei, and Napoli Centrale on Piazza Garibaldi, linked to Sorrento and Salerno by the twice-hourly Circumvesuviana train; see vesuviana.it for details.
Automobiles It's worth renting a car to explore Campania's countryside; be warned, though – in summer, traffic can be bumper to bumper. Hertz has a branch at Naples airport (hertz.com); Praiano is a two-hour drive away.
Boats There are regular ferries from Naples to Sorrento; the faster hydrofoils take about 35 minutes (a speedier option than the Circumvesuviana) and leave from Beverello harbour, off Piazza Municipio (metrodelmare.net).

LOCAL KNOWLEDGE

Taxis Expensive, but you'll find cabs outside stations and on squares. In Positano, the taxi rank is at the top of the village; the boat taxi is down at the right-hand side of the dock. In Sorrento, most sights are walkable.

Siesta and fiesta Opening times vary but, roughly, they're 9am–1pm and 5pm–10pm; in low season, some shops close on Saturday afternoons and Monday mornings. Evenings start late: folk head out to eat at around 10pm.
Do go/don't go Coaches cram the coast road come summer, but the pay-off is the palpable buzz in the air. Spring and September/October are quieter, but the weather is still good. Winter's romantic, but much will be closed.
Packing tips Tackle steep steps with foldable flats you can pop in a bag; hats or scarves to help tame speedboat hair.
Recommended reads *The Volcano Lover: A Romance* by Susan Sontag explores a love triangle in 18th-century Naples; John Steinbeck's 1953 novel *Positano* is set in and around the town; *The Last Days of Pompeii* by Edward Bulwer-Lytton spies on the city's ill-fated inhabitants.
Local specialities Spaghetti alla anything is the star player on Amalfi menus, but it would be a crime not to have it with fresh seafood: we love *vongole* (clams). Sorrentine cuisine naturally focuses on Campania's larder of mainstays – sweet olive oil, plump San Marzano tomatoes and plaited *fior di latte*: a cow's milk mozzarella (nearby Naples is credited with the invention of this

now-staple ingredient – not to mention the classic pizza margherita it commonly adorns). This is also the homeland of sweet liqueurs limoncello and nocino, made from giant cliff-grown lemons, and local walnuts respectively.

WORTH GETTING OUT OF BED FOR

Viewpoint For one of the world's most impressive vistas, head to hilltop Ravello; soak up the views from the gardens of Villa Cimbrone (villacimbrone.com), which cascade picturesquely down the promontory's tip. Afterwards, have lunch at low-key Villa Amore (+39 089 857135): it's not fancy, but the food is great (and so is the scenery).
Arts and culture The Greeks and Romans both left their highly civilised mark on this coast, bequeathing temples, roads and civic architecture. In 79AD, Sorrento had an awesome view of the eruption of Mount Vesuvius and the destruction of Pompeii. Wander the well-preserved ruins of the doomed city, but wear proper shoes – Roman roads are surprisingly ill-suited to sandals (pompeiisites.org). Most of the best treasures dug out from the ash (plus finds from Egypt, Ephesus and Herculaneum) are on show at the Museo Archeologico Nazionale di Napoli (+39 081 442 2149), a Battenberg-pink building atop Santa Teresa hill.
Activities Promenade along Sorrento's marinas and lie on one of the little sundecks, or requisition a boat to jaunt over to pretty Positano – try Mediterraneo Charter (+39 081 807 2947; mediterraneocharter.it) for bespoke day trips. Take your love to a deeper level with TGI Diving Sorrento (+39 081 808 9003): there are plenty of local scuba sites to explore. Fiery temperament and a head for heights? Get the Circumvesuviana train from Sorrento to Pompeii, then buy tickets by the station newsstand for the bus to the top of Vesuvius. Peer into its smoky crater and out across the Bay of Naples (or just enjoy its flora and fauna; see parconazionaledelvesuvio.it for walking routes). Learn to make pasta at the Sorrento Cooking School (sorrentocookingschool.com).
Perfect picnic Take a packed lunch of prosciutto or pastries and head out of town: a mile west of Sorrento, Bagni della Regina Giovanna at Punta del Capo is a landlocked lagoon. Queen Joan II of Naples reputedly bathed in this calm natural seawater pool in the 1600s.
Daytripper On the fabulous island of Capri, you can explore dramatic scenery or rub shoulders with the jet set while you shop in a miniature Milan of boutiques. The hydrofoil takes 20 minutes, but if you hire a speedboat in Sorrento, you can explore secluded beaches en route – try Nautica Sic Sic (+39 081 807 2283; nauticasicsic. com). Scout out your own private hideaway – the little cove near De Filippo's island is stunningly set among the rocks, with nothing but the local fisherman's house in sight.
Walks Follow the Via del Capo from the Corso Italia as it winds around the little cape of Sorrento for surround-vision views of the town. Massa Lubense, a ravishing stretch of coast and country at the tip of the peninsula, is a pretty area of hamlets and lemon groves, crisscrossed by mule trails and footpaths – fantastic for an afternoon's strolling, especially in spring, when the citrus blossom is in bloom.
Shopping Positano is the fashion capital in these parts, with myriad petite shops and galleries selling silk kaftans, Murano glass, local ceramics and designer dresses. The town's famous for artisans, tailors and cobblers who will make beautiful made-to-measure pieces – sometimes while you wait. If you hanker for the days when 'You've got mail' meant ink, parchment and wax seals, visit La Scuderia del Duca (+39 089 872 976) on Amalfi's Largo Cesareo Console for exquisite handmade paper.
Something for nothing Sneak into one of the wood-inlay workshops and observe the traditional craft of marquetry (*tarsia*); try Gargiulo Salvatore at 33 Via Fuoro in Sorrento.
Don't go home without… hiking along the Sentiero degli Dei, a super-scenic route along the Amalfi cliffs; go solo or with a guide (onthegodspath.com). From Praiano, head to Bomerano, then follow the track to the monastery of San Domenico. Go later in the day, and you'll catch sunset, too.

ABSOLUTELY AMALFI COAST

Nothing says 'Amalfi Coast' like a tot of limoncello in a chilled ceramic tumbler. The region is famed both for its ceramics and the sweetly tart nectar expertly prepared from the lemon trees that spring from the rocky cliffs. The genuine article is made with rind, not juice, hence its distinctly sweet flavour, and the drink is slowly supped as a *digestivo* in bars and restaurants all over the coast. Limoncello sorbet is another local favourite.

DIARY

March/April Brass bands parade Sorrento's streets before an incense-waving crowd for Easter. **June–September** Opera, dance, music and theatre performances take over venerable villas and gorgeous gardens for the Ravello Festival (ravellofestival.com). **Late June** The Festa di Sant'Andrea on the 27th sees the statue of Amalfi's patron saint hiked down to the sea, followed by pyrotechnics. **Late July** Boats and fireworks in the bay beneath Maison La Minervetta for the Festival of Sant'Anna on the 26th. **July–September** The Sorrento Summer of Music season pulls in internationally renowned classical and jazz musicians (sorrentotourism.com). **November** The 30th is Sant'Andrea's birthday: cue more statue-toting processions for the patron saint.

Bellevue Syrene

STYLE Pastel-painted villa
SETTING In view of Vesuvius

'Ice-buckets of wine are scattered about:
fuel for more cheerful fantasy about
mischievous Roman gods and Neapolitan
sex goddesses'

It's a fine thing to be sitting here with Sophia Loren in the lobby of a spectacular hotel. The dimensional specifics of each are similarly impressive. Additionally, I have a glass of prosecco nearby, blue water in the middle-ground, a volcano in the distance and, just by my right elbow, a gasp-making cliff-drop of perhaps 300 feet down to a small beach of black sand.

To be truthful, there is a (sliding) sheet of glass between me and bloodily pulped oblivion, and – alas – La Loren is here only in photo-album form: although, unlike Vesuvius, she continues to smoulder (even off the page). Still, as reception areas go, it's not too shabby. The sun shines, oranges and lemons grow like weeds in the perfumed air and I think, as I so often do, of *La Dolce Vita*.

Sorrento's freshly refurbished Bellevue Syrene is the most elegant of the necklace of fading grand hotels garlanding the vertiginous cliffs of the Golfo di Napoli's southern shore. It's only 50km from Capodichino airport, but since half that distance is travelled on the slow,

derrière-clenchingly terrifying SS145 – more ledge than road – it seems more remote… both in space and time.

The ledge is a congealed mass of hot, angry metal in summer, so use a boat or come a little out of season. A grand hotel out of season is, I fancy, as the prosecco takes hold, rather like making love to an ageing beauty. Sophia Loren, for example. The physical attraction remains, but decorum is required; the passion may be muted, but the expertise is assured. The result? A specialised, but nonetheless satisfying, experience. For example, Bellevue Syrene's proprietors have made the calculation that, in the quiet months, it's cheaper to give drinks away than pay someone to serve them. And the happy result is ice-buckets of wine scattered about: fuel for more cheerful fantasy about mischievous Roman gods and Neapolitan sex goddesses.

We – and I mean Mrs Smith and I, not me and Ms Loren – are the latest in a line of odd couples drawn to this magical, haunted place. At the bottom of my cliff, Virgil celebrated completing the *Aeneid* with a party thrown by the Emperor Augustus, dedicating a statue of Amor in a troglodyte Temple of Venus (where they now store butane cylinders). Admiral Nelson began his affair with Emma Hamilton nearby in 1793: she had promoted herself by dancing naked on tables at society dinners. Nietzsche and Wagner had their nasty spat here in 1876. Love, and hate, hang in the air along with the oranges, lemons and popping prosecco corks.

All rooms have a sea view, but we have a suite with a panorama of everything. Decoration is by Marco de Luca, who worked on the High Bohemian B&B La Minervetta just up the road. But while the colourful mayhem of La Minervetta is like an explosion in Tricia Guild's knicker drawer, the Bellevue Syrene's style is monochrome and restrained: layered, competitive whiteness of very high threadcount sheets and superb Richard Ginori china. It is sumptuously austere: a perfect counterpoint for our room's model Riva Aquarama and a schlock bust of Marcus Aurelius suggesting the poles of experience,

sensual and philosophical, available here. A flyer for a car hire company is in Russian and shows a Ferrari.

Like any luxury hotel, Bellevue Syrene has grand restaurant spaces out-of-sync with the stylish intimacy and dominant sensuality of its bedrooms. Eat here one night and enjoy the tinkle of the pianist playing soft rock classics while you sup. In town, Inn Bufalito is a mozzarella specialist that also cooks real Campanian dishes, which we enjoyed. (Possibly ignore the plague of alien industrial balsamic always on offer.) Also tempting is Aurora, a solemn, brightly lit old-school pizzeria where the staff sport dinner jackets and customers are in shorts.

Best of all, saunter down to Marina Grande, among the fishermen's nets and ziggurats of piscatorial crapola, to Trattoria da Emilia. I doubt the menu has changed much since 1947, but since they serve the freshest possible *fritto misto* (the fish are too small to be worth freezing) along with, for Italy, unusually good restaurant bread and jugs of glugging *bianco* – who wants innovation?

'Mrs Smith sits on the terrace, watching a distant *aliscafo* shoot silently across a glass sea to the craggy island of Capri'

And, just beyond the threshold, a thrilling confirmation of the rightness of it all: a black and white photograph, taken in 1955, of Sophia Loren in mozzarella-tight shorts, taking a break at this very spot from filming Dino Risi's *Pane, Amore e…* Loren said everything she did owed a debt to spaghetti, but I think other factors were involved.

Saturday morning in Room 501, the sepulchral quiet is interrupted only by a distant strimmer, a tap-tap-tap from invisible *lavori* and the maddening Eurostar chime, like the Danone ad riff, of our lift coming and going. Mrs Smith is sitting on the terrace in neo-classical repose, watching a distant *aliscafo* shoot silently across a glass sea to Capri, the craggy goat island. I know she is thinking of lunch.

Years ago, we stayed in Franco Zefirelli's old house, the Villa Tre Ville in neighbouring Positano. This global HQ of modern hedonism introduced us to the troubled magic of an area that has attracted poets and lovers since BC and drawn gamblers, chancers, divas, directors, dancers and stars AD. The owners of Bellevue Syrene have just bought Franco's old house and turned it into apartments, establishing another local connection to historic pleasure.

A chair on a vantage point here is a good laboratory to test if the ancient gods still exist. I think they do, but so too do rather younger ones. Maybe if I wait long enough in this sunburnt otherwhere, Sophia Loren will actually turn up. Bellevue Syrene makes *la dolce vita* real, turning a dream into an address.

Reviewed by **Stephen Bayley**, design critic

NEED TO KNOW

Rooms 50, including two suites.

Rates From €250–€750, including a generous buffet breakfast featuring local produce.

Check-out 11.30am, but flexible, subject to availability (free before 2pm; half the daily room rate thereafter). Earliest check-in, 2.30pm.

Facilities Spa with hammam and treatment cabins; sunbathing deck with loungers and umbrellas; gym, gardens, library; free WiFi throughout. In rooms: flatscreen TV, minibar and La Source bath products.

Children Cots for babies are free; children under 12 can share Deluxe Rooms with their parents for €60 a night. A local nanny can be drafted in with 24 hours' notice (€20 an hour), and the restaurant has a menu for tots.

Also Little dogs are welcome – but not in communal areas. According to legend, the spot where Bellevue Syrene is built was once home to that renegade gang of sailor-tempting bird-women, the sirens.

IN THE KNOW

Our favourite rooms The opulent Roccia suite, fashioned from an ancient grotto beneath the hotel, has a small hydrotherapy pool with mosaic tiles, at the foot of a four-poster bed screened with billowing white fabric. Superior Sea Rooms have balconies overlooking the Gulf of Naples, and are decorated with crystal chandeliers, antiques, sprays of fresh-cut flowers, and soft sherbet-y hues: violet, rose, turquoise, tangerine and mint.

Hotel bar No set drinking den, but waiters will seek you out on the terrace, or by the piano in La Pergola, the Winter Garden room; sip a mimosa on one of the comfy sofas. The hotel also has a wine cellar, set in a Roman grotto.

Hotel restaurant Mimmo Iodice's sweeping views and locally inspired menu won't let you forget your seaside setting: seafood-focused dishes include home-made pasta with clams and courgettes. Help yourself to a spread of savoury nibbles, cakes, fresh fruit, wine, juice and various other treats laid out in the Club Lounge from 10am until 8pm. Spring-green Gli Archi opens in winter, serving the main restaurant menu in a series of elegant rooms with white arches, lilac- and green-cushioned chairs, and parquet flooring.

Top table In summer, nab a terrace seat, as close to the sea as possible; come winter, the tables clustered around the piano are hot property.

Room service Sandwiches, salads, cakes and fruit can be ordered between 10am and noon.

Dress code Linen by day; Lanvin by night.

Local knowledge Wander into Sorrento to admire the flower-laden balconies, and to acquaint yourself with some of the region's art and architecture: Roman ruins, the 15th-century Duomo and the 14th-century Church of St Francis.

LOCAL EATING AND DRINKING

Trattoria da Emilia (+39 081 807 2720), a five-minute walk down the road on Via Marina Grande, is traditional and family-run, with simple food, plenty of fish, and carafes of local wine. The owners also run the tiny bar next-door, which is something of a local hero. Set in the cellars of an old monastery, Il Buco (+39 081 878 2354) is five minutes in the other direction, on Rampa Marina Piccola. It may have earned a Michelin star but it's as unpretentious as they come; eat on the romantic cobbled terrace outside, just off the square. Also on the harbour, just a few doors away, Vela Bianca (+39 081 878 1144) has three floors of nauticalia, a fine Neapolitan menu, and superb seafood.

GET A ROOM!

Hotel details 5 piazza della Vittoria, 80067 Sorrento (+39 081 878 1024; bellevue.it).

To book Ring our expert Travel Team (you'll find all our numbers with your membership card on page 5) or go to mrandmrssmith.com/bellevue-syrene.

 A bottle of sparkling white or regional red wine.

Ca'P'a

STYLE Rocky retreat
SETTING Tyrrhenian clifftop

'Our room, Cupola d'Oro, sits underneath
a weathered yellow dome. It is beautiful,
carefully curated, and the sun streams in
through its huge windows in gilt slices'

'My grandparents came here on their honeymoon,' I tell Mr Smith, 'and they were married for 60 years. So something special must happen on the Amalfi…' He pauses, then hurriedly points out an available taxi, over where a tiny figure in a white vest is waving his arms at us.

'There's Vesuvius to the left and the Tyrrhenian Sea to the right; that's Sophia Loren's villa,' says Gennaro. He talks his way around every bend. Coughing and laughing at the same time, he also waves at every car we pass. As the taxi climbs the hill out of Sorrento, we stick our heads out of the windows and inhale tarmac and turf, lemons and waves. And that is it; our senses are perfectly primed for the feast of colour, sound and smell that will make up the next two days.

As a little Smith, I was an occasional tourist to the steeps of the Amalfi. I tell my other half how mozzarella came in plaits, not balls, and how the Neopolitans slurred their words, their gesticulations making up for missed syllables. I reminisce how all the best things to eat around here are green – the olives, the limes, the *granita di menta* and pistachio ice-cream. A vividness of colour is what you notice about this whole area: the lava-rich soils of the Sorrentine peninsula, nurtured by volcanic eruptions, have created an Eden of yucca, cacti and clementines. It's a deep Perrier green, broken up by vertical splinters of white rock and *zabaglione*-coloured cottages tumbling from mountain down to sea.

Any sensible street-numbering system seems long forgotten this far from the main road. The steps down to the hotel are steep, passing between olive groves and high walls with doors and gates leading on to the houses beyond. The Amalfi Coast must breed muscular thighs.

We drop our bags dramatically in a sigh of sweaty relief; we're at a high wall marked 'Casa Privata'. The door slowly opens. I now have an idea how Livingstone must have felt when he pulled back the vines and saw Victoria Falls for the first time. Walled gardens and terraces lead from the house right down to the sea, and we hear workmen and a bonfire in the distance. Syrian oregano gives way to gilded rosemary – each plant has been marked with a copper plaque telling us what we are smelling. The drive had been stimulating, but the gardens of Casa Privata are something else.

True to its moniker, a spell at Casa Privata is like staying in a private house. The owners – Rosa, Max and Marie – spent childhood summers sailing around the peninsula, returning years later to this spot to restore a fisherman's cottage. They carefully preserved frescoed vaulted ceilings, furnishing the six rooms with 18th-century maps and a cube of suitably themed books. Aptly called Cupola d'Oro, our room has a library of Egyptian antiquity and a bed set underneath a weathered yellow dome. It is beautiful, carefully curated (as with the rest of the house), and the sun streams through its huge windows in gilt slices.

Watches removed, we measure time by the iridescence of the sky and the direction of the breeze. Mr Smith

takes off his top and smiles proudly at the sea, as if he'd made it himself. I do exactly the same, and we fall asleep on our sunlit terrace not knowing if it is afternoon, morning or evening.

An honesty bar in a corner of the downstairs sitting room means we tally up our glasses as we take photos of still-life compositions created from lemons and corks. We stop talking every 15 minutes or so, usually when the church bells ring to remind us that we are in Italy, and look up at an evening sky the colour of Campari.

A great energy hits you the second you wake up in Casa Privata, as if your senses need an instant fix. Encouraged by this – and a breakfast spread straight from a farmhouse fantasy – the next morning, in matching shorts and shirts (reminiscent of *The Talented Mr Ripley*), we hit the coastal road, 'buying' nearly half the romantically crumbling villas we pass along this stretch of the coast. We also spot a sign that reads 'Beach: 362 steps'.

'Mouthfuls of monkfish and home-grown tomatoes cooked by the family; the lights of Positano reflected on the sea'

Adopting an expression that says,'We both know where we're going', we soon find ourselves next to the sea, persuading a local fisherman to let us hire his boat. Because I am lazy, and because Mr Smith fancies himself as a pirate, he paddles us past caves and under stone cliff arches while I tell him why there is no seaweed on Mediterranean beaches and what the inside of a squid looks like, until eventually it is time to head back for dinner.

Striped grey benches have been arranged around a little pond. Between mouthfuls of monkfish and home-grown tomatoes cooked by the family, the evening lights of Positano reflected on the sea further along the coast, we ponder that soon we'll have to reset our watches. We take one last walk around the gardens, squeezing each herb we walk past, trying to memorise every aroma and texture. Wishing I could take home a sample of everything we smell, I settle on some seeds for our London window box. At least we'll have our own tiny plot of Praiano-on-Thames.

Reviewed by **Alex Tieghi-Walker**, *Nowness* picture editor

NEED TO KNOW

Rooms Six, including two suites.

Rates €180–€290, including Continental breakfast.

Check-out 12 noon, but flexible if there's availability. Earliest check-in, 10am.

Facilities Landscaped herb and sculpture gardens, private seaside sundeck, library of books and DVDs, free WiFi throughout. In rooms: flatscreen TV, CD/DVD player, minibar, L'Occitane products. In-room massages can be arranged.

Poolside The sea-facing pool is at the cliff edge, bordered by an outdoor lounge area and a line-up of sleek sunbeds.

Children Cots for babies are free; extra beds cost €20 a night. Babysitting can be arranged, but book it early.

Also Pets allowed with prior permission. Stone steps lead down to sunbathing platforms on the cliff and a private patch of rocky beach with a fresh-water shower. Hurling oneself off the rocks and into the water is heartily endorsed.

IN THE KNOW

Our favourite rooms We love spacious Cupola d'Oro for its golden-hued walls, which glow in the sunlight, and its domed ceiling, covered with fresco fragments. From the corner terrace, there are spectacular views out to sea. Families and friends can book out entire floors at a time, with rooms or suites that interconnect. If you're not a fan of publicly wandering around in a towel, avoid the Red Room: the bathroom's a few steps away, outside.

Hotel bar The lounge has vaulted ceilings, pastel hues and gilded mirrors; there's an honesty bar, stocked with spirits and the appropriate receptacles, in the corner.

Hotel restaurant In keeping with the casual, family feel, meals are prepared on request and served either outdoors or in the cosy restaurant area: all whiter-than-white tablecloths, low lamps and hanging glassware. The kitchen offers both Italian and international dishes, with an emphasis on fresh seafood. Outside, there's a wood-fired barbecue tucked in by the pristine hedgerow, ready to flame-grill fish in the summer.

Top table Opt for outside: hit the terrace to be nearer the sea, or sit out on the gravelly part of the garden, surrounded by fragrant foliage under the arbour.

Room service Hot food and snacks can be rustled up until 9pm – just ask.

Dress code Laid-back and linen-clad by day, but follow the owners' lead and stylishly spruce up for the evening.

Local knowledge Drive the coast road to Atrani, a serene little town just beyond Amalfi, flanked by lemon groves and a twinset of hills. The lovely Piazza Umberto I and all the winding, stone-paved streets will be mostly yours, even in high season. Follow the path from the piazza to the top of Monte Aureo, and be prepared for one heck of a view at the top.

LOCAL EATING AND DRINKING

Reached by boat, beachside Da Adolfo on Via Laurito in Positano may have a limited menu, but everything on it is sublime (+39 089 875022). La Cambusa on Piazza Amerigo Vespucci serves traditional Italian food on the beachfront (+39 089 812051). Also in Positano, Le Sirenuse on Via Cristoforo Colombo is where to head for brilliant bivalves – its alfresco champagne and oyster bar has cracking views; alternatively, book a table at its super-romantic Neapolitan restaurant, La Sponda (+39 089 875066). In Praiano, walk down to La Strada, a friendly little restaurant on Via Gennaro Capriglione, for fresh fish, good steaks and excellent Italian wines (+39 089 81308). Serving food in Amalfi since 1872, Da Gemma on Via Fra Gerardo Sasso has had more than a century to master the region's recipes (+39 089 871345).

GET A ROOM!

Hotel details 41 via Rezzola, 84010 Praiano (+39 089 874078; casaprivata.it).

To book Ring our expert Travel Team (you'll find all our numbers with your membership card on page 5) or go to mrandmrssmith.com/casa-privata.

 A bottle of limoncello and a brass keyring from a ship's chandler in Amalfi.

Capo la Gala

STYLE Nautical Neapolitan
SETTING Cliffside cove

'Giant, straight-from-a-cartoon cacti split up the terraces of each room, and palms and pines give you the feeling that you can see out, but the world can't see in'

What's the Italian expression for love nest, darling?' I murmur into Signora Smith's ear as we stand arm in arm on the beach, watching the sun slowly descend into the Bay of Naples. 'Because this is one, *veramente.*'

Behind us is the object of my newfound infatuation, the Capo la Gala, five miles outside Sorrento. The five-star hotel's 22 rooms are beguilingly tucked down a cliff – in and around terraces and rocky outcrops, among lemon trees and soaring pines. We've only just arrived but, having seen that the sunset promises to be splendid, we put off check-in and scamper down through the grounds to take in the finale on the strand.

Mrs Smith turns towards me with a look that begs a lingering kiss; I'm seconds from touchdown when an elderly fisherman, who's gathering his nets just down the beach, calls out: 'Do you know the legend of Caterina and Antonio?' Ahem. 'Where's the language barrier when you need it?' I huff, but Mrs Smith pulls back reprovingly and says: 'Darling, don't be rude.' With that, she engages the man, whose name is Gennaro. 'No, but please do tell us.' Pointing to a pair of stone stacks, he says, 'You see those two seagulls that never stop flying from one stack to another? Those are the postmen.'

I stifle a dig at the Italian mail system because Mrs Smith is already rapt. Gennaro continues in his Neapolitan lilt. 'Caterina was a young noblewoman who fell in love with a fisherman, but her parents forbade this love and locked her in the castle tower. The two lovers wrote messages that were delivered by seagulls, and in the end, decided to choose the most beautiful place they knew of and live there forever in the form of stone.' He waits a beat and then concludes, 'They hoped to spread their feelings to travellers…' A light flush has come over Mrs Smith, who thanks Gennaro profusely, takes my hand, and sets off back towards the hotel. By now it is well into dusk, so I can't be sure about this, but when I last glimpse Gennaro, I am pretty sure he is giving me the thumbs-up sign.

Capo la Gala has been here since 1962. Five years ago, Enzo and Marite Acampora took over the property and renovated it in a style that you might venture to call 'preppie Italian yachtsman'. The interiors are crisp and clean, a coastal dream of blues and whites, interspersed with daring design touches such as the rectangular navy and burnt orange floor tiles in the Marite Suite, laid down in a rick-rack pattern.

Giant, straight-from-a-cartoon cacti split up the terraces of each bedroom, while palms and pines give you the feeling that you can see out, but the world can't see in. Capo la Gala feels like an exclusive seafarers' club; here, it's easy to pretend that you own a yacht and are on shore leave.

The hotel lies just outside the tiny village of Vico Equense, which is laced with narrow streets that smell of clean laundry, orange blossom, lemon and the geraniums that overflow the balconies. Behind the hotel rise the Lattari mountains, named for the gallons of goat's milk produced by the herders living up there. If you could drive over the Lattari from the hotel, as the crow flies, you would come down in Positano, on the Amalfi Coast.

We are impressed that such a small hotel has a well-equipped wellness centre. The next day, I ask for an appointment, and even though it is the staff's day off, Signor Acampora opens the Aquarium spa and persuades his Thai masseuse to come in specially. Afterwards, Mrs Smith and I loll about in the sauna and Turkish bath, and then go down to the seawater swimming pool, which is right on the bay. The feeling of being spoiled continues with our visit that evening to the hotel restaurant, Maxi. It has one Michelin star and the young chef, Daniele, has cooked up a menu of rich Mediterranean flavours, with a tangy twist: seven different olive oils, all from the region, are accompanied by just-baked bread.

It's too bad that we are here in April because from June onwards, the hotel organises daily trips on its own yacht to the nearby islands of Capri and Ischia and down the Amalfi Coast – but it's a good reason to come back. The following morning is spent in Sorrento, where we sample some of the 100 or more flavours of ice-cream at Gelateria David. Then we drive to Forcella, outside Naples, to lunch on the best pizza in the world (in our humble opinion). It's served at La Antica Pizzeria da Michele, and it's a wondrously large creation: thin, crispy, fragrant, and stringy with mozzarella. Although we pass it on the return, we give ancient Pompeii a miss, drawn by the gravitational pull of the Capo la Gala.

After a good interval by the pool, we head back to our terrace, where we kick back, glasses of Campari and soda in hand. As the sea swallows the sun, gradually turning the two stone stacks red, I turn to Mrs Smith and say, 'Do you know the legend of Caterina and Antonio?' And with that, she takes up where she had left off the first evening. Thumbs up to you, Gennaro.

Reviewed by **Mario Mazzer**, architect

NEED TO KNOW

Rooms 23, including one suite.

Rates €160–€470, including a Mediterranean buffet breakfast.

Check-out 11.30am, but guests can usually stay in their rooms until 1pm with no charge. Earliest check-in, 1pm.

Facilities Spa, gym, gardens, DVD library, free WiFi throughout. There are kayaks and bikes to borrow. In rooms, flatscreen TV, minibar and Lorenzo Villoresi bath products.

Poolside The tree-encircled pool is at the heart of the hotel, with wooden decking and a rocky path down to the sea. As well as a hot tub, there's an assortment of terraces, both sun-drenched and shady. A heated pool awaits inside, too.

Children Cots for under-threes are free; extra beds cost €50 for under-nines and €80 for under-12s. Ask three days in advance and a nanny can babysit for €15 an hour.

Also Small pets are welcome. Guests can book the hotel yacht for two-day trips to Capri or Ischia. Aquarium – the marine-themed spa – has treatments along the same lines: settle in for some thalassotherapy or hydromassage.

IN THE KNOW

Our favourite rooms We loved Room 205 for the terrific tiles in its bathroom: white but with bright blue splatterings only an angry person with a brush could produce. Its terrace isn't bad, either – vast, with a spectacular view out to sea. The classic rooms are smaller but their terraces more than make up for it; views are less restricted, too.

Hotel bar Stone-walled, wide-windowed and dressed in navy, the beach-house-style bar above the restaurant wears the sea on its sleeve: model boats, conch shells and wooden decking are everywhere. The long wooden bar is stocked with spirits and the wine list draws heavily from the vineyards of Campania.

Hotel restaurant Nautically decked out in navy blue tablecloths and white Panton chairs, Michelin-starred Maxi sits above the pool, with various dining areas inside and out. Expect fine flavour combinations, such as tuna steak in herb pastry with caponata and candied tomatoes, and ravioli with caciotta cheese and marjoram. Down by the beach, Nerea offers a relaxed osteria-style lunch menu of Neapolitan classics, as well as lighter salads and panini.

Top table Beside the windows in the main restaurant to stare out to sea.

Room service Order in various pastas and puddings between 12 noon and 10pm.

Dress code Pucci and Prada, worn with a tan.

Local knowledge Set off for an afternoon strolling Massa Lubrense, a gorgeous stretch of coast and country at the tip of the Sorrentine peninsula with unrivalled sea views. Peaceful hamlets and scented lemon groves are crisscrossed by mule paths and marked footpaths; it's all best seen in spring, when the lemon and orange trees are in blossom.

LOCAL EATING AND DRINKING

A few minutes' walk away in the centre of Vico Equense, Osteria Nonna Rosa adds modern Michelin-starred cooking to a backdrop of traditional decor and flavours (+39 081 879 9055). Torre del Saracino on Via Torreta serves inventive twists on spag bol – it comes with octopus here (+39 081 802 8555). Up on the hilltop at Sant'Agata, Don Alfonso is two-Michelin-starred and haute, haute, haute (+39 081 878 0026). Nearby on Via Deserto is Lo Stuzzichino, not flashy or frilly, but the food speaks volumes. Try the sea bream, or carb-heavy pasta with potatoes (+39 081 533 0010). Pizza fans shouldn't miss out on a trip to Pizza a Metro on Via Nicotera (+39 081 879 8309).

GET A ROOM!

Hotel details 8 via Luigi Serio, 80069 Vico Equense (+39 081 801 5758; hotelcapolagala.com).

To book Ring our expert Travel Team (you'll find all our numbers with your membership card on page 5) or go to mrandmrssmith.com/capo-la-gala.

 Free spa entry for BlackSmith members (usually €30 each); a 30-minute massage each for SilverSmiths; GoldSmith members get both, plus 10 per cent off a two-course dinner in the restaurant (excludes drinks).

Casa Angelina

STYLE All white now
SETTING On the edge

'This is how I imagine Rupert Everett's house would have looked in the Nineties: all whitewashed walls, clean lines and busts of beautiful women. This is no bad thing'

Too much work and winter-induced malaise means these Mr Smiths are due a holiday. An empty long weekend and some last-minute flights to the Amalfi Coast present themselves, and we pounce. We're on that plane faster than you can say 'Andiamo!'. The second we come soaring into the shimmering haze of Naples Bay, all work stresses dissipate, replaced by thoughts of oranges plucked from the tree, pizzas pulled from the wood-fired oven, and Campari, well, straight from the bottle.

Though we'd planned on renting a car, the prospect of tackling the coast's notoriously zigzagging roads brings out the scaredy cat in me, and we decide to take a taxi. A little flirt with car sickness and a near miss with a giant lemon (actually a lemonade truck) aside, the journey is smooth and pleasant – thanks mostly to the eye-popping view. Panoramas of this glistening gulp of the Med and its dramatic coastline hit us from every angle as we wend our way round the Gulf of Naples down to the southern coast of the Sorrentine Peninsula.

Positano marks our penultimate pitstop before the tiny village of Praiano. Hanging on the craggy landscape, tiers of pale apricot abodes seem on the brink of tumbling into the crystalline sea beneath (Mr Smith goes as far as describing it as 'impossibly sapphire'). The first thing that strikes you about this rugged corner of Amalfi is how astonishing it is that people ever came to live here: incredibly steep and impassably rocky, it is mind-boggling to think the Italians made it this far.

A whitewashed stalagmite of minimalist luxury on this rocky edge, Casa Angelina is invisible from the road, thanks to the near vertical cliff-face. To reach it, our taxi twists its way down a road that a limber mountain goat would find challenging. Before we've made it out of the car and passed Angelina's swishing electric doors, we've had our bags prised from our dragging fists, replaced by glasses of fresh almond milk straight from an ice-bucket.

On initial inspection, Casa Angelina is how I would imagine Rupert Everett's house to have looked in the

1990s: all whitewashed walls, clean lines and busts of beautiful women. And this is no bad thing: the Nineties' look is back, after all (and I imagine Everett's got impeccable taste). Our celestial casa is an art hotel, and colourful contemporary paintings and sculptures by Tim Cotterill, Gina Nahle Bauer and Sergio Bustamante are bright and intriguing. These fantasy-world bronzes, Murano glass sculptures and papier-mâché figures, if not to everyone's taste, make for engaging eye-stops between white spaces and cerulean sky-and-sea views beyond.

Our spacious, light-flooded bedroom also has a small, sea-facing balcony, which we quickly take to with glasses of complimentary champagne. Frankly, we are desperate to get our alabaster bodies into the sun – even if it is by now already 5pm. A quick shower in the well-proportioned, very white, beautifully tiled bathroom, and we're ready for a stroll down to the sea. 'A hike!' declares Signor Smith. The walk is worth it. A trip down in the elevator and then we follow the steps down a meandering, olive-tree-lined path to a secluded beach bar. Negronis in hand, we

plot up and open the floodgates to some serious awe, inspired by watching the Mediterranean sun sink into that mesmerising sea.

Strolling, and pausing intermittently for a little breath to be stolen, is what mostly fills our time in Praiano. Orange-tree-shaded lanes, an aquamarine-sea-facing church – it's a landscape that is unspeakably beautiful. We eat our way through Praiano's handful of restaurants, perhaps peaking with the massive, tasty pizzas from Trattoria San Gennaro. Traveller-beloved tiny towns litter the Amalfi Coast, and Positano, despite being full of Italian tourists and their little pooches, is soul-stirringly pretty and welcoming. Amalfi itself is worth a visit alone for its unparalleled gelato.

When it comes to our last night, our freshly uplifted hearts plummet briefly: it's too nice here. We're sad to be departing Casa Angelina, so we savour our stay down to the very last drop by dining at the hotel's own restaurant, Un Piano nel Cielo. Feeling romantic, full by now with

'Praiano's scenery is some of the most beautiful we've ever seen, food is universally faultless and our is hotel a dream'

great food, wine and sun, Mr Smith and I plump for the tasting menu and a bottle of delicious local Aglianico. From the off – a meltingly fresh monkfish, juicy pancetta and tasty sautéed broad bean salad – each of the seven dishes is among the best we've had on our trip: no small claim in this gourmet's paradise.

Praiano's scenery has been some of the most beautiful we've ever seen, the food is universally faultless and our hotel is a dream. Thinking back to those initial weekend aspirations, we've successfully ticked a lot of boxes. At least 20 oranges were devoured straight from the tree; maybe five chewy yet crispy pizzas were wolfed direct from the oven. Campari bottles slugged? Too many to mention. And as for our trip away... it was one in a million.

Reviewed by **Teo van den Broeke**, *Esquire* Associate Editor

NEED TO KNOW

Rooms 39, including a junior suite. There are also four Eaudesea Experience Rooms, with private-beach access.
Rates €250–€675 (€750–€1,150 for the Junior Suite); rates exclude buffet breakfast (€25 a head).
Check-out 3pm; later check-out is subject to availability and, if it's busy, an extra charge. Earliest check-in, 12 noon.
Facilities Spa with sauna and gym, cigar room, CD/DVD library, free WiFi throughout. In rooms: flatscreen TV, CD/DVD player, iPod dock (on request), minibar, L'Occitane bath products. Higher-category rooms are also graced with B&O entertainment systems, Nespresso machines and laptops. Private yoga classes and personal training can be arranged.
Poolside Inside the hotel, a heated hydrotherapy pool bubbles away under a constellation of fibre optics on the ceiling. Out on the deck, a sun-warmed counter-current pool is surrounded by stylish sunloungers and parasols.
Children Mini Smiths are welcome in low season (November and April), for €110 a night; it's over-10s only in high season. Babysitting costs about €40 an hour – give half a day's notice. The restaurant has a children's menu.
Also A shuttlebus runs to and from Positano five times a day, and the hotel has a fleet of private boats for zooming along the coast. The hotel closes in the winter (mid-November to March), but reopens briefly to bring in the New Year.

IN THE KNOW

Our favourite rooms With views of Praiano from its Starck-designed bath tub, Junior Suite 401 has to be the most reach-for-the-camera impressive; it also has a vast private terrace offering 180° views of Positano and Capri from the comfort of a luxurious lounger. Beside a private beach and with access to their own club lounge, airy Eaudesea Experience Rooms are former fisherfolk dwellings set apart from the hotel, incorporating the cliff face into their whitewashed walls.
Hotel bar The small Moroccan-influenced bar has a terrace on the cliff edge scattered with teak tables and umbrellas. The staff certainly know their way around a mojito (they slug in a dash of limoncello). Drinks are served until 1am.
Hotel restaurant Un Piano nel Cielo ('a floor in the sky') is just that: a top-floor terrace with yet more amazing views of the Amalfi Coast. The indoor area is fitted with wide windows, so you can still admire the vista when the wind's up. The kitchen makes the most of the hotel's coastal setting: expect a high-end, seafood-heavy Mediterranean menu.
Top table Ask for a spot on the edge of the terrace overlooking the ocean – dining doesn't get more dramatic.
Room service Drinks, snacks and light meals can be summoned 24 hours a day.
Dress code White summer wraps to blend in – or vibrant sarongs to stand out. Gigantic sunglasses are de rigueur.
Local knowledge Hire a Vespa from Praiacosta (+39 089 813082) and tour the coast in true Italian style. The nearby village of Nerano is famous for its spaghetti *con zucchini*, so stop there for lunch before heading up to Ravello, the hilltop town famed for its amazing viewpoints.

LOCAL EATING AND DRINKING

A two-minute wander away on Via Gennaro Capriglione, La Brace (+39 089 874226) is a charming family-run trattoria, with home-made dishes, fresh fish and excellent pizza. At night, you can see the lights of Positano twinkling across the bay. Nestling in a quiet cove, a short boat ride from the hotel, Trattoria Da Armandino (+39 089 874087) is another family-run eatery on the seashore with a very local flavour: recipes have been handed down the generations, and diners are often serenaded by local musicians. Meat, wine and views is La Tagliata in a nutshell; this hilltop restaurant near Positano serves plate upon plate of expertly barbecued farm-style fare in simple surroundings (+39 089 875872).

GET A ROOM!

Hotel details 147 via Gennaro Capriglione, 84010 Praiano (+39 089 813 1333; casangelina.com).
To book Ring our expert Travel Team (you'll find all our numbers with your membership card on page 5) or go to mrandmrssmith.com/casa-angelina.

 Champagne and fresh fruit on arrival; a romantic bath drawn for you on your first night; and a gift bag of Casa Angelina's traditional home-made pasta on departure.

Maison La Minervetta

STYLE Technicolor dreamboat
SETTING Sorrentine cliffhanger

'The door opens to reveal a staggering panorama. The view comes at us in full floor-to-ceiling-window glory. A model boat on the sill is all that interrupts the sea'

Whizzing around another hairpin bend, I gasp at the sheer drop from this coastal road to the Med. There's no denying this is a trip already high on drama. A swarm of Vespas zips past. Below us the *gozzi* – brightly coloured wooden boats – bob in the sapphire-blue water. It's everything I dreamed of. Uh oh.

As anyone who works in travel will know, you see a lot of images of sleek minimalist bedrooms and turquoise pools in the course of your day, which, I confess, can blur into one. Yet I distinctly remember the first time I saw a photo of the blue-and-white tiled kitchen at La Minervetta. It was 2005, it had just opened, and my eyes boggled. That shot – and one taken looking over the red parasols on the hotel's terrace down to Sorrento's harbour and out across to that big blue gulp of the Bay of Naples – has been nagging me ever since. The problem with these kinds of fantasies? When you're lucky enough to make them a reality, there's a danger they'll fall short of your expectations. So it is with bittersweet anticipation that we approach La Minervetta.

'Turn now!' I screech, spotting its sign as we climb the hill out of Sorrento. Mr Smith swerves onto a tiny rooftop carpark on the cliff's edge. 'Hang on. Where's the hotel?' Spotting a lift protruding like a pretty white tardis, I twig it's right below us. A small set of stairs tempts us into the hotel's glossy sky-blue lounge.

Ocean-themed objets d'art, witty artworks and mountains of books and magazines confirm this is somewhere considered and cultured. It calls to mind the only internet date I had where the chap who turned up was actually as handsome as his profile picture: it's a huge effort not to jump up and down, clapping my hands, and cry, 'It's as lovely as I'd hoped!' (Looking back, it might have helped if I hadn't done that on the date.) We're here anonymously and I need to play it cool. Too late. Mr Smith is already gushing about how gorgeous it all is.

Clutching the heavy key to our room, our delightful Sorrentine host escorts us down a flight of stairs. La Minervetta isn't a fancy-schmancy five-star hotel where they dazzle you with their big talk of facilities and activities: it's a family-owned boutique bed and breakfast that makes you feel as though you're residing in their stylish holiday home. Our eyes are drawn by a cute collection of quirky finds on the way to our room. But the sharpest intake of breath is yet to come…

We're on a corner, and the door opens to reveal a double-take eyeful of that staggering panorama. The vista comes at us in full floor-to-ceiling-window glory. A model sailboat on the sill is all that interrupts the sea – an unashamed nod to the nautical theme. No wonder they've positioned two armchairs right there, facing out. What else is there to do but flop into one and admire Capri and Vesuvius in full splendour? I reach for my phone, quickly snap a shot, and upload it to Facebook faster than you can say 'I'm not being smug; it would just be selfish not to tell the world how wonderful this room's view is.' In the time it takes for me to freshen up for supper, 13 friends have hit the 'like' button. OK, maybe I am a little smug.

One off-season perk is that this most beloved of destinations is free of the tourists that converge on the Sorrentine Peninsula and Amalfi Coast in summer. We're a week too early for the lift down to the harbour to be running or the pool to be open, but it seems a fair trade-off for people-free peace.

We ditch the option of taking the 300 steps down to the quiet port and instead drive to Bellevue Syrene, a waterside hotel off a piazza in Sorrento's centre. Having parked next to a church, we pass a nun and then a monk, both wishing us *buona sera* – someone up there must want all our dream-holiday wishes to come true. We toast them with a prosecco as a pianist tinkles out a rendition of 'Tonight, I Celebrate My Love' on the baby grand.

You might think having a bed that big in a room with that view would make getting out of it challenging. Or that the five courses we ate quite late last night might prompt a lie-in. But remember: I've been dreaming of eating in *that* kitchen for years. The Breakfast Table I'll Never Forget is

'The Breakfast Table I'll Never Forget is piled high with sticky pastries and biscuits, like a cookery-book cover shot'

piled high with sticky pastries and every possible biscuit, making it look like a cookery-book cover shot. We park ourselves next to an Australian family living in Switzerland, who are just as enamoured with La Minervetta's colourful, quirky decor and relaxed atmosphere as we are.

Next comes another long-awaited lifetime goal: visiting Positano. The Amalfi Coast drive is in itself celebrated, twisting along the rock's edge. We wend our way round the waif-thin roads, narrowly missing big buses that confidently hurtle past. When John Steinbeck visited in the 1950s, it was only populated by a few fishermen and lemon farmers. He predicted in an article for *Harper's Bazaar* it was too unlikely a candidate for development to ever get busy. Ahem.

Tell you what Steinbeck also said: 'It is a dream place that isn't quite real when you are there and becomes beckoningly real after you have gone.' He got that right: it's truly magical. All I'm wishing now? It won't be long until it's very real all over again.

Reviewed by Mr & Mrs Smith

NEED TO KNOW

Rooms 12, including a junior suite.

Rates €180–€420, including full English breakfast.

Check-out 11.30am, but flexible. Earliest check-in, 2pm, but also flexible, subject to availability.

Facilities Solarium, plenty of books and CDs, WiFi throughout (€10 a day), onsite parking. In rooms: flatscreen TV, minibar, Crabtree & Evelyn bath products. Spa and beauty treatments can be arranged.

Poolside The giant outdoor hydro-massage pool on the sea-view terrace opens on 1 May each year, with wooden loungers and towels provided.

Children Under-14s can share their parents' rooms; baby cots are provided at no extra charge, and additional beds are priced at €50 a night (€80 in high season). Babysitting can be arranged (€10 an hour).

Also Reservations can be made for the private beach at La Tonnarella, 200 metres from the hotel. There are stairs leading direct down to the sea from La Minervetta; be prepared for the climb back – there are around 300 steps.

IN THE KNOW

Our favourite rooms Every room is sea-facing, with fantastic views: some have floor-to-ceiling windows, some have Juliet balconies. Two pairs of rooms can be separated from others on the same floor by a third door with its own key, creating a mini-apartment ideal for families or groups of friends (rooms are sound-proofed, too). The junior suite has two balconies and a large walk-in hydro-massage shower – no bath, though.

Hotel bar Sip your prosecco on the terrace or cosied up in the lounge: guests can take drinks anywhere they like. This boutique B&B feels more like a private home than a hotel, and every guest soon locates their favourite spot.

Hotel restaurant No restaurant – breakfast is a sweet-toother's fantasy, served buffet-style at the kitchen table, with hot eggs and bacon, pancakes or omelettes (and more) cooked to order. The hotel's dramatic cliff-clinging location means getting to a restaurant in the fishing village below (Marina Grande) involves a steep climb down the steps.

Top table On the terrace with a splendid view across the Bay of Naples.

Room service Bar service is available 24 hours a day, and there's a mini-fridge in your room for drinks and nibbles.

Dress code Laid-back; nautical but nice.

Local knowledge If you're catching a boat to one of the islands, La Minervetta can pre-book you a parking space in the underground carpark at Sorrento's main port – which is usually full by 9am.

LOCAL EATING AND DRINKING

Bagni Delfino on the Marina Grande (+39 081 878 2038), down the steps from the hotel, is the place for a relaxed waterside lunch of wonderfully fresh fish and seafood. For a more formal lunch, try next door at Taverna Azzurra (+39 081 877 2510). Michelin-starred Il Buco on Rampa Marina Piccola (+39 081 878 2354) is one of the best restaurants in Sorrento; it's a good idea to reserve one of the tables outside on a warm summer evening. The tasting menu is an excellent choice. Have drinks at Photo, a lounge bar turned restaurant just off Piazza Tasso (+39 081 877 3686). In summer, its garden is perfect for cocktails or a glass of wine. Da Gigino on Via degli Archi (+39 081 878 1927) is the best place for a pizza, and has super spaghetti vongole. La Minervetta can also whisk you to and from the charming family-run restaurant Da Filippo (+39 081 877 2448), just outside Sorrento, for a taste of local cooking.

GET A ROOM!

Hotel details 25 via Capo, 80067 Sorrento (+39 081 877 4455; laminervetta.com).

To book Ring our expert Travel Team (you'll find all our numbers with your membership card on page 5) or go to mrandmrssmith.com/la-minervetta.

A bottle of prosecco; GoldSmith members also get a limoncello-tasting session.

espresso
espresso

CAPRI

COASTLINE Grotto fabulous
COAST LIFE Glamour on the rocks

If land-mass equated with reputation, tiny-but-stylish Capri would be the size of Texas. Mighty emperors have fallen for it; literary heroes have hankered after it – Charles Dickens, Oscar Wilde and Graham Greene among them. In the 1950s the island enchanted a host of Hollywood stars: Kirk Douglas, Elizabeth Taylor and Jackie Onassis have all posed on its shores. Not that Capri's charms are in any way faded: enjoy sun-kissed days strolling the flower-framed alleyways and elegant piazzas of Capri Town; explore the genteel villas of famous former residents, and marvel at Capri's captivating caves. As the sun sets, savour one of the island's simplest pleasures: the satisfaction of staying put as boat-loads of doleful daytrippers depart. With serene Capri to yourself after dark, you'll be glad you checked in for the night…

GETTING THERE

Planes Naples-Capodichino on the mainland is Capri's closest airport (gesac.it). Take the Alibus shuttle from there to Centrale station or Piazza Municipale (for the ports); single journeys, about €3 (anm.it). Or grab a taxi.
Trains International routes serve Naples Centrale (trenitalia.com), a short cab ride from Beverello port.
Automobiles There's no need for a car on this pint-sized island. But if you already have one with you in Naples, park in long-stay at the airport (P1), from €12 a day; or near the port from about €16 a day (myparking.it).
Boats Reach Capri by ferry or hydrofoil from Naples; check timetables with Alilauro (alilauro.it), Snav (snav.it) or Caremar (caremar.it). Ferries leaving Calata Porta di Massa take about 80 minutes; you can shave half an hour off your crossing with a hydrofoil from Molo Beverello.

LOCAL KNOWLEDGE

Taxis The original stretch Fiat taxis – candy-striped, open-topped – have mostly been put out of service. You'll see a few restored classics around, but new seven-seater versions are now made specially for the island.

Siesta and fiesta Lunch languidly between 1pm and 3pm, when shops are shut; they reopen from 4pm. In quieter months, eateries close on Mondays as well as Sundays.
Do go/don't go May, June and October offer warm weather and few crowds; in July and August, the holiday season and island prices are at their peak.
Packing tips Mrs Smiths, your glitziest rocks for starlit soirées; Mr Smith will want cashmere after dark; both will need boat-friendly threads and shoes for journeys afloat.
Recommended reads *The Apprentice Lover* by Jay Parini follows the affairs of a young American in Capri; Shirley Hazzard recalls her friendship with writer Graham in *Greene on Capri*; Norman Douglas' 1917 novel *South Wind* is a hedonistic romp through the lives of sybaritic islanders.
Local specialities All things *Caprese* are signature dishes of the isle, including the salad of tomatoes, mozzarella and peppery island-grown basil, and ravioli – plump ricotta- and marjoram-filled pasta pillows in tomato sauce. Fish and seafood are staples: should you tire of *linguine alle frutti di mare*, try *totani ripieni*, aka parmesan-stuffed cuttlefish. Unsurprisingly, given its proximity to Naples, pizza is a fixture on local menus: get yours at historic

family-run restaurant Aurora near the Piazzetta (+39 081 837 0181). *Dolci* include *torta Caprese*, rich with ground almonds and dark chocolate, and lemony, almondy *caprilù*: try some at Buonocore on Via Vittorio Emanuele in Capri Town (+39 081 837 7826), also famed for fabulous ice-cream in home-made cones.

WORTH GETTING OUT OF BED FOR

Viewpoint Mount Solaro is this rock's literal high point, at around 600m: you can walk up, or take the *seggiovia* (a rickety one-at-a-time chairlift), from Piazza della Vittoria in Anacapri. From the top, spy Capri's sugar-cube houses, and the Faraglioni rocks jutting into the Tyrrhenian Sea.
Arts and culture Those who have fallen for the island and made their home here have left an intriguing architectural legacy: Villa Jovis is the ruin of one of three remaining Roman residences built by Tiberius (+39 081 837 4549). Villa San Michele was Axel Munthe's hilltop hideaway: a colonnaded beauty with sculpture-dotted terraces, the estate grounds host sunset concerts on summer Fridays (villasanmichele.eu). Casa Malaparte (closed to the public) is a cliff-straddling Rationalist wonder in brick orange overlooking the Gulf of Salerno. The Museo del Centro Caprense Ignazio Cerio (centrocaprense.org) records the island's prehistory and early inhabitants.
Activities Stubborn landlubbers miss out on much that Capri has to offer: board a traditional wooden *gozzi*, for a sea-level tour around the craggy-cliffed land and its many caves; pick up a launch from the Marina Grande or Piccola. Sercomar (caprisub.com) has flashier seafaring options to hire. Some boat tours offer snorkelling, but if you plan to DIY, try the south coast, pocked with interesting grottoes. For a taster session on regional cuisine, book a private at-home cookery lesson with a native chef through Ciao Laura (ciaolaura.com).
Perfect picnic Pack a Caprese hamper loaded with gorgonzola, salami and olives from Macelleria da Michele on Via Marina Grande (+39 081 837 5254), and take it to the beach across the island at Marina Piccola: this shingle cove has a sea-carved stone arch, shallow waters and a sheltered position that's perfect for picnicking.
Daytripper Take the 20-minute hydrofoil to Sorrento ahead of the lunchtime rush to secure a table on the jetty at Delfino (+39 081 878 2038); post-lunch, retire to a sunlounger on its adjoining bathing deck. Wander into Sorrento; before you head home, pop into classic 1950s

watering hole Fauno Bar for cooling aperitivi (faunobar.it).
Walks Pick up walking maps from the tourist office at 59 Via Giuseppe Orlandi in Anacapri (capritourism.com). A 40-minute stroll will take you to the bathing steps at Punta Carena: this pretty inlet overlooked by a gigantic lighthouse enjoys camera-worthy sunsets. For guided hikes, try Capri Trails (+39 081 837 5933; capritrails.com).
Shopping Capri's roll call of designer stores reads like Milan in miniature: Fendi, Cavalli and co are shoe-horned into boutiques lining Via Vittorio Emanuele and Via Camerelle. Splurge a few hundred euros on bespoke bejewelled sandals, handmade by legendary Capri cobbler Canfora (canforacapri.com). Bottle holiday memories with scent from Carthusia Profumi (+39 081 837 0368; carthusia.com): its fragrances have been distilled from island-grown ingredients since 1948. In Anacapri, unearth pleasingly colourful pottery at L'Oasi Ceramiche on Via Capodimonte (+39 081 837 3646).
Something for nothing There's no charge to roam the cloisters and courtyards of 14th-century Carthusian monastery Certosa di San Giacomo: its clocktower is a showstealer. Afterwards, seek out shade in the Gothic chapel (+39 081 837 6218; 9am–4pm, closed Mondays).
Don't go home without... walking the hairpin-packed feat of engineering that is Via Krupp: descend the cobbled path's ultra-narrow zigzags, which score the cliffs below the Augustus Gardens, and take a breather on the beach at Marina Piccola at its base. Stroll there from Capri Town; return by boat to avoid the steep climb back up.

COMPLETELY CAPRI

The enchanting Grotto Azzurra is Capri's most famous cavern. Lie down in a rowing boat to negotiate the low entrance, and you'll soon see why: sunlight streams through an underwater gap in the rock so that the sea within shimmers sapphire blue; silvery air bubbles cling to submerged boulders. There's a misguided myth this was once the setting for Roman orgies – who knows what really went on in the Emperor's shrine to the sirens.

DIARY

May The Med's sailing season kicks off with Rolex Capri Sailing Week, the yachtie equivalent of the Monaco GP (yachtclubcapri.net). Capri honours patron saint Costanza on the 14th, with processions, blessings and music (cittadicapri.it). **June** Athletes of the sea take the plunge from Marina Grande to swim 36km to the Via Carriciolo seafront in Naples (caprinapoli.com). Around the 13th, Anacapri residents parade their patron saint around town for the Festa di Sant'Antonio (comunedianacapri.it). **September** The Festa di Santa Maria di Cetrella sees processions in traditional dress from Anacapri and two days of musical celebration (communedianacapri.it). **Late December** Capri's answer to Cannes: the Hollywood Film Festival (caprihollywood.com).

JK Place Capri

STYLE Snow-white suntrap
SETTING Stylish-on-sea

'Books, the beach, that view over the Bay of Naples, vintage photographs – it's all ravishing, like a palazzo with hints of hip Hamptons getaway'

Capri: until now, this meant to me the mid-calf trousers favoured in warmer climates (stylish, but hard to pull off; best kept for the tall and the gamine). Now my focus is the small island off the Amalfi Coast. Like the pants, it's chic – very chic. In fact, this romantic idyll in the Tyrrhenian Sea is heavenly. Our journey begins in Naples, the birthplace of pizza. No time for a slice, despite Mr Smith's pleading – it's 'arrivederci' to the grey façades of the mainland city: we have a hydrofoil to catch across the sparkling bay.

Capri, a noble beauty, sits demurely waiting for us like a sphinx. The first thing we spot is the gleaming white Villa Fersen, teetering on the cliff's edge. We have arrived. The hydrofoil pulls into the Marina Piccola; the plank is dropped. Weekend bags are grabbed at the dock by seersucker-clad JK Placers, who have a car waiting, and we are whisked away up a steep narrow road and down a discreet driveway. Like Jacques d'Adelswärd-Fersen's art nouveau villa, JK Place is set into the cliffs – the only Capri hotel built directly on the coast. Our driver gingerly

backs through the gates and a scene reminiscent of *Downton Abbey* unfolds: a stream of staff members spills out of the 18th-century cream villa to line up. Everyone is immaculately dressed head-to-toe in that striped cotton so beloved of Ivy Leaguers, stretching out their hands, nodding and welcoming us. Have Mr Smith and I been mistaken for Roman emperors by these preppy pagans? Oh no, this intimate 20-room hotel has been expecting us: Mr Smith and I have come home.

After a brief encounter with every staff member, we are led into a cerulean-blue library, stocked with design, fashion and architecture essentials – everything you could ever want to read on those inviting overstuffed white sofas. Apple mojitos and plump olives at our fingertips, we flick through Helmut Newton's gigantic *Sumo* biography. 'This is *amazing*,' breathes Mr Smith. A quick gander reveals a DVD hoard that even includes every episode of *The Sopranos* – not that we'll be locked up watching box sets. Capri won't have it: she'll lure us out with her voluptuous green hills, sexy sidestreets and, of course, beautiful locals.

Books, the beach, that view over the Bay of Naples, vintage photographs – it's all ravishing, and all so welcoming. A brief hotel tour includes glimpses of the beautiful southeast-facing pool, the separate spa building (deep-tissue massage, Mr Smith?) and the wraparound deck: JK Place feels like a palazzo ('Another type of trouser', notes the ever-sharp Mr Smith) with hints of hip Hamptons getaway. Ah, the good life.

Drinks drained, we are led to our handsome bedroom, which is a large white space with two French doors opening over the bay. Mr Smith inspects the wet room and a large marble bath while I flop onto a gorgeous white-linen-shrouded four-poster. It may all sound a tad honeymoonish, but it isn't: it is unisexy – logical clean luxury, riffing on a nautical note.

It's time for dinner. Capri is relaxed – but be sure to look good. This is an Italian resort in which to put your best foot forward, and embrace life as a bon vivant – preferably a good-looking one – a place to be chic at all

costs. (If you must slum it in a hoodie, you'd better at least drape said item around your shoulders.) Eventually emerging from our suite, we pad up to the lounge.

Tranquil, I note. 'Cocktail hour,' proffers Mr Smith. We linger over dry martinis in the library before being steered to the small dining room. Intuitive staff strike a masterful balance of friendly but not too familiar. In the intimate restaurant, all six tables are buzzing with lively conversation. Charmingly walked through the Mediterranean menu by the head waiter, we are quizzed on our plans for the weekend over seafood recommendations. Classic risotto proves to be the best we've ever had, and simple starters such as swordfish carpaccio are beyond delicious. As is the wine. And the desserts. It's a decadent place, Capri.

Another wonderful feature of JK Place is its proximity to everything – and there is lots to do on see-and-be-seen Capri. The incredibly helpful concierge is super-informative and the hotel is more than happy to zip you around the

island in its shuttle. Mr Smith and I have a packed itinerary: first off is Villa San Michele in Anacapri, once home to the charismatic Swedish psychiatrist Axel Munthe; crammed to the rafters with artefacts, now a luxury hotel, it is flanked by a glorious Vesuvius-view garden perched above the harbour.

I decline Mr Smith's suggestion of a vertiginous one-man cable car to the isle's peak in favour of trawling the shelves of the renowned bookshop La Conchiglia, and I make off with one of their very own delightful tomes. Next is lunch at the old-school Da Gemma, on a warren-like alleyway in the old town; the kind of place where walls are plastered with faded photos of patrons past and the thin-crust pizza is unforgettable.

Fortified, we tackle a walk to Villa Jovis, perched on the brink of a 300ft cliff at the apex of the island; Tiberius ran the Roman Empire from here and the ruins are fairly intact. Vertigo sufferers beware: it's properly on the edge. Many a gobby slave has no doubt uttered his last from this dramatic spot. Our panorama-enhanced walk back, down winding narrow streets, past enigmatic palazzo gates with wisteria-shrouded pathways, is breathtaking in the fading light.

What a magical place this is, branded forever on our brains. Our lasting impression of JK Place Capri will be its easy, relaxed style, its understated glamour and comfort. But mostly, we'll remember how hard it was to leave.

Reviewed by **Erdem Moralioglu**, fashion designer

NEED TO KNOW

Rooms 22, including eight suites.
Rates €600–€1,400, including buffet breakfast, tax and minibar soft drinks.
Check-out 12 noon, but flexible subject to availability. Earliest check-in, 4pm.
Facilities Spa, gym, library of books and films, free WiFi throughout, shuttle service. In rooms: flatscreen TV, DVD/CD player, minibar. Some of the Penthouse Suites have Jacuzzi baths, and two can be combined into a Grand Penthouse.
Poolside You can bask in a soft sea breeze on the hotel's sun-deck, where a big heated swimming pool allows dips even on chillier days. Staff are on hand to offer up cooling drinks to a soundtrack of light lounge music.
Children JK Place is more suited to couples, although cots are available free for babies, and extra beds can be added to rooms for €150 a night. The spa even offers specialised treatments for under-14s.
Also JK Spa uses bespoke natural products and Ren cosmetics in its body and beauty therapies, which range from chocolate anti-stress massages and facials to tinting and waxing.

IN THE KNOW

Our favourite rooms Interiors maestro Michele Bonan (also responsible for JK Place Firenze) has given JK a splash of nauticalia with a palette of navy blue, ultramarine, cream and white. Number 22 on the second floor faces out onto the sea, and the bath tub is positioned in the middle of the bathroom floor, allowing you to bathe while gazing at the ocean – with the windows open, you can even sunbathe as you soak.
Hotel bar JK Lounge attracts the Caprese glitterati come aperitif o'clock, although it's open all day until midnight. It's great for martinis and strawberry mojitos on the terrace at sunset.
Hotel restaurant Stylish JKitchen is a modern confection of black, white and grey, with tables spilling outside onto a veranda above the sea. Seafood and pasta combine temptingly on the dinner menu, available until 10.30pm.
Top table On the very edge of the terrace, overlooking the Bay of Naples. Or, settle into the library with a super-strong coffee and thumb through the Taschen back catalogue.
Room service Food and drink are available 24 hours a day, with a more limited menu kicking in when JKitchen closes.
Dress code Bright, white and out for the night.
Local knowledge The entrance to the chairlift that takes you up Monte Solaro, the highest point on Capri, isn't far from the hotel, in Anacapri – it's well worth braving the heights for the views at the top.

LOCAL EATING AND DRINKING

Capri Palace Hotel's restaurant L'Olivo (+39 081 978 0111) is the island's only Michelin-starred dining option – it has two. Its bar and beach club Il Riccio, on the cliffs overlooking Capri's famed Blue Grotto, has spectacular views (+39 081 837 1380; booking essential). Enjoy dinner among the lemon trees at Da Paolino on Via Palazzo a Mare (+39 081 837 6102), where Paolino himself has been serving *ravioli caprese* to Hollywood royalty for more than 30 years. Sample home-made Mediterranean dishes and a range of Italian wines on the terrace at Villa Verde on Vico Sella Orta (+39 081 837 7024). Settings don't come more impressive than La Fontelina's (+39 081 837 0845); it's a prime water's-edge lunch spot with views of I Faraglioni – an offshore trio of dramatic rocks. Da Gemma on Via Madre Serafina (+39 081 837 0461) was Graham Greene's favourite eatery; it serves Caprese favourites and ocean-fresh seafood.

GET A ROOM!

Hotel details 225 via Provincial Marina Grande, 80073 Capri (+39 081 838 4001; jkcapri.com).
To book Ring our expert Travel Team (you'll find all our numbers with your membership card on page 5) or go to mrandmrssmith.com/jk-place-capri.

 €50 credit to spend on treatments in the spa.

BASILICATA

COUNTRYSIDE Caves, coves and orange groves
COUNTRY LIFE Going underground

Much of Italy wears its heart on its sleeve – but Basilicata is an enigma. This tiny southern region, tucked into Italy's instep, flanked by the Ionian and Tyrrhenian Seas, is as tough as its *tufa*-rock caves: a gritty tapestry of stone settlements, craggy mountains and arid terrain. Basilicata needs to be strong – it has endured: tussled over by the Greeks, Romans, Byzantines and other sword-wielding ruffians, its locals emigrated in droves, leaving the hills to the goats, and the coasts to the sea turtles. Later, the 1950s were unsettled, too: residents of the Sassi di Matera (Italy's earliest human dwellings) were relocated by the government. Despite this, Basilicata's wild beauty and mystery remains. Potenza, the capital, yields glittering beaches, and Matera is a film star, playing Jerusalem for four famous directors.

GETTING THERE

Planes Basilicata doesn't have an airport, but Palese Airport in Puglia, 15km from Bari's city centre, is about an hour's drive from Matera; just over two hours from Potenza. Papola Casale airport in Brindisi is two hours from Matera. For details of both, see aeroportidipuglia.it.
Trains Bari is the region's main rail hub, linking the national network to local services to Matera (fal-srl.it), as well as further-flung city stops, including Rome (fsitaliane.it).
Automobiles With purple-tinged mountain ranges, fresco-adorned ruins and ravishing coastlines to uncover, having a car is more than sensible, but be extra careful when driving in the small hamlets and towns – streets are narrow and winding, and parking can be a challenge.

LOCAL KNOWLEDGE

Taxis This is a mountainous region, so don't expect cabs on tap. In Matera, it's easier to navigate the winding paths on foot, but if you're weighed down with cases, try Viaggi Lionetti (+39 0835 334033; viaggilionetti.com). Flag taxis by bus and train stations – since they're far from cheap, they're best kept for short journeys.

Siesta and fiesta Shops are open 9am–1pm and 5pm–9pm, and they're shut on Sundays. Locals eat late, so start with aperitifs (Campari and *crostini*, perhaps?) around 8pm, then dine from 9pm.
Do go/don't go Summer is sizzling and sociable, with plenty of festivals; spring is balmy, and more conducive to exploring. The region is also growing in popularity as a ski destination, with three ravishing resorts: Monte Sirino, La Sella-Pierfaone and Volturino-Viggiano.
Packing tips Loose linens, rock-proof sandals, and a blank Moleskine notebook: soon to be filled with lamb recipes and artistic doodles of Byzantine churches.
Recommended reads The Roman poet Horace was born in Basilicata (Venosa, to be precise). If you're feeling erudite, take his *Odes, Epodes or Satires*. Carlo Levi was exiled to Basilicata in the 1930s; his account of the poverty-stricken *sassi* (in his memoirs, *Christ Stopped at Eboli*) prompted enforced relocation by the government.
Local specialities Basilicata's wheat is famous throughout Italy, so expect wonderful just-baked bread. In Matera, the dough is twisted into a cornet shape, and warmed in wood-fired ovens until it's a soft yellow-gold. Pasta

comes in at least 10 regional varieties: try *cavatelli*, or *mischiglio*, chunky tubes served with *cacioricotta* cheese and peppers. *Pezzente* is a salami unique to Basilicata: pork seasoned with chilli, garlic, fennel seeds and pepper. Lamb is also a favourite, cooked to molten succulence with carrots, sausage, breadcrumbs and cheese. Closer to the coast, the emphasis shifts to seafood: try *scapece* (vinegar-splashed fried anchovies).

And... The grapes nurtured on volcanic Mount Vulture are alchemised into the inky Aglianico red wine: take home a few bottles of the robust Aglianico del Vulture; Potenza's Terre dell'Alta Val d'Agri is another favourite.

WORTH GETTING OUT OF BED FOR

Viewpoint Walk to the top of the Piazza del Duomo in Matera and look out over the *gravina* (ravine), listening out for the tinkling of cow bells below. For sea views, climb Monte Pollino in the Pollino National Park, and survey the Tyrrhenian and Ionian coasts.

Arts and culture Matera's 13th-century cathedral has a Byzantine fresco of the Madonna della Bruna and Child, and a depiction of the Last Judgement, too. Explore Matera's troglodyte houses and churches dug out of the rock: the Civita district is the oldest group of buildings, and divides the two Sassi districts: Sasso Barisano and Sasso Caveoso. Visit the Domenico Ridola National Museum, set in a former convent on Via Ridola, for its collection of Palaeolithic and Neolithic archaeological artefacts. Admire the remains of the Temple of Hera at Metaponto (and the vivid orange groves). The Museum of Contemporary Sculpture (Musma) is set in the 16th-century Palazzo Pomarici, with exhibitions spilling into the caves. The underground rock-hewn rooms make for a backdrop as dramatic as the international sculpture haul (musma.it).

Activities Go for golf: there's a brace of 18-hole courses within 10km of each other (rivadeitessali.it): the Riva dei Tessali Golf Club, set in a beautiful pine forest bordering the Ionian Sea, or Metaponto Golf Club, on the Ionian coast. While you're there, Metaponto's beaches are calm and secluded, with shallow, family-friendly waters. Maratea, where the mountains meet the Tyrrhenian Sea, is a more rugged experience. If you'd rather stay on dry land, the rocky terrain makes for dramatic horse-riding, hiking or mountain biking. In the Alta Murgia National Park, explore cave church complexes and winding mountain paths surrounded by blossom and birdsong (parcoaltamurgia.it).

Perfect picnic Pick up provisions such as *pupazzella*, little fiery peppers in vinegar stuffed with anchovies, and cured meats from L'Arturo Enogastronomia, a little deli on Piazza Sedile in Matera (+39 339 390 7068). Take your edible bounty to Matera's rocky ravine, and picnic in a cave overlooking the gorge.

Daytripper Drive to Potenza, which overlooks the valley of the Basento river, and is nestled in the Apennines. Here you'll find some of the area's best beaches, dotted along the north coast of Maratea. There are sea caves to explore too: try the Grotta di Maratea (aka the Cave of Wonders).

Walks Don your hiking boots for the Gallipoli Cognato Park (parcogallipolicognato.it). The lush Cognato forest and its winding chains of terrain trails make for a romantic, if energetic, ramble. Walk from the Basento river up to the summit of Mount Impiso.

Shopping Matera's weekly food markets are the best places to stock up on provisions. Matera new town has plenty of clothes, jewellery and gift shops – keep a lookout for intricate wood carvings and patterned ceramics. In the Sassi itself, shops tend to be tourist-driven and pricey.

Something for nothing Pause for an espresso in Piazza del Sedile, and listen out for students at the music academy practising above – pray for an impromptu opera performance, for the ultimate Italian serenade.

Don't go home without... admiring Maratea's Statua del Redentore – an imposing 72-foot statue of Christ carved from white Carrara marble on Mount San Biagio. It certainly gives Rio's Redeemer a run for its money.

BOUNTIFULLY BASILICATA

Bright red *peperoni di Senise* (Senise peppers) colour the countryside's fields and flavour its typical dishes. The locals love them, and treat them with imagination: fresh peppers give sauces a fiery zing, plump ones are stuffed with meat, or grilled and oil-soaked, and then there's the sun-dried kind: *peperoni secchi* are threaded into garlands and ground into a sweet, spicy powder called *Zafaran*, used as a seasoning.

DIARY

January Matera honours Saint Anthony Abbott, the patron saint of animals and country folk, with the Festa di Sant'Antonio Abate. Also called the 'Feast of Fire', the day is marked with bonfires, music, and dancing in the town square. **May** The tree-chopping ceremony (a pagan fertility rite) is celebrated throughout the region, with an oak tree chopped down and 'married' to a young holly tree in the town squares. **July** The Festa della Madonna Bruna is an annual religious ceremony held in Matera, first celebrated in the 14th century. Following the usual form for sacred parties, there are floats, processions, food and fireworks (festadellabruna.it). **December** The town of Muro Lucano holds a Christmas market on 12 December from 10am until 1pm, in the Piazza Don Minzoni.

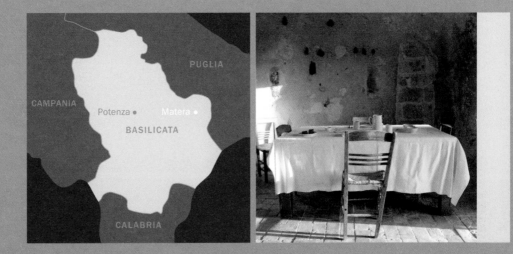

Sextantio le Grotte della Civita

STYLE Boutique bedrock
SETTING Matera's grand canyon

'It's less cave, more soothing sanctuary –
we even have our own dining table, set with
a carafe, pretty glasses and bowl of fresh,
fat cherries. We order wine and get settled'

When I tell my beloved that we're going to stay in a grotto for the weekend, he is less than thrilled. Not just any grotto I enthuse: a super-deluxe made-into-a-glorious-*hotel* kind of grotto. 'Isn't grotto just another word for cave?' grumbles my reluctant troglodyte. I deflect the question by suggesting all sorts of naughty Neanderthal-style games suitable for playing in a 'cave'; he brightens considerably. Thus, a few days later, we land at Bari airport, collect our car and we're soon speeding towards Basilicata, the Southern Italian region just above the arch of Italy's foot, and the rocky, hilly neighbour to Puglia, the country's heel.

Declared a Unesco World Heritage site in 1993, Matera is one of the oldest towns in the world, inhabited since the Neolithic age. The particular area of the town we're going to is known as the Sassi, a series of dwellings cut into the local tufa rock that rises above the Murgia plateau overlooking La Gravina gorge. The roads are narrow and signposts are few as we zip along past buff- and honey-coloured hillside houses.

A bit more zipping back and forth and we have to admit defeat: we have absolutely no idea where the hotel is. Enquiries elicit enthusiastic pointing in the direction we've just come from. Unfortunately this charade is repeated several times up and down the same road until finally a young waiter takes pity on us and walks us to the foot of a broad flight of wonky paved steps. No sign. No indication of hotel-ness, but he assures us this is the way. A shortish climb later, we chance upon a rickety gate, which opens onto a large courtyard. The heady scent of citronella wafts to greet us, and we have found Le Grotte della Civita.

Walking into the reception is instantly soothing. Once accustomed to the sultry glow of candlelight after the glare of the sun outside, we realise that we're standing inside a lofty-domed structure hewn from the surrounding rock. The effect is that of being enveloped in a capsule of calm. Classical music ripples over us and we're presented with a hefty ancient metal key; no impersonal magnetic swipe cards here then.

Our room is immense. Apparently it used to be part of a church; its soaring six-metre high, pock-marked stone ceilings certainly suggests this is likely. The receptionist, now doubling as chambermaid, busies about lighting huge pillar candles in every corner, and our luxurious cavern gradually comes into focus. On one side, the bed, all draped in indulgent layers of lush antique linen that tumble extravagantly to the floor, and an extremely modern scoop of a bath on the other. Beautifully aged pieces of wooden furniture, chests and benches are dotted around, and the overall aesthetic is authentic rustic natural.

A self-confessed style absolutist, I will happily concede that this is less cave, more soothing sanctuary. We even have our own dining table, set with water carafe, pretty glasses and a bowl of fresh, fat cherries. We order a bottle of wine and get settled. Moments later, we're sat outside on our terrace, with swifts and kestrels wheeling silently overhead. To the sound of distant goat bells, we sit back and savour an impromptu welcoming feast of bruschetta, olives and cheese. Watching the blush of early evening sunlight bounce off the hills opposite, it all tastes like nectar (even the somewhat fierce local red wine).

Eventually, the compulsion to explore overtakes us and, because there's no bar or lounge in the hotel, we amble off to see what gives beyond our enclave. The choice of direction is straightforward: left or right. Matera is seemingly composed of one main road along which all things must pass. It spirals the city, winding up towards a tottering church at its peak, from which the houses, like roughly carved building blocks, tumble down. The overriding impression one gets is of a Cubist painting in shades of taupe, sand and khaki.

A typical local trattoria is what we're after, and it's not hard to find one. Friendly and unassuming, La Talpa is set like all the buildings into the rock. Intoxicating smells waft from its cavernous interior and we're particularly keen to sample the local speciality, *purè di fave con*

cicorielle di campo (a broad bean purée with wild chicory), and they don't disappoint. The beloved is particularly enamoured of his traditional *vitello all'aceto balsamico* (veal with balsamic glaze). But this culinary joy is nothing compared to the glee our hotel breakfast elicits the following morning.

Arranged like a buffet, it is a veritable feast. Everything is locally sourced, from the salty pecorino to the butter, ham, apricots and plums. There are sweet almond cakes, savoury biscuits and bitter chocolate cake. Fresh orange juice, a flan stuffed with squidgy tomatoes, and steaming pots of jasmine tea. It seems criminal to leave anything, so we devour with gusto. It takes some time but is the perfect start to a leisurely day.

This isn't a lie-in-the-sun-by-the-pool kind of hotel (there is no pool, and there's not a lot to do in Matera, other than soak up its immense history), but that suits us fine. We wander through the deserted Sassi on the old side of town and visit a mini-museum that shows a cave furnished as it would have been in ancient times; another little display in a musuem on Via Bruno Buozzi highlights the Roman underground system of irrigation so essential to the region. We wend our way through a former church and monastery turned art gallery, Madonna delle Virtù and San Nicola dei Greci on Via Purgatorio Vecchio, and then devote ourselves to the pursuit of more fine food.

Le Bubbole is chosen to play host to our final meal, as it has a rooftop terrace with an enchanting view of the city. What's more, there's an extraordinary full moon, heightening the sense of Matera being an almost mystical place with many tales to tell. Tonight though, it's keeping schtum, and all is well with us, and the world.

Reviewed by **Michelle Ogundehin**, *Elle Decoration* editor

NEED TO KNOW

Rooms 18, including six suites.

Rates €275–€495, including tax and buffet breakfast: a spread of local produce, including yoghurt, mozzarella, provolone, bread, fruit and cakes).

Check-out 11am, but flexible depending on availability. Earliest check-in, 3pm.

Facilities Free WiFi in the reception 'cave', communal areas and rooms on the first level. In rooms: natural, locally made bath products, candles and antique linens; some have sleek freestanding bath tubs.

Children Smith Junior is welcome. Beds for children under six (€15 a day) and older children (€75 a day) can be added to rooms on request.

Also Pets can come along free – just let the hotel know in advance.

IN THE KNOW

Our favourite rooms Suite 13 is a romantic honey-coloured cave with its own balcony, plenty of candlelit alcoves, and a fireplace beside the bath tub. Suites 4 and 8 are fit for families, with plenty of space. Superior Cave Rooms 9 and 15 come with both a bath tub and shower.

Hotel bar None, but you can sample local wines and local produce in the Tasting Room, or on the terrace that faces the splendour of the Murgia National Park.

Hotel restaurant The Tasting Room, set in an ancient church hewn into the rock, is a dramatic setting for a meal (dinner is served only on request). In keeping with the hotel's philosophy, frills and furniture are minimal, food is traditional and local, and service is fuss-free. By night, flickering candlelight lends a romantic glow to the clutch of tables.

Top table Sit in one of the corner nooks carved into the stone walls.

Room service Breakfast is available in room from 8am, and drinks can be ordered until 10pm (ask for olives, taralli or bruschetta if you're hungry).

Dress code Jesuit chic or Italian widow: a white smock or black lace with leather sandals.

Local knowledge Go on a guided tour of the sassi (Matera's rock-cut dwellings). Stop-offs include a typical cave home decorated with traditional furnishings, the church of San Pietro Caveoso, the cavern church of Santa Lucia alle Malve (worth visiting for its frescoes) and the museum of farming history.

LOCAL EATING AND DRINKING

Hotel Palazzo Gattini in Piazza Duomo has an enticing restaurant, Tasch Nisch (formerly known as Le Bubbole). Try to book a spot on the charming city-view terrace; expect seasonal produce and a well-stocked wine cellar (+39 08 3533 4358). The pretty gingham tables at La Talpa (+39 08 3533 5086) on Via Fiorentini provide a romantic setting for the restaurant's traditional treats. Ingredients are sourced from the surrounding countryside each morning, so food is as fresh as it's flavoursome – cavatelli with chickpea purée, porcini, rocket and tomatoes is a typically tasty example. Those needing a sugar rush should visit Caffè Tripoli at 25 Via Giuseppe Garibaldi in Martina Franca (+39 08 0480 5260): we especially love the ice-creams and the cherry and cream *bocconotti* (cakes made with ground almonds and sweet pasta).

GET A ROOM!

Hotel details 28 via Civita, 75100 Matera (+39 0835 332744; legrottedellacivita.com).

To book Ring our expert Travel Team (you'll find all our numbers with your membership card on page 5) or go to mrandmrssmith.com/sextantio-le-grotte-della-civita.

 A bottle of Aglianico del Vulture, a local red wine.

PUGLIA

COUNTRYSIDE The shapely heel of Italy
COUNTRY LIFE *Trulli*, madly, deeply

Sunny southern Puglia has a unique character and charm that's relatively unknown to outsiders; the holidaymaking Italians who flock here in summer keep this laid-back playground of blue sea, golden sands and olive groves strictly a family affair. As at all good Italian get-togethers, food takes centre stage: fresh fish, melons, figs, olive oils and wines keep those alfresco tables piled high with pretty provisions; Puglia also produces almost all of Europe's pasta. Despite seeming Italian down to its boots, this region has a very cosmopolitan past: Greek, Spanish and Norman settlers have all paid visits, leaving behind a quirky mishmash of architectural heirlooms, from Baroque churches and Romanesque cathedrals to whitewashed fishing villages and the stacked-whorl rooftops of Puglia's iconic *trulli*.

GETTING THERE

Planes Between them, Puglia's airports at Bari and Brindisi (aeroportidipuglia.it) handle regular flights from many European cities, including Rome, Venice and London.
Trains Puglia's main towns and cities are connected by rail, but local services are slow (albeit scenic). Intercity services are operated by Trenitalia (trenitalia.com).
Automobiles Puglia is sprawling, and its remoter sights – such as 13th-century Castel del Monte – are accessible only by road; pick up wheels at the airport. Chancing upon tiny, ancient villages as you drive along is part of the fun.

LOCAL KNOWLEDGE

Taxis Trying to hail a cab on the street won't get you anywhere; go to a taxi rank or ask your hotel to order one for you. They are metered and levy small extra charges for luggage and for travelling after 10pm.
Siesta and fiesta Shops open early and close late, with long lunch breaks. Most close on Sundays and Monday mornings, except in resort areas. Banks also break for lunch, reopening at 3pm for an hour. Restaurants only start to fill at 9pm; nightclubs hot up around midnight.

Do go/don't go Fine, sunny weather starts in spring and lasts well into autumn this far south; if you don't fancy sweltering heat and busy beaches, visit in early or late summer for milder conditions and the chance to bag a decent spot on the sand.
Packing tips Summer wardrobe staples – think laid-back southern style, not chichi Capri – and a decent road map.
Recommended reads Francesca Marciano traces a family's patchwork past as they pack up their Puglian home, *Casa Rossa*; follow in Charles Lister's footsteps as he journeys *Heel to Toe*; or taste the Puglian countryside that inspired London's River Café chefs Rosie Gray and Ruth Rogers in *Italian Two Easy*.
Local specialities *La cucina Pugliese* is about full, fresh flavours and robustly rustic recipes: grilled swordfish with sprigs of oregano and a squeeze of lemon; and antipasti such as roasted aubergines and marinated peppers. For ingredients that make Puglia's antipasti dishes sumptuous, visit Cisternino in the Itria Valley: its Monday-morning market is a colourful feast for the senses. Wander past slender salamis and pungent blocks of pecorino, creamy balls of Pugliese burrata, fresh capers and neon-bright

lemons; there'll be a natural abundance of sun-ripened fruit and vegetables, and delicious olive oils. Definitely try the native pasta, *orecchiette*, or 'little ears'. The region's wine ain't bad, either: Salice Salentino, a full-bodied, visceral red, is one of the best.

And... Head to the hamlet of Speziale di Fasano for artisan suppliers of the kind of Pugliese ingredients that foodies are falling over themselves for at the moment. On the main road, the cheesemaking family at Caseificio Crovace Oronzo e Figli will happily talk you through production process; all their creamy fresh burrata, smoked mozzarella and ricotta is made and sold on-site.

WORTH GETTING OUT OF BED FOR

Viewpoint The mediaeval hilltop town of Locorotondo on the Murge plateau gives panoramic views of the sprawling Itria Valley; Selva di Fasano also offers horizon-kissing eyefuls of fields, woods and Adriatic coast.

Arts and culture Puglia's towns are perfect for cultural grazing. With a history spanning more than 2,000 years, Lecce in Italy's stiletto tip (aka the Salentine Peninsula) is known for its splendid Baroque architecture – hence its 'Florence of the South' appellation. Bari and Otranto meanwhile have cathedrals worth bragging about – the latter especially for its mosaic floor. Taranto's Museo Nazionale Archeologico (museotaranto.it) has a dazzling display of Hellenistic jewellery.

Activities The region's flat terrain and grove-lined country roads are ideal for cycling; Puglia in Bici (+39 340 264 4128; pugliainbici.com) will deliver bikes to you, as well as helmets and other gear. Combine cycling and gourmandising and pedal your way through Speziale di Fasano; pause at Tavern Il Cortiletto on Via Lecce (+39 080 481 0758) and pick at fennel-infused *taralli* (mini bagel-type dough rings), then pig out on their speciality calzone. Learn to whip up delicious Puglian dishes or traditional pasta yourself with a local chef at Masseria Torre Coccaro, which has a dedicated cookery school in a converted church (+39 080 482 9310). Rent clubs and tee off at the San Domenico golf course near Savelletri (sandomenicogolf.com), or on Masseria Torre Maizza's private nine-hole course (+39 080 482 7838).

Best beach The beaches on Puglia's Adriatic coast are pine-fringed and gorgeous, interspersed with hidden bays and sheltered lagoons. The village of Torre Canne has a long stretch of soft sand and shallow water for cooling off toes after working on the tan – it'll be crowded in August.

Daytripper The Parco Nazionale del Gargano, in the north of Puglia, contains the deep, dark Foresta Umbra (Forest of Shadows; parks.it). These 11,000 hectares of pine, oak and beech are the last remnants of an ancient forest that once spread over most of Puglia. Gather picnic pickings en route and find a shady spot to spend the afternoon.

Walks Puglia was once a Greek colony, and nowhere is this heritage more obvious than in Ostuni, where pretty whitewashed houses gleam against the cobalt sky and sea. Go along later in the day to join the locals on their *passeggiata* – the see-and-be-seen evening stroll.

Shopping On market days, in addition to groceries, you'll find handicrafts from as little as €10 upwards; best buys are antique local ceramics and tapestries or olive-branch basketry; head to Bari on the first Sunday of the month, Ostuni on the second, Martina Franca on the third and then, for the biggest of the lot, Lecce on the last Sunday.

Something for nothing Puglia produces the lion's share of Italy's olive oil. There are many varieties: cold-pressed extra-virgin oils in particular develop distinctive aromas and delicate fragrances. The olive press of Il Frantolio di D'Amico Pietro near Cisternino (ilfrantolio.it) offers tastings – great for wine buffs in need of a challenge.

Don't go home without... dining at Grotta Palazzese, at 59 via Narciso in Polignano (+39 080 424 0677). Typical Pugliese dishes are served with Adriatic wines in a sea cave that has been used for entertaining since the Duc de Leto first converted the grotto into a hall in the 1700s.

PERFECTLY PUGLIA

Trulli are the circular limestone dwellings, with beehive-shaped roofs and whitewashed walls, unique to the Itria Valley and particularly visible around Alberobello, where the settlements have earned Unesco World Heritage status. Originally built as storehouses many have now been converted into stylish holiday homes (mrandmrssmith.com/self-catering). Set your SatNav for Ceglie Messapica with your camera at the ready.

DIARY

June One of the oldest motorcar races in the world, the Rally del Salento takes place in Lecce; it's a nail-biting event characterised by slippery roads, fast straights and sharp turns (rallydelsalento.com). **August** Divingusto is a weekend-long food festival held in Ceglie Messapica, bigging up Pugliese ingredients and cuisine with stalls, tastings, musical events and cookery demonstrations (divingusto.it). **Mid-July** The Festival della Valle d'Itria – a three-week event in the town of Martina Franca, with opera, classical and jazz performances – starts tuning up in the second half of the month (festivaldellavalleditria.it). **September** Jazz in Puglia brings international artists to Lecce for an all-swinging, all-dancing festival of soul, blues and syncopation (jazzinpuglia.it).

Masseria Fumarola

STYLE *Trullo* to its roots
SETTING Verdant Valle d'Itria

'Arriving at dusk is magical: huddles of immaculate white *trulli* and canopied seating areas are connected by tree-lined paths lit by hundreds of tiny lanterns'

As we zip up the mountain roads towards Martina Franca, Mr Smith is growing increasingly enthused about Puglia's architecture looking, as he so eloquently puts it, 'like boobs'. The hills are dotted with *trulli*, buildings clustered in small mounds with nipple-like peaks. To me they seem quite exotic, Moorish almost, compared to the Italian buildings I've seen before. Naturally, Mr Smith is pretty excited that we will be sleeping in one of these fertile-looking huts together.

The sun is dipping away as we approach the hotel from a winding country road, overlooked by the plump silhouettes of hundreds of *trulli*. Occasionally we slow down to check if any of these rustic piles are worthy of the 'boutique' label. But each weather-beaten hut looks much like the last. When we eventually pull into our destination we feel quite silly for supposing the entrance to our masseria would in any way have resembled those for the vineyards we have been passing. The gate to our hotel is mammoth, and it is no less than thrilling when it starts to roll open to reveal the twinkling lights of Masseria Fumarola.

Arriving here at dusk is magical. The hotel consists of huddles of small, immaculately painted white *trulli* and canopied seating areas, connected by tree-lined gravel paths that are lit by hundreds of tiny lanterns. These peasant-built dwellings have been transformed into a maze of mini luxury hideaways. This, in my opinion, is the best type of boutique hotel: a modest local building that is developed in a way that is both unique and sensitive to its original charm.

Now, I am one of those people who gets overly excited about great bathrooms. So I can't help but let out a sound that betrays how thrilled I am when I see that we have a two-person Jacuzzi. A remote control that opens a skylight right above it – in the very nipple of our rooftop – elicits another squeal. The idea of various small domes in the garden letting out steam into the night sky like so many little teapots tickles me. Mr Smith? He couldn't care less. He is already cruising the Italian MTV options on a flatscreen in the very same colour as the stone walls; it's at the end of a bed sitting inside a grape-crushing well.

I am, perhaps worryingly, not ashamed to say that – like proper Brits abroad – our focus while we're away is on: a) catching the sun; b) eating to our absolute maximum capacity; and c) drinking as much local wine as possible. We exceed even our own expectations at all three and we are soon burnt, bloated and very content.

Having told Mr Smith in plain words that we would be spending our first afternoon by the pool, amid a sea of white loungers across two levels of decking, we agree to dilute my pleasure-seeking mania with a morning exploring Martina Franca. The streets of the old town are beautiful, cobbled and labyrinthine, but getting lost is sweetened by fresh hazelnut gelato, and several macchiato pit stops. As we cross the piazzas, I notice that my bare British limbs are causing a few raised eyebrows. We then notice that the inhabitants of the town are wearing furs, hats and scarves. Spot the Londoner keen to worship the spring sun in Italy.

Italian culture has a holy trinity: food, family and fashion. Masseria Fumarola sings a song of praise to all three.

The relaxed dining room is the setting for culinary magic – *al dente* orecchiette cloaked in seasonal sauces; toothsome grilled meat; delicate cakes and pastries. And you'll never be able to look at beer and peanuts in the same way after sampling the hotel's antipasti: hunks of creamy local cheeses paired with slivers of salty salami. A favourite meal out for us is at family-run Ristorante Sagitarrio, where we feast on regional specialities having fought the locals to bag a table on Saturday night. There are pictures of the owner all over the wall, and I am naff enough to mention his resemblance to Tony Soprano. (This is after a €2 litre of Pugliese wine.)

Masseria Fumarola works so well because it makes the most of what Puglia has to offer. Waking up to a jug of fresh blood-orange juice, cappuccino and local breads, and spending our days surrounded by green woodlands dotted with white huts is a delight. Everything is easy and simple – the hotel, its proximity to the town, even the short drive to the airport. We leave feeling we have had a real holiday rather than just a quick break.

'There's not a stand-out feature to shout about as such – more a plethora of tiny perfections'

At Masseria Fumarola, there's not a stand-out feature to shout about as such – more a plethora of tiny perfections, every one low-key and intimate. Since returning home, Mr Smith and I have both recommended the hotel to many a friend – each time with an air of smugness. For some reason, the place left us with the feeling that we had personally discovered it – not *exactly* the truth. But as someone who sat in the sun by that seductive garden pool, listening to bird chatter as attentive staff brought over freshly made ricotta cheesecake, I feel justified in claiming it as our very special secret...

Reviewed by **Quentin Jones**, illustrator

NEED TO KNOW

Rooms 14, including eight suites.

Rates €75–€140, including buffet breakfast and service.

Check-out 11am but flexible, subject to availability. There's a €20 charge if you leave after 3pm. Earliest check-in, 1pm.

Facilities Gardens, library, free WiFi throughout. In rooms: flatscreen TV; minibar and bathroom stocked with locally sourced products.

Poolside The outdoor pool is partially hidden by a dry-stone wall and encircled by chestnut and olive trees, with a scattering of white canvas deck chairs and tangerine sunloungers.

Children Very little Smiths are welcome; cots for babies are €10 a night. Older children aren't really catered for.

Also Go for an early morning jog or a post-lunch constitutional in the hotel's 15 acres of oak woodland.

IN THE KNOW

Our favourite rooms Book Massaro Vecchio, a junior suite which spans three colourful, conical rooms (bedroom, bathroom and lounge). Highlights include the romantic wrought-iron bed and the sitting room's minimalist log fireplace. Palmento Due, a suite fashioned from the farm's former wine store, has a well-like sunken sleeping area and a mezzanine living space overlooking the bed. The bathroom has a Jacuzzi that looks up to a skylight in the roof.

Hotel bar There's a snug little bar area inside, but the best place to spend sundowner o'clock is outside by the pool. Sample the peppery cold meats and calorific local cheeses: pecorino, ricotta and burrata di Andria.

Hotel restaurant The dining room is simply styled: exposed stone walls, wooden furniture and gingham tablecloths. Forget toast and cereal: breakfast is a spread of fresh fruit, cold cuts and pastries (try the pine nut and mascarpone tart). Come lunch and dinner, there's *grigliata* (an Italian-style barbecue grill) to look forward to.

Top table Sit outside by the swimming pool, or by a window if it's chilly (unlikely in season).

Room service In-room treats are limited to breakfast and *aperitivi*.

Dress code Relaxed as you like: cords and plaid to match the farmhouse theme; linens and silks to keep cool outside.

Local knowledge Visit Martina Franca, 4km away, for its wonderful whitewashed Baroque architecture. Step under the grand historic gateway, Porto Santo Stefano, and into the old town. Basilica di San Martino is worth peeking into for its marble work and statues; the Palazzo Ducale, on scenic Piazza Roma, is equally impressive.

LOCAL EATING AND DRINKING

Bina is a smart, romantic little eatery (white linen, cream-coloured stone walls), a 20-minute drive away on Via Dottor Recchia in Locorotondo (+39 080 431 1784). The menu is brimming with local specialities, including *purea di fave* (bean purée with sautéed chicory). There's no phone, so you can't book at Piazzetta Garibaldi, an understated osteria on Piazza Garibaldi in nearby Martina Franca, that offers honest home cooking and a selection of local wines. However, it *is* worth booking at Trattoria le Ruote (+39 080 483 7473) at 52 Contrada Primicerio – especially at lunchtime, when the reasonably priced, flavoursome dishes lure in a loyal crowd. On Via Quarto, Ristorante Saggitario has no delusions of grandeur, but it does know a thing or two about roasting meat (+39 080 485 8982). Osteria del Tempo Perso, on Via Vitale Tanzarella in Ostuni (+39 0831 304819), has a characterful enoteca – stop by for a tasting.

GET A ROOM!

Hotel details 104 via Villa Castelli, 74015 Martina Franca (Taranto) (+39 080 430 3722; masseriafumarola.it).

To book Ring our expert Travel Team (you'll find all our numbers with your membership card on page 5) or go to mrandmrssmith.com/masseria-fumarola.

 A bottle of Masseria Fumarola's home-made olive oil.

HOW TO... pick your pasta

1 **Looks like** Little ears
Sounds like [or'ē-kyē'ti]
Must be... orecchiette
This traditional Pugliese pasta shape is handmade in homes across Puglia, and matched simply with vegetables; find it also in neighbouring Basilicata.

2 **Looks like** Quills/nibs
Sounds like [pen'ē]
Must be... penne
Tubular, diagonally cut and perfect for soaking up meaty tomato sauces or sucking up creamy concoctions. Penne 'rigate' are the ridged kind, all the better to mop up every last drop of flavour.

3 **Looks like** Helter-skelters/spirals
Sounds like [trot'ōl'ē]
Must be... trottole
Trottole actually means 'spinning top'. The intricate shape originates in Campania and lends itself to slippery, creamy sauces. Often produced as a tricolore pasta, it also makes for pretty salads.

4 **Looks like** Rolled-up tea towels
Sounds like [stro'tsa-pre-t'i]
Must be... strozzapreti
This hand-rolled pasta is named the 'priest strangler' (the exact etymology is unknown, but anti-papal and tax-dodging fables abound). Common in Italy's heartlands of Romagna, Umbria and Tuscany, it's renowned for its unique texture.

5 **Looks like** Wagon wheels/Trivial Pursuit wedges
Sounds like [ro-tel'in'ē]
Must be... rotelline/rotelle
A non-traditional crowd-pleaser that's fantastic for sponging up chunky meat or vegetable sauces.

6 **Looks like** Butterflies or bow ties
Sounds like [fär-fal'ē]
Must be... farfalle
These cheerful plate-fillers first appeared in the 1500s. Their flat surfaces lend themselves to many different uses, but in Italy you'll often find them smothered in garlic, butter and/or cheese.

7 **Looks like** Travel pillows, or nuns' headgear
Sounds like [kap-ə-le'ti]
Must be... cappelletti
From Modena, these 'little hats' are similar to tortellini: stuffed and served in broth or sauced with butter. Or pomodoro. (Versatile little number.) Capelletti in capon broth is traditional at Christmas.

8 **Looks like** Little stars
Sounds like [ste-let'ē]
Must be... stellette
Larder stars to scatter in vegetable soup and stock – delicious as a minestrone-padder, or in viscous chicken *brodo* (add a cavalier splash of red wine, as the Italians do at home).

9 **Looks like** Radiators/front of a Land Rover
Sounds like [rad'i-a-tor'i]
Must be... radiatori
This industrial-looking pasta shape is sturdy enough to take on the chunkiest of sauces: pair with hearty hare ragu and a racy red wine.

Generally, thin pasta = thin sauce.
Thick pasta = thick sauce.
Ridges or funny shapes = chunky sauce.

For more information, visit the National Pasta Association (ilovepasta.org/shapes.html).

ISLANDS

SARDINIA

COASTLINE Crystal-watered yacht spot
COAST LIFE Beach-lazing, ruin-gazing

Taking a *laissez-faire* approach, life on Italy's favourite island focuses on an idyllic coastline of sugar-sand coves and glass-clear waters. Jewel in this Mediterrannean crown is the Costa Smeralda, first crafted into a hip holiday hangout by billionaire spiritual leader the Aga Khan IV in the 1960s. Sardinia's capital Cagliari lies around five hours south, but luckily, there are cultural treasures to discover closer to this classy playground... Put down your drink, tear yourself from the beach and explore the island's rugged interior: an open-air archaeological museum of ancient ruins. It's also Sardinia's store cupboard, where ingredients thrive on vine, tree and herb-strewn hill – complementing an offshore larder of luscious seafood. Whether it's cuisine, climate or culture you crave, prepare for a beguiling blend of surf and turf.

GETTING THERE

Planes Half an hour from the Costa Smeralda is Olbia airport (geasar.com); two hours' drive away is Alghero (aeroportodialghero.it); for the south coast, capital Cagliari has the widest choice of routes (sogaer.it).
Trains The island's slow, slow trains are more scenic than practical (ferroviesardegna.it). The journey from Olbia to Cagliari, for example, takes around four hours.
Automobiles A car is essential if you want to explore the island – book early for high-summer months when demand is at its peak. From the Costa Smeralda it takes around two hours to drive to second-city Sassari.
Boats For the Costa Smeralda, sail to Olbia or Golfo Aranci from Genoa, Livorno, Civitavecchia (Rome) or Naples; Civitavecchia offers the speediest crossing, in under five hours (see mobylines.com, gnv.it or tirrenia.it).

LOCAL KNOWLEDGE

Taxis There are ranks in larger towns. For airport transfers from Olbia, try Marco Desini Taxi (+39 329 661 9205; taxi-costasmeralda.it); for Emerald Coast fares, use Arzachena-based Ragnedda Giov Maria (+39 0789 8028).

Siesta and fiesta There's a fluid approach to downtime on Sardinia: the daytime siesta is not always observed, so you should be able to beach-café-hop all afternoon. Rise late and dine even later – from 9pm onwards.
Do go/don't go Sardinia is renowned for its wet winters: many hotels and restaurants close between November and February. In sunny May, June and July, the flowers are in full bloom and evenings are still cool. Beware mid-August's *Ferragosto*: most businesses will close for several days.
Packing tips Good-quality sunglasses for driving (and blending in on this glamorous island); floaty cover-ups for sunbathing and sightseeing; a mask, snorkel and fins.
Recommended reads Local author Grazia Deledda was the first woman to win the Nobel prize for literature; try *The Woman and the Priest*. *Sea and Sardinia* is DH Lawrence's account of his love affair with the island. Michael Dibdin's thriller *Vendetta* is set between Rome and Sardinia.
Local specialities Shellfish such as clams, mussels and Alghero lobster are prized and plentiful. Sardinia's dry conditions make for excellent wine-making: look out for crisp vermentino whites, especially DOCG-regulated *vermentino di Gallura*; plummy cannonau, aka Sardinian

Grenache, is an intense, antioxidant-rich red; for examples of both, try lauded winery Jerzu (jerzuantichipoderi.it). Sardinian pecorino, aka *fiore Sardo*, is a cheese-counter staple. Even the island's desserts are cheese-laced: *seadas* is a dairy-filled pastry topped with honey and orange zest. Other filled delights include Sardinian pies, called *panadas*, and *culurgiones*, a kind of semolina ravioli.

WORTH GETTING OUT OF BED FOR

Viewpoint On the northern tip of the island, at Santa Teresa Gallura, stroll up to the church on Piazza San Vittorio and go through the archway on the left. From here, you can see if Rena Bianca beach lives up to its white-sands name and spot Corsica in the distance.

Arts and culture Art galleries are rare, but the village of Buddusò has gained a reputation for its sculptures; see pieces in wood and granite outside as well as inside its Contemporary Art Museum (sardegnaturismo.it). Near Cagliari, the Roman amphitheatre (anfiteatroromano.it) and Phoenician-Punic city of Sant'Antíoco (comune.santantioco.ca.it) will impress even the most reluctant of historians. Sardinia's archaeological wonders are many, whether intact, or documented in museums in Cagliari, Sassari, Nuoro and Olbia. The latter is an impressive colonnaded building on the waterfront (olbiaturismo.it/museo.html).

Activities Between the Gulf of Pevero and the Bay of Cala di Volpe, Pevero Golf Club garners pan-European superlatives: don't let the sea views distract you from the pristine par-72 course's 70 bunkers and smattering of lakes (golfclubpevero.net). For aquatic pursuits in the sheltered Gulf of Arzachena, the Water Sport Centre on Cannigione beach offers wakeboarding, wind surfing, water-skiing and sailing (watersportcentre.com). Hire bicycles in Porto Cervo at the bus station from Smeralda Crociera (+39 328 105 4518; smeraldacrociera.it), and dip into a 40km circuit out towards Baia Sardinia, inland via Arzachena and back to Porto Cervo.

Best beach La Celvia on the Costa Smeralda attracts a glamorous crowd with its Caribbean-style beach bars. At La Marinella, four kilometres from Porto Rotondo, a perfect crescent of vanilla sand embraces a shallow bay facing the islands of Soffi and Mortorio. Further south beside the bay of Orosei, Cala Luna is a much-lauded beach: reach it on the hourly boat from Cala Gonone (calagononecrociere.it).

Daytripper Board the boat from Palau and island-hop to Caprera, part of the Maddalena archipelago park (lamaddalenapark.it). Visit the whitewashed villa where national hero Giuseppe Garibaldi spent his last days (compendiogaribaldino.it); once you've explored the museum and gardens, join the sailing crowd for lunch on La Maddalena at La Scogliera in Porto Massimo (open May to October; +39 347 989 3578; lascoglieraristorante.com).

Walks Sun-baked scrubland, cliff-sheltered coves and sci-fi rocks sculpted by wind and sea make for dramatic scenic walks around the Capo Testa headland at the northern tip of the island (comunesantateresagallura.it): start/finish in Santa Teresa Gallura. In the east, Ogliastra attracts outdoorsy types to its craggy limestone hills and cove-pocked coastline (turismo.ogliastra.it).

Shopping Porto Cervo's twin marinas bow to the in-crowd's catwalk tastes, with cave-like arcades housing Gucci, Versace and Prada boutiques. There's a weekly market in most towns: every Thursday in San Pantaleo or Santa Teresa Gallura; Fridays in Palau. Browse stalls for local delicacies, and arts and crafts – especially tapestries.

Something for nothing Around Arzachena, discover the neolithic Giants' Tombs of Coddu Vecchiu, consisting of burial chambers, passageways and impressive dolmens; then marvel at the 3,000-year-old concentric stone circles at the Li Muri Necropolis (comunearzachena.it).

Don't go home without... snorkelling the underwater Costa Smeralda. The Maddalena islands in particular offer warm, shallow waters, and submarine caves hollowed out of limestone cliffs. Orso Diving organises half-day excursions from Porto Cervo (orsodiving.com).

STRICTLY SARDINIA

Tombs? Lookout towers? *Star Wars* props? They date back 3,500 years, and, despite their prevalence, their purpose remains disputed: *nuraghe* complexes of squat beehive-shaped towers dot the island. Check out the Unesco-listed complex of *nuraghi* in southerly Barúmini. In the north, the Nuraghe Albucciu is a slightly squarer version near Arzachena; or discover an impressive cluster at the Nuraghe Palmavera in Alghero.

DIARY

Mid-March Uri's artichoke festival (Sagra del Carciofo) kicks off on the second Saturday of the month with music and dancing; on Sunday, expect themed tastings and a market (comune.uri.ss.it). **April** Celebrate an 18th-century uprising at towns across the island on the 28th, Sardinia Day, with reenactments, folk music and fireworks. **May** The Festa di San Simplicio in Olbia celebrates a local legend, the humble mussel (olbialive.it). **June** Processions of decorated boats mark Olbia's Festa della Madonna del Mare on the 24th (olbiaturismo.it). **Mid-August** Ferragosto on the 15th goes off with a pyrotechnical bang. **October/November** The turn of the month brings the Montagna Produce Fair to Desulo, with food stalls, street performances and more fireworks (comunedesulo.it).

Petra Segreta

STYLE Stylish stone *stazzi*
SETTING Olbia hilltop hamlet

'The hotel appears pure perfection against an azure sky strewn with streaky fluffs of white. A bristling guard of lavender stands to attention as we walk up the drive'

We leave the delightful village of San Pantaleo and begin our approach to Petra Segreta. A winding dirt road snakes through scrubland strewn with hulking volcanic rocks. My BlackBerry shows no reception. Commencing a vertiginous climb, we follow teeny tiny signs directing us to Petra Segreta Resort & Spa, high in the hills above the Costa Smeralda. It is, however, not the happiest taxi journey. Italy is currently losing 2–0 in the football. Our driver is energetically shouting 'Kaput!', motioning a slit throat. As we pull up to the pale timber double gates of our final destination, Italia scores. 'Due-Uno!' By now, all three of us are shouting.

Flying easyJet was our only option to get to Olbia airport, half an hour's drive away – and easyJet is not always, well, easy. And there were air-traffic control strikes. But never mind all that – one glimpse of the low-slung warm bronze stonework of the traditional *stazzi* farmhouse buildings and the hotel appears pure perfection, set against an azure sky strewn with streaky fluffs of white. A bristling guard of flowering lavender stands to attention as we walk up the steep drive to reception, where we are greeted by tinkling jazz tunes, and the attentive and charming Daniel.

Assigned room 202 (you cannot book specific suites), our impressions are that it's cool, calm and well-designed, with white walls, timbered ceilings and solid Sardinian furniture. Double doors lead out to a generous veranda and a breathtaking view over a sparkling Costa Smeralda bay. We turn on the television looking for BBC World – it's Italian Sky. It's probably for the best, and we're nudged out into the Mediterranean gardens past olive trees, wild lavenders and prickly pears, to catch the last rays of sun, poolside.

This pair of Smiths on a post-nuptials escape are in fact at a 'wellness centre'. Indeed, Petra Segreta is a spa hotel, meaning that all the other guests here now – a mere 12, there are only 15 rooms in total – are, like us, couples looking for peace. As such, the atmosphere is pin-drop silence. We talk in stage whispers. 'They charge €3 for filtered water?' and 'Shall we have a cocktail?'

Ordering a gin lemon and a Bloody Mary, we encounter Barbie and Dodo, the resident West Highland Terriers. Unlike most hotel pets I've met, these two cuties aren't jaded by the affections of strangers, and they gamely they offer up their tummies for a rub.

The hotel has the effect of making you want to dress elegantly for supper. How lovely is that? We return to our room to transform ourselves from frazzled travellers to chic women-about-Sardinia. A fly in the ointment is that the bathroom mirror/moody lighting makes for challenging make-up application. And I wouldn't be doing my job as a retail – or in this case, hospitality – adviser if I didn't point out the frustrating socket situation: all plug points are used by the essential lighting or TV equipment, leaving none spare for phones or laptops. Maybe the hotel is just *that* determined that guests properly switch off?

Dining right here at Petra Segreta is definitely preferable. Apart from having heard that the food is a highlight (think lobster Catalana with pan-fried garden vegetables), the

alternative is having to tackle that dirt road again. No thanks – we're here to relax. So our first meal is in the fine-dining room. Although I find the dishes a little fussy for my tastes, with lots of complicated sauce reductions, my craving for great wine couldn't be better satisfied. I'm a fan of red, and having shared my preferences with our waiter, Giorgio, he delivers a wonderful local syrah – a Nero d'Avola d'Alessandro.

Only twice do we venture out of the hotel during our three-day mini-moon, and day two sees us venture north to Baja Sardinia. Arriving in the beach-resort village after a 30-minute drive, we realise it is, well, a resort. Not much rustic allure, purpose-built, with a sandy beach covered with multiple beds. But this is the Italian way – and that lends a certain charm. An entertaining lunch at coast-side L'Approdo makes it well worth the trip.

That evening, we hit the second, simpler-fare menu at Petra Segreta. Delicious! My Mrs Smith has carpaccio of octopus while I enjoy the wafer-thin beef. Spaghetti

vongole and sautéed veal, mushroom with fried potatoes and an arugula salad follow. Tonight's ruby tipple? Cagnulari Alghero from Cantina Santa Maria La Palma – as lovely as the first recommendation.

Porto Cervo, the next morning, is our next excursion: this is essentially Bond Street set in a 1970s mall, selling clothes for Nancy dell'Olio and those dolly-bird Italian TV presenters, and their *signori*. Ralph Lauren and Tod's for him; Dolce & Gabbana or Versace for her. Plenty of these very ladies cavort around Porto Cervo in their five-inch Louboutins, all big lips and big hair. We've heard they even wear their Loubis on the beach. My idea of hell. After discovering a beautiful brand-new Eres boutique (and a bikini each later), we take in more edifying window-shopping care of art-filled Fumi and the Louise Alexander Gallery.

Happy to return to our romantic hideaway, which is as genuine as Porto Cervo is phoney, we decide it's pool time again. Laid-back and unhurried, service full of warmth and charm – this is heaven. And Paolo, the therapist who performs our vigorous full-body massages in the spa, has our health and wellbeing in his mind throughout. He is *properly* good. And should we desire more spa time, Turkish baths, a sauna and Jacuzzis are at our disposal.

For someone seeking a relaxed spa break, Petra Segreta has all the essentials for those fleeing city stresses: an isolated and soothing location, chic look and feel, great service, good weather. But, for me, the real touch of genius? An outdoor running machine. Pounding it in my bikini, Zola Budd style, overlooking the stunning surrounding hilly landscape, I realise this a place where I can enjoy my red wine and still know I am being good to myself. That's Petra Segreta all over.

Reviewed by **Mary Portas**, retail guru

NEED TO KNOW

Rooms 21, including eight junior suites.
Rates €200–€500, including buffet breakfast.
Check-out 11am but flexible, subject to availability and, during busy periods, half a day's room charge.
Earliest check-in, 2pm.
Facilities Spa with sauna and Jacuzzi, fitness area and outdoor running machine, relaxation room, three acres of gardens, free WiFi, free parking. In rooms: flatscreen TV, minibar, free broadband internet access, Etro toiletries.
Poolside Petra Segreta's curvy sun-warmed outdoor pool is fed by a waterfall and lined with hydro-massage jets.
Children This hotel was designed with adults in mind – however, cots can be provided on request for €40 a night.
Also The Wellness Centre spa offers signature Petra Segreta massages in a grotto in the gardens, along with herb-scented Jacuzzi baths and relaxation rituals.

IN THE KNOW

Our favourite rooms Get back to nature in Deluxe Room 201, which has a shaded seating area, its bamboo roof supported by a craggy boulder. Inside, the muslin-draped, white-washed four-poster bed takes centre stage, and sturdy farmhouse-style furniture adds a cosy-cottage feel against a muted palette. Junior Suite 306 is charming and rustic: beamed ceiling, snug sitting area and a private outside lounge.
Hotel bar The Pool Bar, with its shaded veranda, is a peaceful little drinking spot. Sit overlooking the pool and gardens and mark sunset with a glass of moscato. The soundtrack of lounge music is as relaxing as the country-at-dusk views.
Hotel restaurant Il Fuoco Sacro continues the hotel's fabulous farmhouse style; its white walls and ceiling are punctuated with bamboo beams, and tables are fashioned from chunky oak. There's also a terrace overlooking the Gulf, roofed with bamboo and dotted with linen-laid tables and rattan chairs. Renowned Roman chef Luigi Bergeretto is a dab hand with clams. Try his signature *fregola al frutti di mare* – a Sardinian-style seafood risotto.
Top table Sit at the back of the veranda by the rough-cut wall and admire the romantic sea views as you eat.
Room service A selection from the restaurant menu is available for breakfast and dinner.
Dress code Match the restaurant's relaxed mood with cool, crisp linen in stone and putty shades.
Local knowledge Spiaggia del Principe, named after the Aga Khan's preference for this nook of the island, really is a beach fit for royalty. It has two pretty stretches of powder-soft sand, separated by a promontory of blush-pink rock. Petra Segreta's super-helpful staff will point you towards the best local activities and excursions – just ask.

LOCAL EATING AND DRINKING

For delicious *frutti di mare*, pretty terraces and sea views, head for Madai, a chic restaurant, bar and winery just past Porto Cervo in Liscia di Vacca (+39 0789 91056). Chef Elio Sironi – a former fixture of the Bulgari hotel group – heads up the kitchens. If you're after fresh, rustic pizza in a relaxed setting, you can't go far wrong at Il Vecchio Mulino in Arzachena (+39 0789 81943). For a Michelin-starred fine-dining affair, sample Sardinian specialities reinterpreted with gourmet flair at Ristorante Gallura, a deservedly popular restaurant attached to Hotel Gallura in Olbia (+39 0789 24648). People-watch in Caffè Nina (+39 338 368 7288), a small café-bar in the centre of picturesque San Pantaleo.

GET A ROOM!

Hotel details Strada di Buddeo CP130, Frazione di San Pantaleo, 07026 Olbia (+39 0789 187 6441; petrasegretaresort.com).
To book Ring our expert Travel Team (you'll find all our numbers with your membership card on page 5) or go to mrandmrssmith.com/petra-segreta.

A massage each, and the option of booking a special Sardinian tasting menu in the hotel restaurant: created exclusively for Smith members, it costs just €45 a head (worth €75; excludes drinks).

AEOLIAN ISLANDS

COASTLINE Lava at first sight
COAST LIFE Unhurried island-hopping

The seven sisters of the Aeolian archipelago scatter like stars across the Tyrrhenian Sea. Sizeable Salina shines brightly, with a picturesque port, clusters of coastal villages and vineyard terraces that only enhance its wild good looks. Unspoilt beauty runs in the family: explore Stromboli's fiery volcano; venture to the black-sand beaches and thermal baths of sulphurous Vulcano (named after the god of fire) and track down chic bougainvillea-framed hideaways on pint-sized Panarea. Largest of the lot, Lipari has museums, restaurants and shops open year-round, and is as culturally close as you'll get to neighbouring signora-about-town Sicily. At the other end of the scale, diminutive Filicudi and Alicudi are made for deserted beach days. However far you roam, for would-be escape artists, the *Isole Eolie* are an out-of-this-world constellation.

GETTING THERE

Planes The nearest airport is Sicily's Palermo (gesap.it). Charter an Air Panarea five-seater helicopter for private transfers (+39 090 983 4428; airpanarea.com).
Trains Toy sets aside, the Aeolians are locomotive-free: among these mountainous mini isles, sail trumps rail.
Automobiles Traffic restrictions mean you can't bring cars onto any of the islands except Salina from July until the end of the summer season. Bus, boat or walk your way round – if you do want some wheels, hire scooters on Salina from Bongiorno Antonio (+39 090 984 3409).
Boats Hydrofoils connect the islands with Sicily's northern ports, including Palermo and Messina, and mainland Reggio di Calabria; the main departure port is Milazzo, around 90 minutes from Salina (usticalines.it; siremar.it).

LOCAL KNOWLEDGE

Taxis Cabs can be tricky to source, but they come in all shapes and sizes: golf buggies on Panarea; Vespa trikes on Vulcano. On Salina, book the four-wheeled variety through Locantro Daniela (+39 333 462 8215).
Siesta and fiesta Afternoon closing times are a moveable feast from island to island, stretching anywhere between 12 noon and 4pm. Diners gather no earlier than 9pm.
Do go/don't go June to October is high season; outside these months you'll have the archipelago to yourselves. Visitor numbers swell in August, when the weather's warmest – steer clear of crowded Panarea at this time.
Packing tips ATMs are as rare as *lire* on Salina, so arrive with plenty of euros; also take insect repellent to keep buzzing biters at bay. With street lights few and far between, for evening expeditions, it pays to pack a torch.
Recommended reads The film of Antonio Skármeta's novel *Il Postino* was shot on Salina. American author Mary Taylor Simeti lives in neighbouring Sicily: *On Persephone's Island* is a journal of her early days; or enjoy the collated recipes and memoirs in *Bitter Almonds*.
Local specialities Salina's capers are the definitive Aeolian ingredient: look out for them whizzed into *pesto di capperi*, or in *vitello tonnato* (veal with tuna and caper mayo). Also try the islands' own version of canestrato, a Puglian sheep's-milk cheese. Fish and seafood abound – particularly *scorfano* (scorpion fish), served fried or in a fragrant wine-laced, olive-dotted tomato sauce. Sweet

Malvasia delle Lipari wines are also Aeolian finds; look out for passito from Carlo Hauner (hauner.it), worth savouring with peach or almond desserts.

WORTH GETTING OUT OF BED FOR

Viewpoint In south-eastern Filicudi, the Capo Graziano is a rocky headland with uninterrupted sea views. Make the 15-minute journey up to the plateau to explore the prehistoric ruins; look out for the large grinding stones lodged in the earth, used for milling by Neolithic settlers.

Arts and culture Standing sentry over Lipari town is a fortified citadel – a cultural layer cake that records the island's history: there are ancient ruins, Greek and Roman artefacts, a Baroque cathedral with colourful frescoes, and a Norman cloister. For the full history lesson, stop off at Museo di Lipari in the Bishops' Palace (comunelipari.it). On Salina, the Museo Civico is split across three sites: gen up on archaeology and ethnography in Lingua; then drink in the island's viticultural heritage at the Santa Marina wine museum (museietnomessinesi.it). Islanders upped sticks down under in the 19th century, taking their wine know-how with them – as recorded in Malfa at the Museo dell'Emigrazione Eoliana (+39 090 344293).

Activities Explore neighbouring Aeolians with a guided boat trip – perhaps to the Bue Marino cave on Filicudi; the *fanghi* (mud baths) and offshore *fumaroles* (steam vents) of Vulcano; or Panarea and its pretty islets: Salina Relax Boats operates out of Santa Marina (+39 345 216 2308). Air Panarea provides helicopter tours: get an eagle's-eye view of a trio of craters as you zoom over Vulcano, Stromboli and Etna (airpanarea.com). Diving around Salina is suited to experienced subaquanauts; for entry-level paddles, Diving Center La Gorgonia on Lipari runs trips to the reef at Le Formiche (+39 090 981 2616).

Best beach Many of Salina's beaches feature boulders rather than sand: Lingua's is stony and relaxingly remote; find black sands near Rinella that make a good launch for swimmers (follow the paths to the Tre Pini campsite).

Daytripper In beach-friendly weather, set aside a day to hang out on Panarea. Secure your spot early on the caramel sands at Zimmari beach, south of the port at San Pietro: you're a short walk from the Bronze Age ruins at Cala Junco, which is a beautiful teal-watered cove; keep going beyond the village of Punta Milazzese to reach Calcara beach, sometimes called Spiaggia di Fumarole for the thermal springs that bubble just

offshore. For such a diminutive island, it has more than its share of glitzy addresses – focused around San Pietro – including the Bridge Sushi Bar (bridgepanarea.com).

Walks The extinct volcano Monte Fossa delle Felci on Salina is the highest peak across the archipelago and its wooded slopes are now a nature reserve. Hiking trails lead upwards through the canopy before breaking into 360-degree views of Salina's sister islands.

Shopping Opportunities for wardrobe expansion are largely limited to beachwear and the odd jewellery store. On Salina, stock up on capers, wine and other foodie gold at Alimentari Carpe Diem on Via Risorgimento in Santa Marina (+39 090 984 3053). Malfa's Pasticceria Cosi Duci has moreish pastries and surprising jams – try the prickly pear (+39 090 984 4358); while you're in the area, pick up olive oil straight from the farm at Azienda Agricola Fenech (+39 090 984 4041). Lipari's La Formagella is another delectable deli (+39 090 988 0759).

Something for nothing Near Pollara on Salina, a natural amphitheatre of rock embraces the bay that served as backdrop to the film *Il Postino*: descend the steps, and you can dive off the rocks into deep plunge pools below.

Don't go home without… taking an evening boat tour around Stromboli: depart at sunset to see the Sciara del Fuoco (stream of fire) and, if you're lucky, lava jets erupting from the crater, offset dramatically by the darkening sky. Excursions operate out of Scari, but if you want to book – champagne included – go through Sabbia Nera (+39 090 986390; sabbianerastromboli.com).

ABSOLUTELY AEOLIAN ISLANDS

Caper plants tough it out in the wild, growing on the lava of the smaller islands, but in Salina they are farmed. The flower buds, aka capers, are hand-picked and brine-packed; find them in sauces, salads or accompanying fish. The fruit – caperberries (*cucunci*) – crop up pickled and crunchy in antipasti. Capers even warrant their own festival on Salina, held over the first weekend in June, with dinners, wine tastings and foraging boat trips.

DIARY

May The month begins with a celebration (on the 1st) of St Joseph in Leni on Salina, where drums and dancing accompany a feast in the main square (comune.leni.me.it). **June** Salina Caper Festival (see above). **August** On the 15th, pilgrims visit the Santuario della Madonna del Terzito south of Malfa on Salina for the Feast of the Assumption. Around the 21st, Lipari marks the Feast of St Bartholomew with pomp, parties and pyrotechnics. **Mid-September** Five days of screenings and events mark the annual Salina Doc Fest (salinadocfest.org). On Filicudi, a decorated procession of boats heads to the candlelit Bue Marino sea cave for Filicudi tra Miti e Leggende (a festival of island myth and legend). **Early October** Salina hosts a week-long food and drink festival – *buon appetito!*

Hotel Signum

STYLE Family-run farmhouse
SETTING *Il Postino* country

'Simple, without being spartan; one window framing a Mediterranean view, another revealing olive and lemon trees'

Travel is a mixed bag. With it come many delights, great adventure, a measure of disappointments, small mercies and insights, some of which only make sense when you're back home.

Let's start with the delightful part: Hotel Signum, in the commune of Malfa, is a 20-minute winding drive around the mountain from the main port of Santa Marina on Salina. It looks out across the Tyrrhenian Sea to neighbouring Panarea and the smoking Stromboli – the perfect picture of a volcano.

In a way, the sea journey to Signum prepares you well: these are the waters and islands of Odysseus' epic voyage. Salina is a dream. An island in the Aeolian group just above Sicily, it was formed by two volcanoes, which the locals describe as breasts (of course they do!). Ms Smith swears she can also make out a Cyclops.

After enjoying the exquisite delights of Puglia, we've driven across Basilicata – around the arch of Italy's heel – through Calabria, and crossed the Messina Strait to Sicily. Catching the hydrofoil to Salina, we get a weather warning at the ticket office: *'Il mare e mosso!'* Fortunately this turns out to be nothing more than hand-waving melodrama – a national pastime: considering it's October, the crossing is surprisingly smooth, and we watch with anticipation as Salina finally hoves into view.

Our three-hour transit has become an adventure. The taxi we have taken from the port stops, and the driver points down a track. We walk down scented laneways, passing houses with cherry tomatoes drying in bunches on verandas. In small increments, our state of mind has shifted to local time – over sea, on road and with that final perfumed walk to Hotel Signum's door.

Simple, without being spartan; one window framing a Mediterranean view, another revealing olive and lemon trees. The detail has been handled with a light touch, with an ease that belies the amount of informed thought needed to achieve this effortless-looking style.

In the bathroom, traditional tiles add a splash of colour. A roughly moulded soap looks like a large lozenge of butter, and is cupped in a glazed blue-and-white butterfly-motif dish. Olive oil is the main ingredient, as it is for the body wash, enhanced with a zing of *cedro* (ancient lemon). Wild rosemary and mint plucked from this very island make the shampoo another pleasure.

Ms Smith has found a fluffy robe and she is lying on the bed perusing the spa menu. I'm contemplating lunch. We've been here all of 30 minutes and we feel right at home. Soon we're being seated in the dining room by Signum's sommelier Vincenzo Minieri. It's late in the afternoon and we're the only table, but we feel welcome and relaxed: the mark of a great hotel.

One dish in – a fist-sized mozzarella di bufala, by itself, on a plate, next to a salad of blood-red cherry tomatoes tossed with wild herbs – and we decide to eat in-house for our entire stay. A bottle of local olive oil is chosen from a sideboard holding a selection of Sicilian varieties.

I pour a little over the mozzarella, add a pinch of salt, and cut into it. Immediately it oozes. We groan with glee as we dunk pieces of crusty bread into the milky, virgin slurry.

Seafood, vegetables, grains and pulses make up most of Michele Caruso's menu. Food is deceptively simple but cooked with supreme skill. Spaghetti is tossed with a little oil, *bottarga* (dried tuna roe), wild fennel and breadcrumbs; couscous is served with finely chopped mussels and tomato; fish stew is flavoured with eggplant, anchovies, olives, tomato and capers. Vincenzo doesn't miss a beat. We're in his hands and his wine choices are perfect.

After lunch, we make a pact. I book a couple of hours with Vincenzo in the Signum cellar pulling out bottles of rare, foot-crushed Etna Rosso and planning wines for the following days of our stay, while Ms Smith signs up for a treatment in the Signum Spa.

The spa area is a secret stone garden with pools of geothermal water connected by channels and various

'Ms Smith emerges from the spa glowing, and scented with the sweet herbs, capers and citrus of Salina'

igloo-shaped buildings for different treatments. Water trickles down a moss-laden wall. Ms Smith emerges glowing, and scented with the sweet herbs, capers and citrus of Salina.

The island itself also offers much to see. We catch the local bus on occasion, but mostly we amble through Malfa's stone and terracotta laneways. Ms Smith even manages a dip in the warm Mediterranean and a has close encounter with some local marine life. One evening, we stroll to a little bar in the piazza to drink Salina's fabulous sweet Malvasia, and watch Milan play Juventus.

The many photos we took that show much of what I've described still don't come close to capturing the essence of this magical place. As Italo Calvino put it, aromas and flavours are elements you cannot transmit vicariously or convey electronically. And that is why we travel.

Reviewed by **Stefano Manfredi**, chef

NEED TO KNOW

Rooms 30, including three suites.

Rates €130–€400, including Continental buffet breakfast.

Check-out 11am. Earliest check-in, 3pm – earlier if the room's free.

Facilities Spa, gardens, library, free WiFi. In rooms: flatscreen TV, minibar, artisanal bath products.

Poolside Lined with loungers and lemon trees, Signum's curved infinity pool is the perfect lookout point, with views across the sea to Panarea and the volcanic island of Stromboli.

Children Welcome, although the atmosphere is one of peaceful relaxation.

Also Hydrofoils ferry guests to Milazzo in Sicily from Salina between 6:30am and 7pm each day. The journey takes around an hour and a half. The Signum Spa makes use of mineral-rich geothermal waters, with natural therapies such as rose salt, a 'thermal stove' modelled on an ancient steam bath in Lipari, and a 19th-century copper bath tub.

IN THE KNOW

Our favourite rooms Each room is individually decorated. Rooms 11 and 12 both have private terraces with sea views, and are located slightly away from the rest of the rooms, offering more privacy and seclusion. Room 34 is the most spacious in the hotel.

Hotel bar Drinks can be served anywhere in the hotel until midnight, from morning coffee on the terrace to in-room nightcaps. Locally grown fruit and herbs, including lemons, oranges and mint, are regulars in Signum's cocktail shakers.

Hotel restaurant Dishes are simple, flavour-packed and classically Aeolian; chef Michele Caruso serves up excellent (and generous) seafood dishes and pasta in the largely alfresco restaurant: sample home-made bucatini with *ragu bianco di mare*. His four-course tasting menu of island specialities comes highly recommended. Let the hotel know at lunchtime if you want dinner that night.

Top table Be sure to request a sea view when booking dinner. On chilly nights, make it a window seat.

Room service Drinks, snacks and sandwiches can be brought to your boudoir all day until 11pm.

Dress code Utterly relaxed during the day – sarongs and beach shorts. Things get a little more formal in the evening.

Local knowledge Sweet white Malvasia wine is produced in Salina's vineyards – ask Signum to organise a winery trip for you, perhaps including a stop-off at a caper farm to see the island's other speciality in production. The hotel can organise diving trips and boat excursions around Salina and the other islands; if you'd prefer to go unguided, ask about borrowing one of the fishermen's boats. There are also some tennis courts available, about 5km away.

LOCAL EATING AND DRINKING

For lazy lunches, Portobello in Santa Marina (+39 090 984 3125) serves up fine seafood and classic Italian dishes. The restaurant at Capo Faro resort (+39 090 984 4330) deals in relaxed but romantic dinners with a heck of a view. When you want a change from fresh fish, head round the corner to Pizzeria a' Lumeredda' on Via San Lorenzo (+39 090 984 4130) for a simpler supper. An immaculate all-white outdoor bar, Santa Isabel Lounge (+39 090 984 4018) is a two-minute stroll from Hotel Signum, and great for sunset G&Ts. In Lingua, around 10km away from the hotel, A Cannata on Via Umberto (+39 090 984 3161) has a sunny terrace where you can try penne *alla salinara*, with peppers, pine nuts, capers and olives. Also in Lingua, Da Alfredo serves the best granitas on the island.

GET A ROOM!

Hotel details 15 via Scala, 98050 Malfa, Salina (+39 090 984 4222; hotelsignum.it).

To book Ring our expert Travel Team (you'll find all our numbers with your membership card on page 5) or go to mrandmrssmith.com/hotel-signum.

 A picnic lunch; members staying in a Deluxe room will also get one free entry pass for the spa (worth €25).

SICILY

COUNTRYSIDE Dame Etna
COUNTRY LIFE Exotic, eruptive, erudite

Shrugging off size limitations to reveal bustling cities, dramatic coasts and mountainous countryside, this have-it-all island is Italy in microcosm. Drive around and you'll be soothed by palm trees and scented orange groves one minute, and exhilarated by exotic architecture the next: Greek, Roman, Byzantine, Arab, French, Spanish, Austrian and Brit invaders have all planted their flags. Dominated by Mount Etna – Europe's largest active volcano – the east is Sicily's most built-up sweep. Punchy capital Palermo crowns the north coast with a glut of gutsy galleries and ornate churches linked by a spaghetti-tangle of mediaeval streets. Due south, serene sandy beaches and pretty fishing villages quietly partner flourish-filled Baroque towns. Whether you venture up or down, on this isle, it's easy to enjoy *un poco di tutti*.

GETTING THERE

Planes There are three main airports: Palermo (gesap.it), Trapani (aeroportotrapani.com) and Catania (aeroporto.catania.it). For the south coast, Catania is 30 minutes nearer by car than Palermo, a little over two hours away.

Trains It's possible to take the train from mainland cities to Messina, via the train ferry from Villa San Giovanni in Reggio Calabria; island intercity trains link Messina, Palermo, Taormina, Catania and Siracuse (trenitalia.com).

Automobiles Thanks to mountain hairpins and a carefree regional attitude to bumps and scrapes, driving in Sicily is not for the faint-hearted. But wheels are essential for exploring, and well-maintained motorways link major towns.

Boats The shortest ferry crossing (20 minutes) leaves the mainland at Villa San Giovanni for Messina (carontetourist.it). Sailings from Naples and Salerno take over eight hours; there are occasional services to Sardinia (tirrenia.it).

LOCAL KNOWLEDGE

Taxis Cabs are cheap and easy to find in Palermo and the major resorts. For fares around Palma di Montechiaro, try Licata-based Agenzia Cafa' Viaggi (+39 0922 770031).

Siesta and fiesta Banks and most shops close between 12 noon and 4pm, and outside big cities you're unlikely to find anything open then. Head out to eat around 10pm; in more rural spots, be prepared for earlier closing times.

Do go/don't go Like a typical Italian mamma, Sicily is generally warm but occasionally tempestuous. The months that top and tail summer are ideal as the sun isn't too scalding and the beaches are less crowded.

Packing tips Bring an extra bag to fill with spices, oils and condiments from local markets. And some anti-nausea tablets – those inland mountain roads really are dizzying.

Recommended reads Giuseppe Tomasi di Lampedusa's classic *The Leopard* chronicles a noble family's decline; uncover the mafia world in *Midnight in Sicily* by Peter Robb and *Boss of Bosses* by Clare Longrigg. Seeking guiltier pleasures? Try Mario Puzo's *The Godfather* or *The Sicilian*.

Local specialities Ricotta is a regional obsession, at its sweetest in tubular pastries called *cannoli*. Snack on *panelle*, fritters made with chickpea flour, or try a *brioche con gelato* – the island's take on an ice-cream sandwich, found in abundance in Palermo's *pasticcerie*. Sicilian winemakers' output is largely sun-sweetened dessert wines such as Marsala and moscato, although sunny climes produce some robust reds and super-dry whites – try some chardonnay and Santa Cecilia nero d'avola from famed family winery Planeta (planeta.it).

And... Sicily's explosive star attraction dominates Parco dell'Etna; well-marked trails highlight the volcano's safe areas (parcoetna.it). Make the most of a short visit with guided 4WD tours by Volcano Trek (volcanotrek.com).

WORTH GETTING OUT OF BED FOR

Viewpoint Distinctive terraces of white rock descend towards the sea not far from Agrigento at the Scala dei Turchi. You can easily climb onto them from the beach. Your reward? A view over the bay that's all shades of blue.

Arts and culture Sicily's cultural treasure trove is laden with archaeological wonders, be it the Valley of the Temples in Agrigento (valleyofthetemples.com), or the Greek ruins and Doric temple at Segesta (segesta.org). Art lovers will fall for Palermo's aesthetic charms: take a guided tour of the Teatro Massimo opera house (teatromassimo. it). Seek out sculptures by Laurano and da Messina paintings at Palazzo Abatellis (+39 091 623 0011). More contemporary pieces line the walls at the Galleria d'Arte Moderna (galleriadartemodernapalermo.it). In the south, Modica and Ragusa are beautiful Baroque towns.

Activities Saddle up for a trek near the Valley of the Temples with riding school Maneggio Centro Ippico San Benedetto in Favara (+39 338 315 5745). For scuba diving off the south coast, book a trip from Agrigento to the marine reserves around Linosa and Lampedusa: try Padi-approved Moby Diving Center (mobydiving.it).

Perfect picnic Historic hilltop town Erice, north of Trapani, has fine-looking fortresses, superlative views and a surfeit of *pasticcerie*. Pick up a sweet picnic of nutty pastries and marzipan from Maria Grammatico on Via Vittorio Emmanuele (+39 0923 869390); spread your rug in the Balio Garden, and enjoy your feast with view of the sea speckled with in-the-distance Egadi islands.

Daytripper Head inland to Piazza Armerina, which has a fortress and a cluster of photogenic churches crowned by a domed cathedral in its historic quarter. It's an ancient ruin 5km out of town that steals the show, however: Unesco-listed Roman villa Casale is a sprawling complex of relatively intact rooms and courtyards famed for their mosaics (villaromanadelcasale.it). Stop for lunch at Al Fogher on Contrada Bellia (+39 0935 684123).

Walks Wander Palermo's ancient alleys and gaze at crumbling 15th-century palaces and Baroque churches, then pause for a cappuccino in a pretty piazza. For walks on the wilder side, the peaked Parco delle Madonie in the north of the island is well set-up for visitors, with hiking trails amid rugged countryside rich in wildlife (+39 0921 684011; parcodellemadonie.it). In the south, the Cavagrande del Cassibile is a nature reserve in the form of a woods-and-waterfall-lined canyon: it's worth hiking into the valley for a picnic and swim in the cavernous freshwater pools (parks.it/riserva.cavagrande.cassibile).

Shopping Browse the colourful Ballerò market in Palermo, or pick up cheap-chic Italian labels along the city's Via Sant'Agostino. In the rustic south, weekly markets offer the main retail fix: on Thursday mornings in Licata; Friday bright and early in Agrigento. Caltagirone, inland, is known for its colourfully painted ceramics – both in its many boutiques and incorporated as artwork on buildings.

Something for nothing The island's north-west is wine country, riven with terraces of gnarly vines, and between Trapani and Marsala another industry flourishes, too: salt. For a scenic drive, follow the salt road or Via del Sale, which crosses arid plains topped with salt mounds and white-washed windmills.

Don't go home without... tasting Marsala wine straight from the cask in its birthplace: you'll find the restored barrel cellars at Carlo Pellegrino in the centre of town – take a tour and get up close with gold, amber and ruby versions of this fortified dessert wine (carlopellegrino.it).

STRIKINGLY SICILY

Seaside, sightseeing, sunsets… there are things you want on your holiday tick-list, and things you don't: funding organised crime, say. To help you avoid lining the pockets of Sicilian gangsters, the Addiopizzo movement was set up by a group of students with the aim of promoting businesses who refuse to pay the Mafia's 'taxes' (*pizzo*). Visit addiopizzo.org to identify which cafés, restaurants and shops to spend your cash in.

DIARY

February/March Sicily enjoys a final pre-Lent fling with island-wide carnivals on Shrove Tuesday: the parades, street fairs and fireworks are particularly colourful at Sciacca (carnevaledisciacca.it) and Acireale (carnevaleacireale.com). **March/April** At Easter, Il Ballo dei Diavoli (dance of the devils) takes place in the Norman town of Prizzi, performed by costumed villagers (comune.prizzi.pa.it). **June** The Taormina Film Festival (taorminafilmfest.it) sees screenings in the town's atmospheric Greek amphitheatre. **Mid-August** Piazza Armerina residents come over all mediaeval for the Palio Normanni (comune.piazzaarmerina.en.it). **September** On the 22nd, the procession of the Madonna di Lampedusa – on an island off Sicily's south coast – also involves fireworks and concerts.

Azienda Agricola Mandranova

STYLE Farm here to eternity
SETTING Palm-studded hillside

'We can see the farmhouse poking above landscaped foliage sprinkled around the pool. Beyond that, olive groves amble down hillsides in glorious non-uniformity'

There's an Italian restaurant near my house that comes with its own Mr Shake-Hands Man. Few things better symbolise Italian hospitality: his sole job, it seems, is to greet visitors with a warm handshake and a beaming grin. It makes you feel happy. Likewise, as we roll up the drive of Azienda Agricola Mandranova, our hotel in Sicily, a gentleman welcomes us with a beckoning wave, firm grip and the kind of magnanimous smile that provokes instant soppiness. We discover he is Giuseppe; I get a sudden urge to ask him to be my uncle.

If I had a pound for every hotel website I've seen with a guffy line declaring it a 'home away from home!', I wouldn't be a journalist any more. But this Italian retreat nails it: it's smiling Giuseppe upon arrival who sets the tone, letting guests know that they matter. Although there are a handful of other cars in the drive, variously hired at Catania or Palermo airports, we can't see anyone else.

One of the perks of Mandranova's remote, rural location on Sicily's southern coast is the obligatory adventure en route. Italian motorways are some of the best in the business. While other roads dip and dive, tracing the undulation of the land, Italian ones follow a remarkably level course. At various points you find yourself careering into mid-air supported by gargantuan pillars as the parched Sicilian countryside sprawls beneath you. Moments later, you're ploughing through mountains, emerging on the verge of dramatic escarpments coated with terraced vineyards. We get rather carried away. The basic directions instruct us to turn left somewhere near the southern coast. Mesmerised, we opt for an hour-long three-point turn around south-western Sicily.

And when we arrive… that smile. Giuseppe takes us on a brief tour of this magnificent farmhouse. Blanketing the hefty acreage are the thousands of the olive trees that yield Mandranova's prize-winning oil. Whereas other corners of this island seem scorched and lava-scarred, here there is a lush richness. The farmhouse is the centrepiece, an imposing white-walled building staggered in height and arranged with a distinct geometric beauty – a softer take, perhaps, on the ancient Temple of Concord at Agrigento, half an hour to the west.

Our tour ends abruptly when we reach the swimming pool. Perched above the hotel on a hill, it is dug from the rock around it – a natural water-storage tank inherited from the Moors. From this vantage point we can see the farmhouse just poking above the landscaped foliage sprinkled around the pool. Beyond that, cascades of olive groves amble down hillsides in glorious non-uniformity, framed by craggy peaks and soft cambers – the Sicilian countryside has a beautiful ability to roll and jut almost simultaneously. We notice the sun making a break for the horizon, and then spy a couple of deckchairs by the pool. Giuseppe, you've been great, but we have loafing to do. We fetch a bottle of fruity Bacca Rossa red from the house, the first of many, and recline with happy grins.

As evening arrives, Mandranova's guests begin to loiter around the stone patio next to the farmhouse. They know what's coming. Us newbies get involved, chatting gamely with about eight others, lolling around on wicker chairs beside wrought-iron tables candlelit with lanterns. If you ever need an indication of taste, lighting is the giveaway. At this hip hotel, everything is just right: a selection of trees around the terrace is artfully spotlit from their lower trunks, and golden yellow beams soar from the base of the farmhouse, dissolving as they reach the upper storeys.

Giuseppe drifts from table to table, charming pants off. His English has an almost lyrical quality. His favourite word is 'beautiful', pronounced 'bee-yooootiful' in the manner of a pining sigh. Half a dozen tables are laid, waitresses are dipping in and out of the amber glow of the interior dining room, distributing twinkling goblets. When the guests settle down for supper, tables are shuffled together, and it starts to feel like a dinner party. We are with a honeymooning couple and a middle-aged pair who say 'cool' a lot.

And then the scoop. Giuseppe might be the face of the operation, but his wife Silvia is the mastermind, plotting

a gastronomic tour de force from the kitchen. First up is perfectly al dente, dainty penne in pesto. Next is swordfish baked and basted to disintegrate on your tongue. Almost everything is lubricated with the best olive oil I have ever tasted, from the fruit of trees that grow just yards from our tables. I could drink the stuff neat. Then chocolate cake, subtly spiked with chilli for a gorgeous, light heat. And, of course, lots of wine. Giuseppe and Silvia's two teenaged sons help serve up. Predictably, they are both dreamboats, studying economics in Palermo when not matching Silvia recipe for recipe. You almost want to take them home to your mother.

The family and guests josh and chat and get drunk. It really does feel like you are having supper at a friend's rather spectacular house. Our cups runneth over, and we retire to bed. Like the rest of the hotel, our room isn't ostentatious, instead it is charming and elegant in a simple way; buzz-speak would have it as 'rustic chic'. Old wooden doors open onto restored majolica floors under beamed ceilings. Tiled showers have superb rainfall heads. Crisp stucco walls and cherry-wood beds. That's the secret formula. A grinning Giuseppe upon arrival, ceramic tiles and exposed wood, tastefully illuminated trees, perfectly al dente pasta. Italian hospitality at its best: simple things done very, very well.

Reviewed by Benji Lanyado, journalist

NEED TO KNOW

Rooms 14, including six suites.

Rates €140–€280, including breakfast.

Check-out 11am, although later check-out may be possible. Earliest check-in, 2pm; reception closes at 7pm.

Facilities Library of books, music and films; pool table. In rooms: air-conditioning, bottled water and bath products by Culti; flatscreen TVs in suites. There's no WiFi, but an internet connection is available between 9am and 11am.

Poolside The square little infinity pool (once part of the ancient natural irrigation system) looks down over the olive trees and fields beyond from its hillside perch above the farm. The violet-hued water does wonders for the skin, thanks to its sulphur content. Sunlounger twinsets sit cosily around the pool's stone-paved edges.

Children Kids are welcome, but the hotel's more geared to grown-ups. Cots are free; older children can stay in parents' suites on the sofa bed for €15 a night. Babysitting with staff (€10 an hour) and children's menus can be arranged.

Also There's a two-night minimum stay. Visit between Septembèr and November if you want to catch the olive harvest. Guests can also sign up for daily cookery classes given by Mandranova's owner Silvia, using garden-grown produce.

IN THE KNOW

Our favourite rooms L'Arancio takes its name from the colouring of the original floor tiles and has a romantically draped wrought-iron four-poster. L'Oliva is a deluxe suite with a huge but cosy sitting room leading onto an attractive master bedroom, a small single bedroom and two bathrooms (shower in one, tub in the other). There are beautiful original encaustic floor tiles, and there's an antique bed adorned with carved cherubs and a rich maroon coverlet.

Hotel bar There's no actual bar, but guests can take drinks until 11pm in either of the two living rooms or on one of the stylish mint-green plastic sofas set in the gardens.

Hotel restaurant The Mandranova restaurant is where co-owner Silvia serves up traditional Sicilian dishes such as *torta di mandorle* (almond cake) and *timballo di anelletti* (Sicilian ring pasta with peas and aubergine), all made with fresh-from-the-garden ingredients. Don't be surprised if the hotel's dogs settle by your feet throughout the meal.

Top table In summer, ask for a table alongside the casale (main house), so you can dine alfresco by candlelight.

Room service Tapenade, local cheeses, Sicilian wines, bread and, of course, olive oil can be delivered 9am–8pm.

Dress code Floaty, rustic and relaxed: channel Palermitani gentility on a country break.

Local knowledge For ocean-bound fun, ride the *Tornado* – Mandranova's 38-foot boat – along the coastline, stopping at an island for lunch and spotting dolphins on the way, before returning to Port Licata to take in the daily fish market.

LOCAL EATING AND DRINKING

Half an hour down the coast in the petite port of Licata is one of Sicily's culinary headliners: La Madia has netted a brace of Michelin stars thanks to homegrown chef Pino Cuttaia, whose punchy, playful menu draws from his childhood memories of the area. Pine-cone-smoked fish is one of his most flavoursome signatures (+39 0922 771443). In Agrigento, Locanda di Terra on Via Francesco Crispi (+39 0922 29742) celebrates slow food with a focus on artisinal produce, including Girgentana goat's cheese and Sicilian vegetables. Nearby, Spizzulio is a lovely little enoteca-style bar, with more than 300 different bottles in its cellar, as well as lots of tasty local cheeses and cured meats (+39 0922 20712). In San Leone, family-friendly Trattoria Caico at 35 via Nettuno (+39 0922 412788) has excellent fresh fish.

GET A ROOM!

Hotel details Km217/SS115, 92020 Palma di Montechiaro, Sicily (+39 393 986 2169; mandranova.com).

To book Ring our expert Travel Team (you'll find all our numbers with your membership card on page 5) or go to mrandmrssmith.com/mandranova.

 A bottle of Azienda Agricola Mandranova's own extra-virgin olive oil.

(something on the house)

Smith Look out for this Smith member extra icon at the end of each hotel review.

As a BlackSmith member, you're automatically entitled to exclusive added extras: it's our way of saying thank you and ensuring your stay is as enjoyable as possible.

Activate your free membership now (see pages 4–5) to take advantage of the offers listed below when you book one of these hotels with us. For more information, or to make a reservation, visit mrandmrssmith.com or call our expert Travel Team – you'll find all their numbers on page 5.

AZIENDA AGRICOLA MANDRANOVA Sicily
A bottle of Azienda Agricola Mandranova's own extra-virgin olive oil.

BABUINO 181 Rome
A bottle of Franciacorta (sparkling wine from Lombardy).

BELLEVUE SYRENE Amalfi Coast
A bottle of sparkling white or regional red wine.

BORGO SANTO PIETRO Tuscany
A free massage each.

CA MARIA ADELE Venice
A bottle of Valpolicella.

CA' P'A (CASA PRIVATA) Amalfi Coast
A bottle of limoncello and a brass keyring from a ship's chandler in Amalfi.

CAPO LA GALA Amalfi Coast
Free spa entry for BlackSmith members (usually €30 each); a 30-minute massage each for SilverSmiths; GoldSmith members get both, plus 10 per cent off a two-course dinner in the restaurant (excludes drinks).

CASA ANGELINA Amalfi Coast
Champagne and fresh fruit on arrival; a romantic bath drawn for you on your first night; and a gift bag of Casa Angelina's traditional home-made pasta on departure.

CASTIGLION DEL BOSCO Tuscany
A wine-tasting tour for two.

FOLLONICO Tuscany
A bottle of Icario Rosso.

FONTELUNGA Tuscany
Welcome drinks for two and a bottle of cold-pressed extra-virgin olive oil.

HOTEL SIGNUM Aeolian Islands
A picnic lunch; members staying in a Deluxe room will also get one free entry pass for the spa (worth €25).

IL SALVIATINO Florence
A half-hour wine or olive-oil tasting session.

I QS Venice
Tickets for two to a local exhibition or gallery, such as the Palazzo Grassi.

JK PLACE CAPRI Capri
€50 credit to spend on treatments in the spa.

JK PLACE FIRENZE Florence
A bottle of spumante and a surprise gift.

LAGACIO MOUNTAIN RESIDENCE South Tyrol
Welcome drinks on arrival; 10 per cent off spa treatments; and a 10 per cent discount on equipment and rentals from the hotel's Alta Badia ski shop (altabadiaskirental.com).

LOCANDA AL COLLE Tuscany
A bottle of prosecco or wine. In addition, SilverSmith members also receive a gift of Erbario Toscano products; GoldSmith members receive a box of Erbario Toscano scented oils.

MAISON LA MINERVETTA Amalfi Coast
A bottle of prosecco; GoldSmith members also get a limoncello-tasting session.

MAISON MATILDA Treviso
A glass of prosecco each and free parking.

MASSERIA FUMAROLA Puglia
A bottle of Masseria Fumarola's home-made olive oil.

PALAZZINA GRASSI Venice
A bottle of prosecco and a selection of *cicchetti* (Venetian appetisers) made by the chef.

PALAZZO BONTADOSI Umbria
Two tickets to the Museum of Montefalco, an art collection in a 14th-century church; a tour and tasting at Colle Ciocco Winery; and 20 per cent off at Umbrian linen and interiors boutique Tessitura Pardi.

PALAZZO SENECA Umbria
A bottle of Umbrian red; late check-out (when availability permits). Members staying three nights or more will receive a three-course lunch (including wine and mineral water) at the Granaro del Monte restaurant; book a suite, and you'll get a spa treatment each.

PALAZZO VECCHIETTI Florence
A bottle of wine and a basket of *biscotti di Prato* (almond biscuits). Guests staying three nights or more also get two tickets to the Uffizi or Accademia, or an afternoon with a personal shopper.

PETRA SEGRETA Sardinia
A massage each, and the option of booking a special Sardinian tasting menu in the hotel restaurant: created exclusively for Smith members, it costs just €45 a head (worth €75; excludes drinks).

RESIDENZA NAPOLEONE III Rome
A bottle of Anagallis wine from the Ruspoli family's vineyard in Chianti, plus late check-out (when availability permits).

SEXTANTIO ALBERGO DIFFUSO Abruzzo
Wine tasting on arrival; a tour of the village; and free mountain-bike and snowshoe hire. Members staying three nights or more also get dinner for two: a four-course tasting menu, including wine, water and coffee.

SEXTANTIO LE GROTTE DELLA CIVITA Basilicata
A bottle of Aglianico del Vulture, a local red wine.

STRAF HOTEL & BAR Milan
A free drink of your choice at Straf Bar, and a platter of seasonal fruit.

VILLA ARCADIO Lake Garda
A bottle of local wine in your room; or, for members staying three nights or more, a three-course dinner for two (excluding alcoholic drinks) on one night of their stay.

VILLA ROSMARINO Riviera di Levante
Two glasses of local wine.

 To browse all offers available at each of the 800+ hotels in the Mr & Mrs Smith collection, go to mrandmrssmith.com/smith-card-offers.

(travel tools)

AIRPORTS

Alghero (+39 079 935282; aeroportodialghero.it).
Bari/Brindisi (+39 080 580 0200; aeroportidipuglia.it).
Bergamo (+39 035 326323; sacbo.it).
Bologna (+39 051 647 9615; bologna-airport.it).
Bolzano (+39 0471 255255; abd-airport.it).
Cagliari (+39 070 21121; sogaer.it).
Catania (+39 095 723 9111; aeroporto.catania.it).
Florence (+39 055 306 1300; aeroporto.firenze.it).
Genoa (+39 010 60151; airport.genova.it).
Innsbruck (+43 512 225250; innsbruck-airport.com).
Milan Linate (+39 02 232323; milanolinate.eu).
Milan Malpensa (+39 02 232323; milanomalpensa1.eu).
Naples (+39 081 789 6111; gesac.it).
Olbia Costa Smeralda (+39 0789 563444; geasar.com).
Palermo (+39 091 702 0111; gesap.it).
Perugia (+39 075 592141; airport.umbria.it).
Pescara (+39 895 898 9512; abruzzoairport.com).
Pisa (+39 050 849300; pisa-airport.com).
Rome Ciampino (+39 06 65951; ciampino-airport.info).
Rome Fiumicino (+39 06 65951; rome-airport.info).
Trapani (+39 0923 842502 aeroportotrapani.com).
Venice Marco Polo (+39 041 260 6111; veniceairport.it).
Venice Treviso (+39 0422 315111; trevisoairport.it).
Verona (+39 045 809 5666; aeroportoverona.it).

FERRIES & YACHT CHARTERS

Alilauro (+39 081 497 2222; alilauro.it), Caremar (+39 199 116655; caremar.it), Metrò del Mare (+39 081 497 1036; metrodelmare.net), Nautica Sic Sic (+39 081 807 2283; nauticasicsic.com) and Mediterraneo Charter (mediterraneo charter.it) all serve the Bay of Naples and the Amalfi Coast.
Snav (snav.it) and Tirrenia (+39 02 2630 2803; tirrenia.it) both operate ferries to Sicily and Sardinia.
Ustica Lines (+39 0923 873813; usticalines.it) and Siremar (+39 091 749 3111; siremar.it) cruise to Sicily and the Aeolians.
Trasporti Marittimi Turistici Golfo Paradiso (+39 0185 772091; golfoparadiso.it) for Riviera di Levante boating.
Italy Yacht Charters (+39 06 9818 1706; italyyachtcharters. com) for sailing-boat hire all around the country's coast.

TRAINS

Trenitalia (trenitalia.com) is the national rail network.
Circumvesuviana (vesuviana.it) links up various towns in the vicinity of Vesuvius, including Naples and Sorrento.
Ferrovie Appulo Lucane (fal-srl.it) handles regional services in Puglia and Basilicata.
Ferrovie Sardegna (arst.sardegna.it) looks after Sardinia's train routes.
The Man in Seat 61 (seat61.com/Italy-trains.htm) has a comprehensive beginner's guide to Italian rail services, rolling stock, timetables and ticketing.
Rail Europe (raileurope.com) is the go-to site for booking train tickets all over the Continent.

MAPS, MOTORING AND MORE

Benelux (+39 010 650 7280; beneluxcar.com) has a fleet of shiny BMWs, Mercedes and Audis for hire.
Happy Rent (+39 06 4202 0675; happyrent.com) will kit you out with vintage scooters or smart cars in Rome.
CLM Viaggi (+39 338 423 7249; clmviaggi.net) can arrange Tuscan motor tours, cooking classes and more.
Tuscany Scooter Rental (+39 055 912 1976; tuscanyscooterrental.com) lets you sightsee by Vespa.
Praiacosta (+39 089 813082; praiacosta.com) in Praiano can arrange scooter or cycle hire on the Amalfi Coast.
Il Centro Ippico Oxer (+39 339 533 4468; escursioniacavallo.it) organises horse-riding in Umbria.
Parks (parks.it) is the definitive list of Italy's most glorious green spaces, with in-depth guides to each.

UP, UP AND AWAY

Air Dolomiti (+39 045 288 6140; airdolomiti.it) is a domestic airline linking northern Italy with southern hubs Rome and Naples, plus Frankfurt, Munich and Vienna.
Air Panarea (+39 090 983 4428; airpanarea.com) charters helicopters and planes in the south, as well as providing transfers over to the Aeolian Islands.
Heliair (heliairvenice.com) lets you admire Venice's waterways as you hover above them in a helicopter.
Wind Jet (w2.volawindjet.it) flies between Venice, Rome, Milan, Pisa, Palermo and more.

TOURIST BOARDS

Abruzzo (regione.abruzzo.it).

Amalfi Coast and Capri (regione.campania.it).

Basilicata (regione.basilicata.it).

Liguria (regione.liguria.it).

Lombardy (regione.lombardia.it).

Puglia (regione.puglia.it).

Rome (regione.lazio.it; turismoroma.it).

Sardinia (regione.sardegna.it).

Sicily and the Aeolian Islands (pti.regione.sicilia.it).

South Tyrol (altabadia.org).

Tuscany (regione.toscana.it).

Umbria (regione.umbria.it).

Veneto (regione.veneto.it).

WINING AND DINING

Chianti Classico (chianticlassico.com/aziende) lets you explore the wineries of Chiantishire, check tasting times and view all sorts of pub-quiz-worthy production stats.

Divina Cucina (divinacucina.com), the site of author, gastro-tour organiser and Tuscan food evangelist Judy Witts Francini – visit the blog for superb recipes.

National Pasta Association (ilovepasta.org) is dedicated to Italy's premier foodstuff, with a sauce-matching guide.

Cotto e Crudo (cottoecrudo.com) is an Anglo-Italian blog compendium of seasonal, eco-friendly and vegetarian recipes with a largely Italian approach to cooking.

Slow Food (slowfood.com) is a global movement spread across 153 countries, dedicated to preserving local culinary tradition – find out more on this informative site.

BAGS, BIKINIS AND BEDROOM ESSENTIALS

Coco de Mer (UK: +44 (0)20 7836 8882; US: 1 310 652 0311; coco-de-mer.co.uk). Luxury massage oils and grown-up toys crafted from jade and pearls.

Figleaves (UK: 0844 493 2932; US: 1 866 751 2589; rest of the world: +44 (0)20 3170 0169; figleaves.com). Labels such as Freya and Damaris, delivered to your door.

Heidi Klein (heidiklein.com) sorts holiday wardrobes out with sleek swimwear and accessories for Mr and Mrs.

Kiki de Montparnasse (+1 888 965 5454; kikidm.com) is a purveyor of naughty night attire and chic loungewear.

Mandarina Duck is a Milanese maker of practical, stylish travel luggage; see mandarinaduck.com for stockists.

Myla (+44 (0)870 745 5003; myla.com) has a seductive collection of slinky smalls and bedtime toys.

TRAVEL APPS

PLANNING

Kayak is fantastic for finding flights and booking hire cars.

Mr & Mrs Smith: Plan and Play helps you plot the perfect escape, and entertains you while you're there (forgive us, but we're not going to miss an opportunity to plug our free iPhone app). Find beautiful boutique hotels, check out the latest offers, play Truth or Dare, send stay-extending get-out-of-work emails, and lots of other fun stuff.

TripIt keeps all your travel documents in a single itinerary: share it, add photos or maps, and access it anywhere.

ON YOUR WAY

PackTM lets you organise your packing list by bag, create templates to suit each type of trip, and calculate how much stuff you'll need for however long you're away for.

ProntoTreno is a helpful pocket guide to Trenitalia's timetables and ticket prices, letting you buy tickets on your phone, and check for service disruptions.

Turbcast is the ultimate weapon in battling a fear of flying.

World Weather tells you what the weather's up to right now anywhere on the planet and will take a stab at what it'll be like tomorrow too – handy for planning your packing.

ON THE GROUND

Odyssey Translator: Italian Travel Pro is the perfect tool for all your language-barrier-hopping needs.

Star Walk tells you everything you ever wanted to know about the universe: just point your phone at the night sky.

Tipping Guide lets you know whom to tip and how much, wherever you are in the world, with a gratuity calculator that even factors in how happy you are with the service.

Uffizi guides you straight to every masterpiece in Florence's most famous museum, then gives you the lowdown on each one.

WiFi Italia finds your nearest WiFi hotspot within 25km – and tells you whether or not you have to pay for it.

XE is the big daddy of real-time currency converters.

GUIDES, GAMES AND OTHER GIZMOS

Alpine Ski 3D is a tree-dodging ski game that lets you scope out the slopes before you go.

Eataly – the Recipes shows you how to make 1,000 Slow Food dishes, with a seasonality guide and a mini wine encyclopaedia.

i-MiBAC Top 40 is the Italian Ministry of Culture's nifty free guide to the country's most visited museums and archaeological sites – with handy mobile ticketing technology: just flash your phone for entry.

(who are Mr & Mrs Smith?)

Our reviewers are a hand-picked panel of people we admire and respect, all of whom have impeccable taste, of course, and can be trusted to report back to us on Smith hotels with total honesty. The only thing we ask of them is that they visit each hotel anonymously with a partner, and on their return, give us the kind of insider lowdown you'd expect from a close friend.

REVIEWERS WHO'S WHO

Stephen Bayley CULTURE CONNOISSEUR

The design critic was always more comfortable in hotels than at home. His father, an undercarriage salesman, hoiked him up and down the country in school holidays, and receptions and bars were more familiar than domestic drawing rooms. Room service menus were bedtime reading. He has ever since considered hotels his special subject. Factor in some more maturely acquired notions of hedonism, voyeurism, travel-lust, romantic anticipation and greed, and he's just about the perfect Smith undercover operative.

Oli Beale COMPLAINT-LETTER CREATIVE

Never mess with a hungry copywriter – a lesson Richard Branson learned in a public way when Oli Beale's letter to the Virgin boss swept the internet at the start of 2009. Oli lives and works in London, writing adverts for a leading agency and tweeting from @olibeale. He combines his two greatest passions of travelling and complaining whenever possible. And we never tire of reading the result – see it for yourself at bit.ly/ComplaintLetter.

Immodesty Blaize BURLESQUE BEAUTY

A Fellini-esque bombshell, Immodesty is Europe's premier showgirl and 2007's Reigning Queen of Burlesque. She has dazzled audiences across the world with her opulent shows and hourglass curves. Dior, Cartier and Damien Hirst have all enlisted her glamorous moves. An expert on the art of the showgirl, Immodesty's documentary *Burlesque Undressed* recently screened on TV and in cinemas in over 30 countries. She also lays claim to bringing the bonkbuster genre back with her novels *Tease* and *Ambition*.

Chris Cox MIND MEDDLER

This entertainer likes to fiddle with your thoughts while maintaining that he can't really read minds. Heralded as 'one of the most exciting entertainers in Britain' by *The Guardian*, Chris is far too modest to ever use quotes about how amazing he is. He's toured the world with his shows, staying in swanky pads from Auckland to Vegas, Mexico to Dubai. Originally from Bristol (but without the accent) he now lives in North London where, he laments, the coffee is far too expensive.

Ian D'Agata ALL-ROUND GRAPE GUY

An award-winning wine writer and restaurant and hotel reviewer in the Italian press, D'Agata celebrates the grapes of Italy and Bordeaux in Stephen Tanzer's *International Wine Cellar* as well as for *Decanter* and *Wine Press*. A lecturer on Italian Food and Wine Cultural History in the Food Sciences Master's program at NYU, he authored *The Ecco Guide to the Best Wines of Italy*, which is published by Harper Collins.

Joe Dunthorne NOVEL NARRATOR

During his early days as a writer, when postmodernism still seemed like the hot ticket, Joe wrote a series of damning, future-set reviews of books he had not yet written. He'd like to say this has come in useful when reviewing hotels for *Mr & Mrs Smith* but it hasn't. And for that we can be thankful, says Joe. Nowadays, he writes fiction and poetry, mainly set in the present day, and mostly not about himself. *Submarine*, his first novel, was turned into a major film. His second book, *Wild Abandon*, has just been published.

Martha Freud BRIGHT YOUNG THING

With a past in the creative departments of the film and fashion industries, Martha set up her own company designing and making furniture and lighting. She was soon hailed as a 'young meteor' by *Vogue*, and one of the 'rising stars of the UK's creative industries' by *The Independent*. Despite living in London her whole life, she has travelled much of the world, and only wishes that her cats enjoyed travelling it as much as she did.

Rufus Hound FUNNY MAN

Declaring himself the sort of chap who 'smells pleasant and often wears a suit, but is happier not to', this moustachio'd chancer has stayed at some of the planet's finest hotels. Hound has tried most things, including getting married to his Mrs Smith in the Little White Wedding Chapel in Las Vegas, Nevada. but he claims perennial joy is found in dark rum and dark rooms. A Smith hotel, claims the titular mutt, is like Aladdin's lamp: 'Unique, exquisitely crafted and inhabited by those whose job, seemingly, is to grant your every wish.'

Quentin Jones MODEL CREATOR

Since graduating from Central St Martins with an MA, a model for a decade, Quentin has since worked as an illustrator, an animator and more recently, a film-maker, collaborating with fashion luminaries such as Chanel and *AnOther Magazine*. With both parents architects, Quentin grew up surrounded by extraordinary buildings. This helped her cultivate a ruthless aesthetic eye – one that is often travelling, but never on a break.

Benji Lanyado BUDGET-TRAVEL BLOGGER

The Guardian's budget travel columnist and a regular contributor to *The New York Times*, Benji believes most of his friends quietly hate him because of this. He spends his spare time feverishly updating his three Fantasy Football teams, writing (mostly) rubbish on a variety of blogs, and hunting down salt-beef sandwiches where he can get them. He dreams of one day representing Finsbury Park in a cross-London disco-thrusting competition.

Natasha Law FINE FIGURIST

Best known for her painting and ink line drawings of women, Jude Law's elder sis is beloved by art critics and fashion folks alike. Since graduating from Camberwell College of Art, Natasha remained in London, working for a wide range of clients such as *Vogue*, Browns, Beatrix Ong, Harrods and Mulberry. Based in Peckham, where she lives with her husband and three children, she's celebrated for her sexy illustrations – so who more suitable to escape in the name of undercover Smith reviewing duty?

Sarah Maber MEDIA MARVEL

The Times Weekend's assistant editor Sarah Maber began her career as a junior reporter on the *Dorset Echo*, before moving to London and losing her country burr working on *Cosmopolitan*, *Marie Claire*, *Red* and *Psychologies*. There she discovered the delights of the press trip and, now, only a bed the size of Liechtenstein and a walk-in wet room will do. She became a mother in 2009 and again in 2010, and now intends to introduce her brood to the world of five-star boutique hotels.

Stefano Manfredi ITALIAN CUISINE EVANGELIST
A chef born in Italy and reared in Australia, Stefano inherited a love of eating and drinking grappa in the morning from his father; the cooking gene came from his mother's side. He's run Italian restaurants in Sydney since 1983 and cooked as a guest chef in restaurants and resorts all over the world. He's no slouch: as well as cheffing, he has a weekly food column in *The Sydney Morning Herald* and he oversees the kitchen gardens at Manfredi at Bells in the NSW seaside hamlet of Killcare. Most recently, he opened a Milanese osteria in the Star City Casino on Sydney's waterfront. His friends think he has no life but he wouldn't swap this one for quids.

Giuseppe Mascoli PIZZA-LOVING PHILOSOPHER
Retired at birth in 1958, Positano-born Giuseppe has since obtained a master's degree at the LSE and a Doctorate in Philosophy from Urbino. This expat Neapolitan's hobbies include owning a group of restaurants, including Franco Manca pizzerias and London private members' club, Blacks, and publishing a magazine, *The Drawbridge*. He declares his full-time occupation is International Playboy, although he does have a most respectable Mrs Smith, artist Bridget Hugo, also his co-author on his review.

Mario Mazzer INDUSTRIOUS DESIGNER
As an architect and designer based near Venice, Mario knows a thing or two about beauty: together with his novel-writing wife, Rita de Simone, he travels around the world in search of inspiration from the finer places. Some of Mario's contemporary furniture has been displayed at the London Design Museum, and he has received honorable nods from the likes of the *i-D* mag's Annual Design Review.

Adam McDougall SILVER-SCREEN CELEBRATER
One of the dreamers behind a London independent charity-funding cinema and roaming pop-up screens in parks and pools across the country, Adam hops between directors chairs for the Lexi in Kensal Rise and its pioneering mobile movie division, the Nomad, all over the land. Escape, magic, memory – that's the remit of cinema. Similar measures by which to assess the merits of a boutique hotel? Sure. His one request? Please turn off your mobile phone.

Adrian Moore ALPHA CONCIERGE
After dropping out of a tiny Liberal Arts college in New England, travelling the world and ending up penniless in the UK, Canadian-born Englishman Adrian Moore ended up working in the luxury hotel industry as a glorified dogsbody. Named top concierge by *Monocle*, Paris' Hottest Food Blogger by *Woman's Wear Daily*, and Paris' 'Bad Boy' blogger by *Newsweek*, Adrian balances his life between working as concierge at one of Paris' top luxury hotels, writing, and sucking the marrow from the bones of the City of Light.

Erdem Moralioglu FROCK STAR
Born in Montreal to a Turkish father and an English mother, the fashion designer launched his now coveted London-based ready-to-wear label Erdem in 2005. His unique prints and patterns soon made him a red-carpet regular – he can count Gwyneth Paltrow, Alexa Chung and Julianne Moore as fans. He left Canada to study at London's Royal College of Art (where he met his Mr Smith, Phil Joseph), then after graduating relocated to New York before returning to set up base in Bethnal Green, where he now lives with his twin sister, Sara.

Michelle Ogundehin DECOR DOYENNE
An internationally renowned authority on interiors, style and design, Michelle is editor-in-chief of *Elle Decoration*, director of MO:Studio, her own interiors consultancy, and a trustee of the Victoria & Albert Museum. Manchester-born Michelle studied architecture at London's Bartlett School, before heading to New York for two years. She then shuttled between Los Angeles and London for a couple more, and now lives between the Big Smoke and Brighton.

Jack Peñate GUITAR-POP PRO
South London born and bred, singer-songwriter Jack Peñate was signed in 2006. Since then, he's had various top 10 chart hits as well as his fair share of sold-out tours. The indie pop musician is now a regular on the festival scene and has travelled the world, stopping off to film videos in Jordan and play gigs in Orange County. As someone who lives on the road, he knows a good night's sleep when he sees one – although pinning him down to enjoy one on a two-night trip to Venice was no easy task.

Mary Portas THE QUEEN OF SHOPS

Regarded as one of the foremost authority figures in retail, Mary is creative director at one of London's most respected brand communication agencies, Yellowdoor. She is recognised throughout the trade as the *Queen of Shops*, after her BBC2 television series. Since 2005 Mary has been commissioned to write a weekly column in *The Telegraph,* reviewing the state of the nation's shops, and has been enlisted by the Government to inject life into Britain's ailing high streets. For her reviewer trip she took a mini-moon with her Mrs Smith Melanie Rickey, fashion features editor of *Grazia* magazine.

Tom Robbins INTREPID EDITOR

A former investigative reporter at *The Sunday Times*, Tom Robbins swapped hard news for holidays, becoming travel editor of *The Observer* and then *The Financial Times*. Although the day job demands spending time in many of the world's most lavish hotels and restaurants, his real love is heading to remote corners of the world to indulge his passion for skiing. He's also the author of *White Weekends* (Bantam Press), a guide to the best short ski breaks.

Alex Tieghi-Walker ZEITGEIST CAPTURER

Raised in Wales until his family decamped to Venice, Alex then spent his time on vaporetti drawing life on the canals. After driving up California's coastline aged 18, he worked for *Wallpaper** until taking a degree in Spanish and Italian literature at Durham. Not one to stray far from Italy, he returned with a peppermint-coloured bike and cycled from Portofino to Rome, eating and pedalling his way through Umbria and Le Marche. A *Nowness* picture editor, he now lives in a tall house behind the Oval, where he sketches architectural blueprints and pens food reviews.

Matteo Torre FERRARI FRONTMAN

As with most people whose birthplace was Piacenza, Mattei loves food (especially his mother's), football, and everything that has an engine, makes noise and goes fast. A London-based Italian who has lived in Milan and Paris, he travels all around Europe celebrating the world's most beloved red Italian sports car. He spends his holidays on a vintage Harley Davidson with his wife Sofia on the rear seat and a Michelin Guide in his pocket.

Teo van den Broeke MAG MAN

Teo's Italian obsession took root aged 10 when studying the Romans opened his mind to the joys of eating lying down. After three years studying fine art (Italy cropped up a few times), then writing for *Wallpaper** (where frantic calls to Milan were not uncommon), his most recent magazining is as associate editor of *Esquire*. These days, he's a regular on the Italian peninsula and as long as he's got a Campari in one hand and a Neapolitan pizza in the other, he's a happy ragazzo.

Dan Vernon BAFTA BAGGER

As a film-maker, Daniel spends his time tracking down characters in far-flung destinations: from the freezing darkness of the Arctic to the howling moors of Bodmin and the arid Arizona desert, he has stayed in his fair share of hovels, and knows luxury when he sees it. The holder of a BA (Hons) degree in Three-Dimensional Design, he's also stayed in an extensive array of B&Bs all over the UK and Ireland, but so far nowhere beats his Michelin-starred-chef-equipped honeymoon hideaway in Madagascar.

Gary Walther FREELANCE SCRITTORE

Veteran travel writer and editor Gary has visited 59 countries so far and has been the editor-in-chief of four luxury travel and lifestyle magazines. From 1990 to 2000 he built *Departures* into one of America's premier magazines. In 2000, he launched Expedia Travels; in 2004, he transformed *SpaFinder*; in 2008, he revamped *ForbesLife*. But we cherish our American cousin most for his Cobble Hill wine cellar tip-offs and for adding extra fizz to Smith tales, as our NY-based reviews editor.

Danny Webb AWARD-WINNING THESP

As fans of *Valkyrie*, *Robin Hood*, *Henry V*, *Being Human* and *Dr Who* can attest, Danny Webb is recognisable as one of Britain's most prolific character actors. His theatre work has included touring as Hamlet for nine months and starring in prize-winning West End productions such as *Dead Funny* and *Art*. In 2011 he received an Olivier Best Actor award for *Blasted*. Danny has been exposed to varied hotel experiences dependent on budgetary restraints, from actors' digs in Leicester to oriental splendour in Taipei.

(what's in a name?)

People ask why we're called Mr & Mrs Smith. Well, naming ourselves in honour of the classic dirty-weekend pseudonym was our knowing wink to couples seeking the sexiest stays. We were born in 2003, after Londoners James Lohan and Tamara Heber-Percy followed the advice of – ahem – 'a trusted guidebook', and set off for a romantic country weekend at what had promised to be a beautiful boutique hotel…

It didn't live up to the hype. After a less-than-seduction-packed weekend, they returned to London determined to create a discerning hotel guide dedicated to preventing wasted escapes. They assembled a small team of friends passionate about their campaign and, when our first UK/Ireland book became a bestseller, we took our recommendations online in 2005 and, soon after, created a dedicated Travel Team to help people plan and book their escapes.

Mrandmrssmith.com is now one of the most visited hotel-booking sites in the world, and the Smith team has grown to encompass offices in London, New York and Melbourne. Our aim, as ever, is to ensure boutique hotel lovers never squander a second. Properties big on personality and high in quality – whether they're chic B&Bs or modern-minded grandes dames – are still surprisingly hard to find for those who demand the whole shebang: considered looks, intimate feel, home-from-home comforts, snappy service and a first-class breakfast. We track down the most special hotels and hippest holiday houses, visit them ourselves and take pride in being the first port of call for style-savvy travellers all over the world.

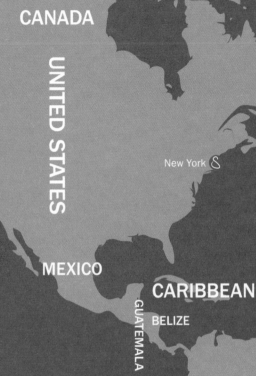

(where in the world)

ICELAND

SWEDEN

CANADA

UK

DENMARK

IRELAND
NETHERLANDS

London

GERMANY

BELGIUM LUXEMBOU

UNITED STATES

FRANCE

SWITZERL.

AUSTRIA F

PORTUGAL

SPAIN

ITALY

New York

MOROCCO

MEXICO

CARIBBEAN

GUATEMALA

BELIZE

BRAZIL

URUGUAY

ARGENTINA

 Smith HQ

mrandmrssmith.com

Welcome to the world of Smith, where you'll find everything you need to plan your escapes – or remember them by.

Complete your guidebook collection, order CDs, or buy travel accessories (and lots more besides) from Smith's online shop and, because you're a member, you get discounts too. Don't say we aren't good to you.

THE SMITH BOOKSHELF: OUR LATEST GUIDES

South-East Asia Featuring sumptuous beach hideaways in Thailand, Malaysia and Bali, chic Indochine retreats in Laos and Cambodia and slick city boltholes in Singapore and Vietnam, this is the ultimate hotel collection for the style-conscious globetrotter looking for adventure out East.

France Taking you on a tour from Paris to Provence via Poitou-Charentes, our France guide features scintillating reviews by a tastemaker panel of perfumers, restaurateurs and designers. Every hotel on our hitlist of much-loved classics and glamorous newcomers wins the Smith stamp of approval for its looks, location and that certain *je ne sais quoi*.

Australia/New Zealand We've combed white-sand beaches, climbed snow-capped mountains, camped in sun-drenched deserts and scoured cosmopolitan cities in pursuit of the sexiest hotels down under, whether you're looking for adrenalin-soaked adventure in Queenstown, or a private-island escape in Queensland.

UK/Ireland: Volume 2 Updated with new entries for 2011, this is the definitive guide to the most amazing places to stay in the British and Emerald Isles, from Belfast to the Brecon Beacons and Edinburgh to East Sussex; this best-of collection includes boutique B&Bs, luxurious spa retreats, country hideaways and secret city havens.

GIVE A LITTLE LOVE

Treat someone special to stay at any hotel in the Smith collection, with a Mr & Mrs Smith *Get a Room!* gift card. Gift vouchers have never been more seductive: they're smartly packaged in a sleek black box, and are perfect for surprising partners, family or friends – who might even invite you along.

Holiday Houses

San Lorenzo Mountain Lodge

TUSCAN VILLAS FOR TWO · PUGLIAN TRULLI · STYLISH CITY STAYS

(pack it in)

Fellini DVDs

beach towel   backgammon s

flip-flops   watercolours   erotica   binocular

SLR + zoom lens   SatNav device   lipstic

corkscrew

your best singing voice

home-spa products   Italian phrasebook

three coins for the Trevi fountai

multi-purpose sarong/scarf/shawl

playing cards

Renaissance art guide

smartphone + charger

wine-tasting notebook

your best singing voice

stilettos

sunblock

sketchbook

condoms

massage oil

passport

bottle opener

sun hat

sunglasses

hangover remedies

driving licence

massage oil

scented candles

fully loaded e-reader

canvas tote bag

swimwear

iPod + speakers

(applause)

Grazie...

There is an army of people who have worked tirelessly to bring this book to the shelf: Adrian Houston and his assistant William Scott for inspiring interiors shots and for doing photographic justice to the Italian landscape, his PA Susi Coben and his Hasselblad cameras; Bloom (and Ben White especially) for creating the brand and for making this book worthy of the most stylish of coffee tables; Ed Bussey, Peter Clements, Paul Portz and Ian Taylor for their strategic insight; Peter Osborne and Sam Millar of Osborne & Little for the beautiful wallpaper prints; Clive, George, John, Keith and Mark at EMC Ltd; Emma Strandberg at Il Salviatino and Lorenzo Bambi, Angela Berti and Claudio Meli from JK Place Firenze for their help with our cover – and Hannah Lohan for styling it; Andria Mitsakos and Erika Vives for championing Smith Stateside, and Rowena Fitzgerald for doing the same down under; Annabel Goldie-Morrison for kickstarting the marketing machine; Jori White (as ever, part of Smith's extended family); the developers for keeping our website ticking over; Amber Spencer-Holmes and her team for looking after our members; Peggy Picano-Nacci and the hotel relations family; Rebecca Honey and the Smith Travel Team for making people's hotel dreams into Frette-linened reality. Finally, we'd like to thank all our properties; Smith's crack squad of hotel hunters for unearthing the hippest hotels in Italy for this book; wordsmiths Sophie Dening, Rufus Purdy, Kelley Sullivan and Gary Walther; all our reviewers, for telling their tales; and, as always, all the other halves who accompanied them on their adventures, or provided support and inspiration.

Mr & Mrs Smith

(the small print)

CONDITIONS OF PURCHASE

Any copy of this book is sold subject to the condition that it shall not, by way of trade or otherwise, be lent, resold, hired out or otherwise circulated, without the publisher's prior consent, in any form of binding or cover other than that in which it is published and without a similar condition including these words being imposed on a subsequent purchaser. All rights reserved. No part of this publication may be reproduced or transmitted in any form or by any means, electronic or mechanical, including photocopy, recording or any other information storage and retrieval system without prior written permission from the publisher. For full terms and conditions, visit mrandmrssmith.com/legal.

DISCLAIMER

Please be advised that opening times and room availability of hotels will vary from time to time; users of this book are advised to reserve accommodation well in advance. All rates given are per room, per night, based on two people sharing, are inclusive of tax, and do not include breakfast, unless specified. Contact details are liable to change. Opinions expressed in this book are those of the individual reviewers and do not represent the opinions of the publishers. The publishers shall not be liable for any deficiency in service, quality or health and safety at any particular hotel. All complaints or claims for redress must be made directly to the hotel concerned. Although the publishers have made reasonable endeavours to ensure that the information contained in this book is accurate at the time of going to press, they shall not be liable for any loss, expense, damage, disappointment or inconvenience caused, in whole or in part, by reliance on such information. If accidental errors appear in print, the publishers will apply the corrections in the following edition of this book. The user of the information does so at his or her own risk. The publishers are not in any way responsible for the conditions of the hotels, venues or services, or third-party acts or omissions at any hotel, venue or service.

HOTELS

Inclusion in the Mr & Mrs Smith collection is by invitation only; hotels cannot buy their way in. Hotels featured by Mr & Mrs Smith have paid a fee towards the management of the membership and marketing programme conducted by Spy Publishing Ltd. Mr & Mrs Smith is funded by private investment.

MEMBERSHIP TERMS AND CONDITIONS

Member extras for Mr & Mrs Smith cardholders are subject to availability and may be changed at any time. The publishers cannot accept responsibility in cases where a hotel changes ownership and discontinues offers promised to cardholders by previous hotel owners. Cardholder offers are valid once for each booking made. If two cardholders share a room in a hotel, they are entitled to one instance of the offer only. The Smith membership card is non-transferable and may be used only by the card's signatory. Holders of the membership card recognise and accept that they visit any hotel voluntarily and entirely at their own risk.

LONDON
Barley Mow Centre
10 Barley Mow Passage
London W4 4PH
United Kingdom
t +44 (0)20 8987 6970
f +44 (0)20 8987 4300

NEW YORK
580 Broadway
Suite 1202
New York NY 10012
United States
t +1 (212) 600 2040
f +1 (212) 219 2605

MELBOURNE
Level 1
137 Flinders Lane
Melbourne VIC 3000
Australia
t +61 (0)3 9419 6671
f +61 (0)3 9650 7290

Editor-in-chief Juliet Kinsman
Editors Lucy Fennings, Anthony Leyton
Contributing editors Sarah Jappy, Caroline Lewis, Kate Pettifer
Copy editor Stewart Wild
Head designer Gareth Thomas
Design assistant Andy Lang
Production Jasmine Darby .
Project management Laura Mizon
Font designer Charles Stewart and Co
Wallpaper Osborne & Little
Reprographics EMC Ltd
Branding consultant Bloom (bloom-design.com)
Printed and bound by C and C Printing. Printed on paper from a sustainable source

Photography Cover and all hotel images by Adrian Houston (adrianhouston.co.uk), except those on pages 77–78, 83, 100, 106, 140, 207, 210, 216, 226–227, 239–240, 274 and 282 – all courtesy of the hotels. Destination images provided by Getty Images and iStockphoto.

Hotel partnerships Mary Garvin, Katy McCann, Carla Silverman
PR and marketing Aline Keuroghlian, Sabine Zetteler
ISBN 978-0-9565347-1-2

First published in 2011 by:
Spy Publishing Ltd
Barley Mow Centre
10 Barley Mow Passage
London W4 4PH

British Library Cataloguing-In-Publication data.
A catalogue record of this book is available from the British Library.

THE SMITH TRAVEL TEAM

Our team of boutique hotel experts and travel consultants is available round the clock; so if you're looking to make your escape, give them a call...

UK 0845 034 0700
US/Canada 1 800 464 2040
Mexico 55 4624 2406
Brazil 11 3957 3947
Australia 1300 896 627
New Zealand 0800 896 671
Elsewhere in Asia +61 3 8648 8871
Rest of the world +44 20 8987 4312

(index)

To book any of the hotels featured, visit mrandmrssmith.com